The Criminal
Justice System

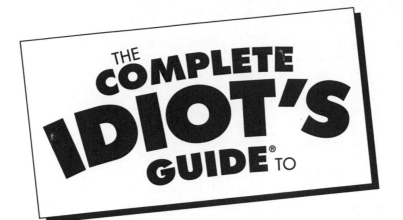

THE
COMPLETE
IDIOT'S
GUIDE® TO

The Criminal Justice System

by Robin Sax, J.D.

ALPHA
A member of Penguin Group (USA) Inc.

For instilling in me the passion to pursue my dreams and to forge my own path to them, thank you, Mom and Dad. I love you to pieces.

ALPHA BOOKS

Published by the Penguin Group

Penguin Group (USA) Inc., 375 Hudson Street, New York, New York 10014, USA

Penguin Group (Canada), 90 Eglinton Avenue East, Suite 700, Toronto, Ontario M4P 2Y3, Canada (a division of Pearson Penguin Canada Inc.)

Penguin Books Ltd., 80 Strand, London WC2R 0RL, England

Penguin Ireland, 25 St. Stephen's Green, Dublin 2, Ireland (a division of Penguin Books Ltd.)

Penguin Group (Australia), 250 Camberwell Road, Camberwell, Victoria 3124, Australia (a division of Pearson Australia Group Pty. Ltd.)

Penguin Books India Pvt. Ltd., 11 Community Centre, Panchsheel Park, New Delhi—110 017, India

Penguin Group (NZ), 67 Apollo Drive, Rosedale, North Shore, Auckland 1311, New Zealand (a division of Pearson New Zealand Ltd.)

Penguin Books (South Africa) (Pty.) Ltd., 24 Sturdee Avenue, Rosebank, Johannesburg 2196, South Africa

Penguin Books Ltd., Registered Offices: 80 Strand, London WC2R 0RL, England

Copyright © 2009 by Robin Sax

International Standard Book Number: 978-1-59257-884-9
Library of Congress Catalog Card Number: 2009924902

11   10   09   8   7   6   5   4   3   2   1

Interpretation of the printing code: The rightmost number of the first series of numbers is the year of the book's printing; the rightmost number of the second series of numbers is the number of the book's printing. For example, a printing code of 09-1 shows that the first printing occurred in 2009.

Printed in the United States of America

Note: This publication contains the opinions and ideas of its author. It is intended to provide helpful and informative material on the subject matter covered. It is sold with the understanding that the author and publisher are not engaged in rendering professional services in the book. If the reader requires personal assistance or advice, a competent professional should be consulted.

The author and publisher specifically disclaim any responsibility for any liability, loss, or risk, personal or otherwise, which is incurred as a consequence, directly or indirectly, of the use and application of any of the contents of this book.

Most Alpha books are available at special quantity discounts for bulk purchases for sales promotions, premiums, fund-raising, or educational use. Special books, or book excerpts, can also be created to fit specific needs.

For details, write: Special Markets, Alpha Books, 375 Hudson Street, New York, NY 10014.

Publisher: *Marie Butler-Knight*
Editorial Director: *Mike Sanders*
Senior Managing Editor: *Billy Fields*
Senior Acquisitions Editor: *Paul Dinas*
Senior Development Editor: *Phil Kitchel*
Senior Production Editor: *Janette Lynn*
Copy Editor: *Krista Hansing Editorial Services, Inc.*

Cartoonist: *Steve Barr*
Cover Designer: *Bill Thomas*
Book Designer: *Trina Wurst*
Indexer: *Heather McNeill*
Layout: *Ayanna Lacey*
Proofreader: *Mary Hunt*

Contents at a Glance

Contents

Appendixes

Introduction

Some people think of the law as boring and tedious, at best, and just a bunch of incomprehensible legalese, at worst. But few would say that about criminal law. Just review the nightly TV listings: crime—and its investigation and prosecution—has a gut-level, real-life drama that captures the interest and hearts of nonlawyers and lawyers alike.

TV crime shows are entertaining, but their ability to educate is iffy—at least, if you want a comprehensive understanding of the criminal justice system. That's where this book comes in. In the following pages, I give you an insider's view of the whole system—not with the arcane detail of a textbook, but rather focusing on what's important, what's useful, and what you need to know to understand how the system really works.

We'll look over the shoulders of the police as they investigate a crime, find out why and when they get search and arrest warrants, and find out why they always give those Miranda warnings to a suspect. We'll discuss the elements of different crimes: you'll learn the difference between larceny and burglary; what makes a killing manslaughter, second-degree murder, or first-degree murder; and why it matters so much whether the prosecutor decides to charge a misdemeanor or a felony.

After the defendant is charged, the trial begins. We'll cover the actual trial process, from bail to jail. We'll walk through how a case makes its way into court; discuss the roles of judge, jury, and all those other people in the courtroom; and examine the defendant's constitutional rights, the victim's bill of rights, and everything in between. And of course, we'll talk about sentencing.

But one thing this book won't do is make a lawyer out of you, or serve as a substitute for one. The United States has 52 different court systems (the 50 states, the federal courts, and the District of Columbia), and each has its own laws and procedures. Throughout the book, I strive to give you a general or consensus view, but I can't cover all the variations in procedures, codes, and laws of all the different court systems. Those differences, and the individual details of each defendant's case, matter a lot—and so this book cannot and should not be considered legal advice.

Here's a quick roadmap of how I've organized this book:

Part 1, "The Criminal Justice System and Its Classifications of Crime," is the foundation for everything else to come. This is where I cover the difference between civil and criminal law, the relationship between state and federal crimes, and why some cases go to state courts and some to federal courts.

Perhaps the most important purpose of Part 1 is to explain why the criminal justice system is in place—what it is trying to accomplish, who it is trying to protect, and how it does this. Part 1 also gives the basics about how crimes are defined and the different classifications of crimes, which will prove useful as we move into the discussion of specific crimes in Part 2.

Part 2, "Elements of Specific Crimes," is the nuts and bolts of the acts we know as crimes. We take each one apart, inspecting its elements in the context of the real world. The best way I know to help you understand these elements is to draw on my own experience as a prosecutor, so you'll see lots of examples as we go through these elements.

Part 2 covers all the well-established crimes, including murder, rape, and burglary. But it also covers more modern crimes, like stalking, identity theft, and elder abuse. We cover the gamut.

Part 3, "From Crime to Trial," starts with the wail of a police siren in the night. A crime has been committed, and this part takes you through the investigation, the limits on the police as they search for evidence, and what's required for an arrest. This is also where I cover the charging process—how a case gets filed, what makes a case not get filed, who decides what crime to charge, and all the steps once an investigation becomes an official criminal case.

Part 3 also explains the rights of the accused during and after the investigation, from the Miranda rule, to fair line-ups, to the right to a lawyer. It also covers the major defenses available to a person accused of a crime, such as insanity, self-defense, and entrapment.

In **Part 4, "The Trial Process,"** we step into the courtroom. I introduce the whole courtroom cast, arraignment, bail, preliminary hearings, and jury selection. I outline each stage of the criminal prosecution and discuss the options available to prosecutors, defendants, and judges. A courtroom can be a scary place, especially when everyone but you seems to know exactly what is going on. Part 4 demystifies the process, showing you the "method to the madness" and revealing its roots in our U.S. Constitution.

Part 4 also gives you a firm grounding in the rules about what does and doesn't get admitted into evidence. But we dig a bit deeper than just the rules and get into why the various rules, like hearsay and privilege, are there in the first place. We close Part 4 with the jury—how the judge instructs jurors in the law, how they deliberate, what happens when they have questions, and of course, their verdict.

Part 5, "The Post-Trial Criminal Justice System," brings us full-circle as we re-examine the purposes of criminal law and how they affect sentencing and punishment. The job of the criminal justice system doesn't end with the jury's verdict. The entire system would be rendered meaningless if there were no consequences for convicted defendants or recourse for victims. This section reviews the range of sentencing possibilities available, both traditional and creative, from probation to prison, to the death penalty.

Part 5 also takes a look at the juvenile justice system. It covers why we have one, who's a juvenile, what the differences are from the adult system, and why some juveniles are tried as adults—along with a lot else.

Part 5 closes the book where it should, with a very important but sometimes overlooked topic: the rights of victims. It examines the victims' right to be informed about "their" case, to be present at trial and other proceedings, and to be heard. I share with you one of the most moving victim impact statements I've ever heard, and discuss how and why these statements are used. Victim restitution, which means reimbursement for damages a crime has caused, is also covered, as are witness-protection programs.

Throughout this book, you will see the following special features:

For the Record

These give you an insider's view of the system, its players, and how it all really works.

Objection

Here you'll find red flags, pitfalls, and other things to look out for in the criminal justice system.

def•i•ni•tion

These sidebars define and explain the legalese and other specialized terminology that can interfere with even the most brilliant person's understanding of what is going on.

Hearsay

These little gems explode myths and misconceptions about the criminal justice system as it is depicted on TV and in books, movies, and other popular sources. I had a lot of fun with these, and I think you will, too.

Acknowledgments

Certain individuals have had absolutely nothing to do with this book but nevertheless have had a life-changing impact on my professional life, which is deeply intertwined with this text. In mostly chronological order, they are: my parents (Rikki and Stan Sax), for everything, including bringing me into this world and being the best parents ever; my sister, Heather (and brother-in-law, Scott), for allowing me to vent when I have taken on more than I can chew; my Aunt Vic (and Uncle David) for supporting my endeavors and always offering a dinner date as a reprieve from working; Sharon Kerson, my sixth-grade English teacher, who taught me how to write a five-sentence paragraph; Richardson Lynn, my academic mentor and cheerleader at Pepperdine Law School; Harry Caldwell, my trial advocacy teacher who has been a mentor, hero, and friend; my husband, Andy, who always supports my endeavors and has taught me how to enjoy life; Jason, Jeremy, and Hannah, who always make me laugh and smile, and have taught me so much; Erica Sanchez and Kristen Green, who have always been there to care of Nanner when I needed to write; Dolly and Bill Katzenstein, for always reading (with a smile) anything I put in front of them, and for making a son who will always be "student of the week" (whose picture hangs on every wall playing hide-and-seek); Dr. Mark Goulston, for keeping me sane and balanced even in the most harried of times; and the best home-girls in the world—Stephanie Cornick, Joanna Cowitt, Stacy Dittrich, Mandi Dyner, Beth Golden Christopher, Stacy Dittrich, Dana Guerin-Frohlich, Kathryn Jacoby, Susan Murphy-Milano, Tamara Miller, Robyn Ritter Simon, Rebecca Simon, Eva Jabber Stodel, Mary Stone, Jillian Straus, Ellie Zexter.

This book would not be possible without the tireless efforts of Rex Browning, who is a genius with words and is skilled at probing me to answer even the most difficult questions; Paul Dinas, the world's best editor, who always has an abundance of ideas and unfailing courtesy and flexibility; and Jaime Williams, research assistant extraordinaire—you rock! My warm and grateful appreciation goes to Claire Gerus, professional angel, gifted editor, and friend. Thank you all for everything—this book would not be possible without you.

Trademarks

Part 1

The Criminal Justice System and Its Classifications of Crime

What is the criminal justice system? Where did it come from? How does it work? Why are there separate civil and criminal justice systems? What cases go to state court, and which to a federal court? And how does it all apply to you? Part 1 answers these questions and more.

Part 1 explores the differences between the civil and criminal parts of our justice system. You'll also learn how the different systems use juries, the level of proof required in each, and what constitutional rights apply where. Finally, Part 1 explains how crimes are classified. What's the difference between a felony and a misdemeanor or between first- and second-degree murder, and between murder and manslaughter? How does the criminal justice system draw a line between a specific intent to do something, versus a general intent that it happen, versus reckless indifference to whether it happens or not? And why does it matter? You'll find out here.

Defining Crime

In This Chapter

- ◆ The origins of our criminal justice system
- ◆ The origins of our definitions of specific crimes
- ◆ Federal law vs. state law—which applies, and when?
- ◆ Federal courts vs. state courts—what cases go where, and why?
- ◆ The three basic elements of a crime

Since humans first gathered together in societies, we have understood the need to create systems to deal with wrongdoing. The concept that wrongful conduct harms society is at the core of our current criminal justice system, and is why the state and federal governments prosecute criminal wrongdoing instead of leaving it to individual victims.

History of the Criminal Justice System

Many of the first codes of law, however, including that of Rome, did not see wrongdoings as acts that threatened or harmed the social order itself. Instead, offenses were viewed as bad actions against individuals. As a result, the codes of law allowed only the injured individuals to collect compensation from those who wronged them.

Later in Europe, political and religious doctrines began to influence the code of law, a process that entire books have been written about. Out of this mixture of ideas came a more structured legal system. A second conception of wrongdoing emerged, and certain offenses were considered crimes that threatened the social order—crimes against society itself instead of just wrongdoing against individuals. These offenses included most wrongdoing that we consider crimes today, such as robbery, murder, and rape.

For the Record _____

A separate justice system, called the civil justice system, allows individuals to make claims against persons who have caused them damage or injury.

In the earliest criminal justice systems, a person accused of wrongdoing was brought before dukes, lords, or other preeminent people in society, who then decided the guilt or innocence of the accused. Later, these social elites started appointing judges to hold the trials for them; in turn, judges began to bring in citizens to help with the decisions—the forerunners of our juries. Eventually, the criminal justice system started to resemble what we know today.

Criminal vs. Civil Law

The difference between the civil and criminal justice systems is that the criminal justice system focuses on defining, investigating, and punishing wrongdoing that is considered damaging to society, not just to individual victims. The goal is to protect society by deterring such conduct through the threat of capture, conviction, and sentencing. The system also tries to protect society by removing criminals from the population for a period of time, during which attempts are made to *rehabilitate* them.

def•i•ni•tion _____

Rehabilitation is the attempt to assist a convicted person to change his ways and to turn from a life of crime to one of a law-abiding citizen. How successful the rehabilitation efforts of the criminal justice system have been, and how they might be more effective, is a matter of ongoing debate within the system and society-at-large.

Keeping Things Civil

The civil justice system allows individuals to make claims against other individuals who have caused them damage, such as by breaching a contract, selling them a defective product that causes injury, or trespassing on their land. But the criminal justice system also deals with people who have caused harm—so what's the difference?

A successful civil proceeding results in a judgment—usually a monetary judgment—paid directly to the injured party by the person or corporation who injured him. In contrast, a successful criminal proceeding results in a conviction of the wrongdoer and a sentence that usually includes jail time and/or fines paid to the state treasury. Sometimes the sentence includes restitution to the victim(s).

The civil justice system becomes involved primarily when one individual files a lawsuit against someone else. All that is required is filing a complaint, paying a court filing fee, and formally delivering the complaint to the defendant (called service, or being served).

The Impact of the U.S. Constitution

For the criminal justice system, however, a lot must happen before charges are filed. The process starts with the discovery or report of a possible crime. The criminal system's rules and statutes control how the police can respond, how investigations must occur, and what evidence must exist before an individual may be charged. We explore these processes and procedures in detail in the chapters to come.

Many of these criminal procedures stem from and are controlled by the rights that the U.S. Constitution guarantees to individuals. A few of these apply to the civil justice system as well, such as the right to due process and to be free from governmental discrimination. However, some of the best-known rights in the federal Constitution apply only in the criminal justice system.

The articles of the Constitution tell us that we are entitled to a trial by jury. They tell us that one state cannot act differently toward us than the state we live in. And they are the basis for the Supreme Court's authority to reject state or federal laws that violate the Constitution.

Possibly even more important to the criminal justice system than the articles in the main text of the Constitution are its amendments. The first 10 amendments, known as the Bill of Rights, were passed as part of the original Constitution and embody many of the most important rights of a person suspected of committing a crime. Imagine yourself as the accused:

The Fourth Amendment places a heavy burden on police before they can search your property or arrest you.

> *The right of the people to be secure in their persons, houses, papers, and effects, against unreasonable searches and seizures, shall not be violated, and no warrants shall issue, but upon probable cause, supported by oath or affirmation, and particularly describing the place to be searched, and the persons or things to be seized.*

The Fifth Amendment saves you from being charged with the same crime twice, protects you from being forced to testify against yourself, and promises you full and proper legal process before you can be convicted and punished for a crime.

> *No person shall be held to answer for a capital, or otherwise infamous crime, unless on a presentment or indictment of a grand jury, except in cases arising in the land or naval forces, or in the militia, when in actual service in time of war or public danger; nor shall any person be subject for the same offense to be twice put in jeopardy of life or limb; nor shall be compelled in any criminal case to be a witness against himself, nor be deprived of life, liberty, or property, without due process of law; nor shall private property be taken for public use, without just compensation.*

The Sixth Amendment mandates that you be provided a speedy trial and guarantees you the right to a jury and legal counsel at that trial.

> *In all criminal prosecutions, the accused shall enjoy the right to a speedy and public trial, by an impartial jury of the state and district wherein the crime shall have been committed, which district shall have been previously ascertained by law, and to be informed of the nature and cause of the accusation; to be confronted with the witnesses against him; to have compulsory process for obtaining witnesses in his favor, and to have the assistance of counsel for his defense.*

The Eighth Amendment protects you from unreasonable bail and fines, and from cruel and unusual punishment.

> *Excessive bail shall not be required, nor excessive fines imposed, nor cruel and unusual punishments inflicted.*

Prove It

In addition to these constitutional protections, the requirement that the prosecution must prove the defendant's guilt—rather than the defendant having to prove his innocence—further assures that innocent persons will receive justice. As even most schoolchildren know, a defendant is presumed innocent until proven guilty, which means the prosecutor must present enough evidence to meet the state's *burden of proving* the defendant guilty.

def•i•ni•tion

The prosecutor's **burden of proof** means that the prosecutor must prove that the defendant committed the crime—the defendant does not have to prove he didn't do it. Of course, a defendant who has evidence of his innocence, such as an alibi, may offer it. But if the prosecution's evidence doesn't meet the burden of proving each element of the alleged crime, the defendant will be found not guilty—even if he offers not a single witness or scrap of evidence in his defense.

Another key difference between civil and criminal law is the level of proof required. In civil law, a fact is considered proven if it is shown to be true more probably than not. This "barely better than 50/50" standard is called the "preponderance of the evidence" standard, and it is the lowest standard in both the civil and criminal justice systems.

A few facts in the civil justice system, such as the elements of a civil fraud claim, must be proven by "clear and convincing" evidence. The clear and convincing standard of proof is a medium burden—more than "preponderance of the evidence" but less than the level of proof that the criminal justice system requires.

In criminal law, the prosecutor must prove each element of a crime "beyond a reasonable doubt." This is a much higher burden than either civil standard, and I delve into exactly what it means in a later chapter. For now, know that this stringent level of proof is a key part of how the criminal justice system does all it can to "get it right." When dealing with an accused's liberty and possibly even life, "more likely than not" doesn't cut it. If there is a reasonable doubt in the jurors' minds—or even in only one juror's mind—the defendant cannot be convicted.

The Origins of Our Definitions of Specific Crimes

Today state and federal statutes provide carefully worded, specific definitions of individual crimes and of the factual elements that must be proven to obtain a conviction for that crime. This specificity has not always existed, however.

As I said earlier, the Romans and others had general codes of law that embodied what most people understood as right and wrong. But with the development of courts and trials, the real source of law came to be the decisions handed down in individual cases by the judges, also known as case law. This is the traditional form of law-making that the United States took from England when the new country was formed.

Case Law

Case law consists of decisions judges write after they have heard a case. Such decisions typically set out the judge's reasons for reaching the decision and the facts and prior decisions on which it is based. These decisions are published and serve as legal precedent. Judges facing similar legal issues in the future are guided by earlier decisions on the subject.

Hearsay

Some people think any judge can interpret the law as he or she likes. But courts are not only "guided" by precedent—they are often bound to follow it. Lower state courts must follow the precedents of their state's higher courts, and lower federal courts are bound to follow the precedents of the appellate or appeals court in their circuit or region. All courts are bound by decisions of the United States Supreme Court on issues involving the federal Constitution or federal laws. We look at the different court systems later in this chapter.

If you've ever read a court decision—and I've read thousands—you can probably guess the problem with case law. What rule was the basis for the court's decision? What was its rationale? How does either apply to the current case (and every case is at least a little bit different)? How can we even find other decisions that might be on point? In addition, different judges at one level often issue conflicting decisions, all of which stand until the next-highest court resolves the differences.

Statutory Law

These difficulties with law as defined by individual cases left citizens uncertain of what was legally required of them. And so another source of law developed—statutory law. Statutory laws are often based on case law but ultimately are legislative: elected bodies in the state or federal government set out the law in statutes. Courts are bound to follow statutes, with a handful of important exceptions, such as when the *statute* violates the state or federal Constitution, when a state law contradicts a federal law, or when the procedure followed in the statute's enactment was not proper.

State legislatures and the United States Congress enact statutes. The Patriot Act, passed by Congress in 2001, is a well-known example of a recent federal statute. Government agencies issue *regulations* that set forth the rules and procedures for implementing statutes. Laws enacted by city and county governments are called *ordinances*. All these forms of laws help define elements of the criminal justice system.

Statutes are often organized into *codes* based on subject matter, making it easier to locate and understand them. The Bankruptcy Code and the Tax Code are examples of federal codes. The Criminal Codes of the various states similarly collect or "codify" the definitions or elements of the different crimes, as well as the possible punishments.

def•i•ni•tion

A legislature enacts a **statute,** a government agency promulgates a **regulation,** and a city or county passes an **ordinance.** All have the force of law. A **code** is a collection of statutes on a particular subject matter, such as a criminal code or a bankruptcy code.

Statutory criminal law is constantly changing to stay up-to-date with our rapidly changing society. An example is California's enactment in 1990 of the first statute to define and criminalize stalking behavior. While some criminal laws come from Congress, by far the most come from the states. Because these laws, statutes, and ordinances are enacted at the state, county, and city levels, they can be more accurately tailored for the communities they affect.

The last, but far from least, source of laws governing the criminal justice system is the Constitution of the United States. As I mentioned earlier, the Constitution takes precedence over all other laws, state or federal, and safeguards some of our most precious freedoms.

Applying Federal vs. State Laws

Federal criminal law usually deals with crimes that occur across state lines, involve federal government agencies, or otherwise impact society at a multistate or country-wide level. So using the U.S. Postal Service to commit fraud would invoke federal law because it involves using a federal service to commit a crime. Other examples are bringing drugs into the United States from a foreign country and failing to pay federal income tax. Any crime that involves federal property, such as national monuments or parks, also is a federal crime. The mere crossing of state lines in the course of committing a state law crime doesn't necessarily turn it into a federal crime, but can if it causes a federal criminal statute to become applicable. In that case, both state and federal criminal statutes usually apply and there is dual jurisdiction.

State laws enacted by individual states generally apply only to conduct within that state's borders. For example, conduct that is a crime in Nevada might not be a crime in Michigan. Usually, the differences lie in the specific wording of the elements of the crime. For example, theft is a crime in all states, but the precise monetary dividing line between misdemeanor theft and felony theft varies from state to state.

Sometimes both federal and state laws apply to the same conduct. This can produce some fascinating questions of whether the federal law preempts the state's law—fascinating, that is, to lawyers and perhaps the accused. For our purposes, let's stick with the basics: federal law takes precedence if the state's law conflicts with it or if the federal statute says it supplants the state's laws on the subject. Otherwise, both apply, which usually happens when the state law goes beyond the federal law, such as by imposing greater restrictions or harsher sentences.

The Courts of the Criminal Justice System

Hand in hand with the question of whether state or federal criminal laws apply is the question of what court system will hear the case. Within the criminal justice system are two separate and independent court systems, each with different judges, courthouses, prosecutors, procedures, evidentiary rules, and so on. The two systems come together in basically one place: the very top. The United States Supreme Court hears appeals from both systems. Yet for all the differences between the court systems, far more similarities exist, as we'll see.

State Courts

State courts hear cases in which a violation of a state law or the state Constitution has occurred within state lines. Since the bulk of criminal laws are state laws, most criminal trials are heard in state courts. A case begins with a trial in the lowest state court, usually called a district, superior, circuit, municipal, or simply trial court. This is where the prosecutor and defense attorneys examine witnesses, present physical evidence, have expert witnesses testify, and argue the facts of the case to the judge and jury. The judge instructs the jury in the law, and the jury then decides whether the evidence proves that a crime has been committed. If so, the judge convicts and sentences the defendant.

A defendant convicted at the trial court level may appeal that conviction to the next court level, generally called a court of appeals. In the appeal, the convicted defendant generally may not reargue the facts of the case, but must show that some error of law or procedure made the conviction improper. Examples of such errors include evidence that should have been excluded, an error in the judge's instructions on the law to the jury, and juror misconduct.

> ### Hearsay
>
> An appeal isn't a "do-over." The trial court determines the facts of the case, and the appellate court doesn't reconsider them unless there was virtually no evidence to support them. This is the major difference between trial and appellate courts—the trial court is concerned with the facts and the law, and the appellate court is concerned only with the law. For this reason, there are no witnesses or juries at the appellate level.

If the intermediate appellate court concludes that some legal error arose during the trial court proceeding, it may send the case back to the trial court for a complete or partial retrial. Or the intermediate court may overturn the lower court's decision completely and enter a judgment of not guilty. This occurs primarily when the appellate court concludes that some critical piece of evidence, such as a confession, should have been excluded, and without it, there isn't sufficient evidence to convict the defendant.

The next and highest level in the state court system is also a court of appeals, generally called the state's supreme court. Whereas each state has several intermediate courts of appeal spread across the state, each state has only one supreme court. A defendant has the right to appeal a conviction to the first court of appeals, but may only request an appeal to the state's supreme court. The supreme court itself decides which appeals it will hear. Why?

The functions of the two courts of appeal—the intermediate court and the supreme court—are related but different. The role of the intermediate court is to ensure that every conviction is re-examined (if the defendant chooses) by a second court, to be as sure as possible that the right law and legal procedures were applied.

The role of the supreme court, on the other hand, is to provide an additional level of review when particularly important legal issues are involved, and to resolve differing or evolving interpretations of the law among the intermediate appellate courts. If a request for review to the state supreme court is denied, the decision of the intermediate court of appeals becomes final—as far as the state court system is concerned, at least.

One final level of review is possible for state court cases: the United States Supreme Court. For most such cases, the United States Supreme Court has the discretion to decide whether to hear the appeal. For some cases, however—those in which the defendant claims his conviction violated the U.S. Constitution—Article III of the U.S. Constitution mandates that the Court must hear the appeal.

One famous example of such a state court case is that of Clarence Earl Gideon. In 1962, the 51-year-old Gideon was in a Florida jail cell, convicted of breaking and entering. In pencil, he wrote a letter to the United States Supreme Court arguing that his conviction violated the U.S. Constitution because he didn't have a lawyer to defend him—his request that the state appoint one, since he couldn't afford one himself, had been denied. The Supreme Court agreed with Gideon, and the right to counsel has become a hallmark of both the federal and state criminal justice systems ever since.

Federal Courts

When a federal criminal law or the U.S. Constitution is violated, the case enters the federal court system. Like the state court system, the federal system is organized into three levels of courts. The trial court is known in the federal system as the district court. The second level, the intermediate court of appeals, is called simply the United States Courts of Appeal. These appellate courts are geographically organized into 13 groups called circuits.

For the Record

The largest by far of the 13 federal circuits is the Ninth Circuit, which hears appeals from federal district courts in California, Idaho, Montana, Nevada, Oregon, Washington, Hawaii, Arizona, and Alaska, as well as from the territories of Guam and the Northern Mariana Islands. When Congress formed the Ninth Circuit in 1891, it contained only 3.3 percent of the country's population; it now contains more than 19 percent.

As in the state court system, the United States Courts of Appeal have no juries and do not review the facts as found in the district court. Instead, judges usually sit in panels of three to review the law and procedures followed at the trial, as in the intermediate level of the state court system.

Requests for review of United States Courts of Appeal decisions go to the United States Supreme Court and are separated into the same two categories as those from the state courts. Cases in which the defendant claims the conviction violated the United States Constitution are heard as a matter of right; all others are heard according to the Supreme Court's discretion.

Hearsay
How often have you seen a lawyer or defendant glare into the TV or movie camera, shake a fist, and declare, "We'll take this all the way to the Supreme Court if we have to!" The fact is, the defendant or lawyer rarely controls this. Most cases do not meet the requirements to be heard as a matter of right, and the Supreme Court's caseload allows it to accept only a very small percentage of the many cases that request discretionary review.

The United States Supreme Court currently consists of nine judges. They and the judges of the state supreme courts are the only judges referred to as "justices." The decisions of the United States Supreme Court are the highest law of the land—at least, temporarily. The Court's interpretations of the U.S. Constitution can be altered, but only by a constitutional amendment or a later decision of the Court itself. However, the Court's interpretation of a state or federal statute may be altered simply by passing a new law.

An early example of a Supreme Court decision that was altered by constitutional amendment occurred in response to the Court's 1793 decision is *Chisholm* v. *Georgia*. The Court held that the individual states did not have the same immunity from suit (called "sovereign immunity") as the federal government did. The states quickly responded with the Eleventh Amendment, deleting such cases from the jurisdiction of the inhospitable federal courts.

Special State Criminal Courts

Juvenile courts were developed at the end of the nineteenth century to handle issues involving juvenile offenders and neglected and abused children. Juvenile courts are part of the state court system, and state statutes designate the age limit for "juveniles." In most states, the juvenile age limit is 18 years, although a few states set the age at 16 years. The juvenile court can decide that a case should be tried in a regular state court, even if the defendant is technically a juvenile. Otherwise, the juvenile court tries the case and determines the verdict. The main difference between juvenile court and regular trial court is the degree to which juvenile courts focus on rehabilitating minors instead of punishing them.

Traffic courts are another specialized court that operates at the city or municipality level. The only purpose of traffic court is to hear cases about traffic tickets. Most of us just pay the fine, but we have the right to go to traffic court to contest the charge. For some serious citations, appearing in court is mandatory. For example, a DUI citation mandates a court appearance and will probably be heard in a regular court instead of traffic court.

The Three Basic Elements of Every Crime

We all have a basic understanding of what a crime is—killing someone, stealing something, assaulting someone, things like that. In our criminal justice system, however, the precise definition of a crime really matters.

First, both the U.S. Constitution and fundamental fairness require clear notice to people of what conduct is prohibited, before an individual may be deprived of his liberty—and maybe life—for engaging in it.

Second, before the defendant may be convicted, the prosecutor must prove all the parts of the definition and the jury must find the defendant guilty. If proof of just one element of the crime is missing, it doesn't matter how strong the evidence of the other elements is—the defendant must be found not guilty.

Various state statutes may define the same crime a bit differently, but three general elements are part of every definition of a crime:

- ◆ Act
- ◆ Intent
- ◆ Causation

First, there must have been some kind of prohibited act. This is important because it means that you can't commit a crime simply by thinking something—you must actually act. You can dream about stealing your neighbor's BMW and cruising with the top down all you want. But unless you actually steal it, or do something in preparation to steal it, you probably haven't committed a crime.

For the Record _____

It is much more common to see crime as an action rather than a failure to act. Failure to act can be criminal, but only when there is some legal duty to act. Examples include a parent failing to protect a child from starvation or exposure, or a company misleading investors by not correcting misinformation in its prospectus.

Second, there has to be criminal intent or a "guilty mind." The criminal justice system refers to this element as the *mens rea* of the crime. This term is taken from a Latin phrase that, loosely translated, says "the act does not make a man guilty unless the mind also is guilty." The level of criminal intent often determines not only the kind of crime, but also the sentence for a conviction.

Determining intent requires peering into the defendant's mind, and this is always a troublesome part of the prosecutor's burden of proof. However, the criminal justice system isn't about punishing people who accidentally commit wrongs. It seeks to punish, and thus deter, intentional wrong-doing. Of course, we will see in later chapters exactly what "intentional" means varies depending on the crime.

Specific intent applies when the defendant purposely intended the result of the crime. For example, first-degree murder requires the specific intent to kill the victim. *General intent* requires the defendant to intend to commit an act and either know or not care that the act would likely cause injury to the victim.

Objection

Confusing intent with motive is easy. Motive is the reason someone commits a crime. Intent is the mental decision to commit the crime. To take an example from the headlines, Scott Peterson's intent was to murder his wife, Laci Peterson; his motive was apparently to free himself from his marriage.

Criminal negligence is extreme carelessness rather than intent. It occurs when the defendant exercises an unintentional but extreme lack of care toward the harm that will probably result from his actions.

Strict liability requires no intent or mental state. If you do the prohibited action, you're guilty—period. This applies to crimes such as traffic offenses and bigamy. For example, you may not have noticed the stop sign as you drove past it, but you will still get a ticket.

Causation is the last of the three basic elements in almost every definition of a crime. The prohibited act must have actually caused the harm to the victim. If something intervenes that prevented the harm, no crime occurred. If something intervenes that itself caused the harm instead of the defendant causing harm, no crime occurred.

For example, let's say that a husband wants to kill his wife's lover, so he cuts the brake lines of the lover's car one night. The next day, the lover pulls out of his driveway without looking or even trying to brake and is T-boned by a bus and dies. If the jury finds that the sole cause of the death was the lover's careless driving, that act intervenes. The chain of causation between the husband's action and the lover's death has been broken, and the husband cannot be convicted of murder.

As we will see as we dig more deeply into the criminal justice system and the elements of individual crimes, such distinctions matter. They can affect the defendant's guilt or innocence, the sentence, and even whether that person lives or dies.

The Least You Need to Know

- The civil justice system allows individuals to obtain reimbursement from those who injure them; the criminal justice system seeks to protect all citizens by deterring crime with convictions and punishments for those who commit crimes.

- One key difference between the civil and criminal justice systems is that the former requires proof by a "preponderance of the evidence," while the latter requires proof by the much higher, "beyond a reasonable doubt" standard.

- The federal and state court systems are separate and distinct. The former handles federal crimes, and the latter handles state crimes.

- Both court systems have a lower court where trials take place, an intermediate appellate court that reviews challenges to the procedures and laws applied in the trial court, and a supreme court that generally has discretion to chose the cases it reviews.

- The definition of virtually every crime includes three elements: an act, an intent, and causation.

Chapter 2

Categories and Classifications of Crimes

In This Chapter

- ◆ Different severities of crime
- ◆ Different kinds of crime
- ◆ Different kinds of criminals
- ◆ Classification by intent: *mens rea*

Let's start this chapter with a little history, with a dash of Latin thrown in for fun. Don't worry—this won't be on the test.

Historically, there were two main classes of crimes: *mala in se* and *mala prohibita*. Mala in se crimes were those considered evil or inherently wrong. *Mala in se* means literally "wrong in and of itself" or wrong "per se." (See? You already knew some of that Latin!) These crimes usually involved a high level of vileness, depravity, physical violence, or dishonesty. Examples include murder, rape, robbery, and arson.

Mala prohibita crimes, on the other hand, were acts made criminal not so much because they were evil, but because the government or courts considered the conduct inappropriate for an ordered society. Examples of mala prohibita crimes included recklessly shooting an arrow into the air (without aiming at anyone), using illegal drugs, and gambling.

Today life is not so simple. The criminal justice system has many different classes of crimes based on such factors as the severity of the harm; the perpetrator's intent or degree of preplanning; and who or what is harmed: people, property, society, and so on. Understanding this classification system is essential to understanding our system of justice.

Classification by the Severity of the Crime

Not all crimes are viewed as equally serious, based on the law—or as viewed by the general public. Even within one category of crime, there is often a continuum from less serious to more serious. Take theft, for example. Is there a difference between shoplifting a jar of baby food, stealing a car, robbing a bank, and bilking thousands of investors in a fraudulent investment scheme? All involve theft and all are criminal, but most of us feel there are differences among them—and so does the law. Classifications try to capture those differences.

There are three general categories of crimes: infractions, misdemeanors, and felonies. Infractions are the least serious. They are punishable by fines only, not jail time, and the fines are usually less than $1,000. Examples of infractions include traffic tickets, citations for disturbing the peace, and citations for possessing less than an ounce of marijuana (in California, at least).

Misdemeanors are a step up in severity and can involve jail time, as well as fines for punishment. Jail time for a misdemeanor, however, is generally less than a year and is served at a local county jail instead of a state prison. Common misdemeanors include petty theft (usually less than $500), driving under the influence, and simple assaults and batteries.

For the Record _____

County jails are temporary holding places for people either serving light jail terms or awaiting trial. State prison is where persons convicted of felonies are incarcerated, for periods up to their entire lives. Because of the longer sentences, prisons have some amenities that jails lack, such as religious facilities, exercise areas, libraries, educational facilities, and computer areas.

Felonies are the most serious category of crimes and are punishable by higher fines, longer sentences, and even death. Jail time is from a minimum of one year up to life, and is served at a state or federal prison instead of a local county jail. Although the fines for felonies are usually higher than for misdemeanors, the length of the prison sentence most clearly distinguishes felonies from misdemeanors. Examples of felonies include murder, rape, arson, burglary, and larceny.

The prosecutor can charge a few crimes, called *wobblers*, as either a misdemeanor or a felony. Typical factors considered by the prosecutor in making this choice include the gravity of the victim's injury or property loss, and the accused's criminal record. This charging discretion is discussed more in Chapter 11.

def•i•ni•tion

Wobblers are crimes that can be charged as either a misdemeanor or a felony, at the discretion of the grand jury or the prosecutor.

Classification by the Nature of the Crime

Another way the criminal justice system categorizes crimes is by the nature of the crime: against whom or what is it targeted, and what kind of harm results? Let's look at the major such categories of crime.

Crimes Against Persons

Crimes against persons are usually easy to identify: murders, rapes, kidnappings, assaults, and other people-on-people crimes. These are the crimes that tear at our heart, bring shivers to our spine, and twist our gut—even when we encounter them in a TV show or movie, let alone in real life. Crimes against people are often the most disturbing to law-abiding citizens. How could one human being be so callous or cruel to another? Can such a person ever really be rehabilitated?

Although homicide, assault, and rape make up the traditional cornerstones of crimes against persons, modern life and our modern criminal justice system have expanded the category. Now included are such crimes as child abuse, domestic violence, elder abuse, stalking, and *hate crimes*.

def•i•ni•tion

A **hate crime** is any crime motivated by an intent to target persons in a particular class, such as race, religion, gender, national origin, sexual orientation, handicap, and so on. A hate crime is not itself a distinct crime, but rather escalates the sentence for the underlying crime.

Since the category of crimes against persons seems so clear, it is a good place to note that drawing the line between categories of crimes is not always easy. Take carjacking as an example: carjacking is the theft of an occupied car. Some people would argue that the purpose of a carjacking is to steal the car and, thus, that it is a crime against property. Others might just as reasonably emphasize that the removal of the occupant, often forcefully, is necessary to achieve this purpose, so carjacking is a crime against a person. The bottom line is that it is a crime against property only when the property is taken without causing fear or using duress or other acts against the will of the victim.

For the Record

Many police stations organize detectives by specific "tables" separated by types of crime. However, the "tables" classification at the police station is not necessarily the same as the "textbook" categories discussed here. For example, the Los Angeles Police Department classifies Major Assault Crimes and Robbery/Homicide as separate units. The Santa Monica Police Department separates by type of victim, such as Juvenile Crimes, Domestic Violence, and Gangs.

Crimes Against Property

Modern crimes against property stem from the historical crime of larceny. Larceny, simply defined, is taking property from its owner without the intent to return it. Again, the complexity and developing technology of current society has required a modernization of the concept of larceny. Today many more things are recognized as "property"—and there are many more ways for criminals to "take" it.

We now recognize, for example, a variety of intangibles as property, such as our identities, the privacy of our medical records, and a business's trade secrets and trademarks. Criminal law also recognizes the rapidly expanding category of "paper" and electronic property, or property that represents or allows access to money or other property. Such property includes bank checks and account information, ATM cards, and credit or debit cards. This has led to "paper cases" such as tax fraud, health insurance or Medicare fraud, identity theft, immigration and other documentation forgery, and welfare fraud.

Also included in the category of crimes against property are *white-collar crimes.* This is a catchall category for a bundle of nonviolent business crimes. These vary from deliberate evasion of expensive regulatory requirements to false financial statements, Medicare fraud, money laundering, and securities fraud.

def•i•ni•tion

A crime can be considered a **white-collar crime** for one of two reasons. One is that the type of offense is associated with business activities. The other is that the perpetrator is of a high socioeconomic status; occupies a position of trust; or is a business, professional, or academic person.

Crimes Against Habitation

Crimes against habitation are an offshoot of crimes against property. The most common examples are burglary, arson, and vandalism. Although these crimes are targeted at property and so might be considered crimes against property, they also threaten the security and privacy of the persons living in the targeted property. Even if the inhabitants escape physical injury, they often experience traumatic feelings of insecurity, invasion, and violated privacy.

Crimes Against Society

Crimes against society are also referred to as crimes against public order and safety. An extreme example is terrorism, which the Federal Criminal Code defines as violent or life-threatening criminal acts intended to intimidate or coerce the population or the conduct of the government. Other crimes that fall under this category include rioting, loitering, vagrancy, pornography, drug use, and use of firearms.

Crimes against society often require balancing the safety of society with constitutional freedoms such as the First Amendment's right of peaceable assembly and free speech. For example, in 1957, the Supreme Court decided to protect society by ruling that obscene materials are not protected under the First Amendment as free speech:

> *Congress shall make no law respecting an establishment of religion, or prohibiting the free exercise thereof; or abridging the freedom of speech, or of the press; or the right of the people peaceably to assemble, and to petition the government for a redress of grievances.*

As our society develops and new social phenomena appear, laws and court rulings shift to maintain the balance between individual freedoms and public safety. For example, 16 years after the obscenity case, the Supreme Court looked at the issue again. This time it decided that a new definition of obscenity was needed, to make the distinction between free speech and obscenity more workable.

Crimes Against Justice

Crimes against justice either disrupt or corrupt the justice system. Some of these crimes, such as contempt and perjury, take place in court. Contempt, or contempt of court, is an actual ruling after someone disrespects the court or fails to obey a court order. Perjury is a crime against justice because it is lying after taking an oath to tell the truth in some aspect of a civil or criminal justice proceeding. A witness can commit perjury in court during testimony, or outside court if creating a written statement.

Some crimes against justice occur outside court. Paying off public officials, or bribery, is one of these crimes, as is obstructing justice. Obstruction of justice can take many forms, such as keeping a witness from testifying. Other crimes against justice include resisting arrest and escaping from custody. Ultimately, any action that attacks the honesty, effectiveness, and dignity of administering justice is a crime.

Victimless Crimes

Victimless crimes are those in which a law is broken but no one is considered to have been harmed by it. Probably the most common victimless crime is a traffic violation. It could be argued that violating traffic laws is a crime against society because it creates a hazard. In fact, many victimless crimes might also be considered crimes against society.

Sometimes a crime is victimless because the only person impacted is the person breaking the law. Drug use, gambling, and prostitution are often talked about as victimless crimes, but in reality, the impact of these crimes reaches far wider, affecting families, business associates, and society as a whole.

Another kind of victimless crime happens when breaking the law is consensual. For example, some states still have laws prohibiting homosexuality. Engaging in consensual homosexual relations would be considered a crime in those states, but it would be victimless because no one was harmed.

Classifications of the Criminal Actor

The "criminal" or "perpetrator" is, of course, the person or persons who actually committed the crime. These are called the principals of the crime. But things get trickier when other persons assist but do not actually participate in the commission of the crime, or when a corporation gets thrown into the mix. For each crime, any number of people other than the principals may have some responsibility.

Accomplices are often what the law calls "accessories before the fact." Such a person may assist in the preparations for the crime, aid or facilitate the actions of the principles, or give them necessary approval for the commission of the crime. An accessory before the fact is liable for the crime just like the principal who commits it.

> **Hearsay**
>
> Can a corporation—the entity itself, as distinguished from the officers and executives running it—be guilty of a crime? The answer is yes. But because it is not a person, it can be punished only by fines, not jail time.

Another person who may be liable for a crime despite not personally committing it is someone who solicits or incites the criminal act. A person who hires a hit man to kill another person is an example of one who solicits the crime.

A co-conspirator may also be guilty of the crime committed by the principal. A conspirator is one who forms an agreement with another person to break the law. For example, Charles Manson was convicted of the Sharon Marie Tate and Rosemary LaBianca murders through the joint responsibility rule of conspiracies.

Yet another type of person who may share responsibility for the crime is an "accessory after the fact." Such a person might receive, comfort, or assist the perpetrator in fleeing, covering up the crime or otherwise avoiding prosecution. To share responsibility for the crime, the accessory after the fact must *know* that the person she is assisting committed a crime. The most recent televised example of this is in the case of missing 2-year-old Caylee Anthony. If Caylee's grandmother knowingly assisted Caylee's mom in getting away with the young girl's murder, then the grandmother will also face murder charges.

Classification by Intent: *Mens Rea*

Many people assume that a criminal must specifically intend to do the crime to be guilty of committing it. However, the criminal justice system recognizes various different mental states, or *mens rea*, that may be associated with the commission of a crime: no intent, negligence, recklessness, general intent, and specific intent. The mental state affects what crime has been committed, the "blameworthiness" of the crime, and its punishment.

Not every crime requires that there be an intent to harm or to injure someone, or even negligence. Sometimes the very act of doing something can make the person liable for a crime. This is called strict liability, or liability without fault on the part of the actor. An example of a strict liability crime is selling alcohol to a minor. Regardless of whether the person selling the liquor knew the customer was a minor, was negligent in failing to check, or had no reason to suspect that the customer was underage, the very act of selling alcohol to the minor is enough to hold the seller criminally responsible.

def•i•ni•tion

Mens rea is the mental state or level of intention with which a crime is committed.

These mental states are a necessary part of criminal responsibility:

- **Specific intent**—carrying out an act with the goal of achieving a specific harm.

- **General intent**—comes into play when there is a general awareness that a certain act could cause harm, but a specific harm or outcome is not contemplated.

- **Malice**—arises when an act is done intentionally, with reckless disregard for the harm or outcome that may result.

- **Criminal negligence**—is involved when a perpetrator recognizes that his actions may result in a crime but still does the act, with a gross lack of care or disregard for the potential harm.

- **Strict liability**—arises when there is no requirement for an awareness of the factors that would constitute crime.

Summary of Mens Rea, or Intent Required for Major Crimes

Specific Intent	General Intent	Malice	Criminal Negligence	Strict Liability
Solicitation	Rape	Arson	Involuntary manslaughter	Statutory rape
Conspiracy	Mayhem			
Attempt	False imprisonment		Battery	Bigamy
First-degree murder				Selling alcohol to a minor
Assault				
Burglary				
Larceny				
Robbery				
Embezzlement				
False pretenses				
Fraud				

The prosecutor has the burden of proving the required *mens rea*, or mental state of the crime, just as he or she must prove all the other elements of the crime. Because the mental state of the accused is inherently subjective, it can be difficult to prove and is often a part of the prosecutor's case that the defense challenges.

Consider an example of when it can be difficult to prove intent. Burglary requires that the person breaking into the house intends to commit a felony once inside. If nothing is actually missing, however, it can be difficult for the prosecutor to prove that the defendant intended to commit the felony of stealing something. Similarly, larceny is theft with the intent to permanently deprive the owner of the property. Again, it can be

Objection

It is easy to confuse motive with *mens rea*, but they are two different concepts. Motive is the reason for committing the crime, whereas *mens rea* is the mental state or degree of intention with which it is committed.

hard for the prosecutor to prove this intent if the defendant has a plausible claim that she planned to give the property back at some point.

The Least You Need to Know

- ◆ Crimes are classified by their severity into infractions, misdemeanors, and felonies.

- ◆ Crimes are further classified by the harm they cause, such as harm to a person, to property, or to society.

- ◆ Responsibility for a crime rests not only with the person who commits it, but also with people who incite or assist in the crime or in preventing arrest and prosecution.

- ◆ An element of each crime is the mental state, or *mens rea*, with which it is committed.

Part 2

Elements of Specific Crimes

Now that we know how the criminal justice system is organized, it's time to hit the streets and see what the system deals with—crimes. The criminal justice systems sets very specific elements for each crime, and each element must be proven before an accused may be convicted of the crime. Not just the act matters—also relevant is the intent behind the act, as well as the victim, the location of the act, and even the time of day it occurs.

We start with crimes against persons: murder, rape, assault, abuse in all its forms, stalking, and more. Then we delve into crimes against property—burglary, larceny, embezzlement, identity theft, and so on. (Did you know, for example, that you can be guilty of burglary without stealing anything?) Next, we cover crimes against society (like drug trafficking and drunk driving) and crimes against justice (like bribery and perjury).

Crimes Against Persons: Homicide

In This Chapter

◆ When is a homicide murder, and when is it manslaughter?

◆ The different levels of murder

◆ The different levels of manslaughter

◆ How the criminal justice system defines life and death

No crime intrigues people more than murder. Murder is the basis for most mystery novels, TV cop shows, and crime movies. A new murder usually becomes the headline story on the local evening news. People are fascinated with what makes people kill, how they kill, how they're caught, and what punishment they get.

Homicide, speaking generally, is the unlawful killing of another person. As with many general categories of crime, however, the criminal justice system breaks down the general crime into many specific subcategories. Each is different, with certain elements that the prosecutor must prove and specific consequences for the defendant if convicted. Explaining the different kinds of homicides in our criminal justice system is the goal of this chapter.

The Difference Between Murder and Manslaughter

What separates murder from manslaughter is what the law calls "malice afore-thought." Given that the penalties for murder can be much more severe than for man-slaughter, this is a very important concept in our criminal justice system.

Hearsay

Malice aforethought, as it is used in the criminal justice system, does not always require malicious intent to do evil or cause harm, as one might expect from the common mean-ing of the term. For example, Michigan physician Dr. Jack Kevorkian clearly had good intentions and a "kind" heart when he assisted terminally ill patients to commit suicide, yet under the law, he had malice aforethought and was convicted of murder.

In the criminal justice system, several different forms of malice aforethought are rec-ognized as sufficiently heinous to be worthy of a murder conviction:

◆ Intent to cause death or great bodily harm

◆ Knowledge that death or great bodily harm will occur

◆ A gross indifference to the value of human life

◆ A death that follows a person's intent to commit a felony

When a person has intent to cause death to another person, he clearly has demon-strated malice—even if he bears no personal malice toward his victim. For example, a gang member who shoots a rival gang member because it is a rite of gang membership has acted with the intent to cause death or great bodily harm, even if he did not per-sonally know the victim.

Similarly, a person who shoots a gun in the middle of a crowded mall during the holiday season may not have specifically intended to kill anybody, but he definitely had knowledge that his act would cause another person's death or great harm. And if he fires wildly, without aiming, he is acting with a gross indifference to the value of human life. In these examples, malice aforethought is present—unless it can be shown that the act of killing was justified (self-defense) or excused (insanity).

Murder by the Numbers

Most states separate the law of murder into first and second degrees. However, each state determines its own murder law based on unique laws and statutes. Therefore, a few states (Minnesota, for example) have more than two degrees of murder.

The significance of separating murder into degrees is in the sentencing. In many states, a first-degree murder conviction exposes the defendant to the risk of the death penalty. Therefore, for the defendant, this distinction can literally mean the difference between life and death.

First-Degree Murder

What distinguishes first-degree from second-degree murder is whether the murder is "willful, deliberate, and premeditated." The "willful" and "deliberate" parts are usually easy to prove—that the person intended to kill is enough.

So the question of whether a killing is a first-degree or second-degree murder often turns on whether the person killed with "premeditation." *Premeditation* is the mental state of cool and deliberate thought about the murder, hence the expression "cold-blooded killer."

A *capital murder* is a first-degree murder that qualifies for capital punishment—the death penalty. These involve not only all the elements for first-degree murder, but also certain aggravating circumstances as defined by the state's penal laws. Such aggravating circumstances may include the death of a public official, multiple killings, and murders coupled with particularly heinous circumstances such as torture.

def•i•ni•tion

Premeditation is a concept with many names in the criminal justice system. Law books, penal codes, and statutes may refer to it "purposeful," "knowing," "deliberate," or "with intent." All reflect the premeditation required for murder in the first degree.

Hearsay

A person who has a premeditated mind-set is generally assumed to have spent more time and thought in planning the murder than a person who commits a killing with only malice. Whether this is actually true is debatable; in some states, just pulling a trigger is sufficient to be considered a premeditated act. Therefore, a person who kills someone, even if it is as fast as the blink of an eye, is considered to have killed with premeditation.

Second-Degree Murder

Second-degree murder is any murder with malice aforethought but without the "willful, deliberate, and premeditated" mind-set of first degree murder. An easy way to think about it is the way a prosecutor often does. First, I ask whether there was malice aforethought—that puts it in either the murder or manslaughter category. If there was malice aforethought, I ask whether there was premeditation, which separates first- from second-degree murder. Finally, I ask whether there were aggravating circumstances, which makes it a capital murder.

Felony Murder

Do you remember that one kind of malice aforethought I listed was "a death that follows a person's intent to commit a felony"? This is a particularly unusual form of malice aforethought because it may apply even when the killing is completely unintentional.

Felony murder applies when someone is killed in the course of an attempt to commit a dangerous felony. For example, if a gang robs a bank and flees in a high-speed car chase (yes, it's probably on a Los Angeles freeway and on TV), the driver and the rest of the gang will be liable for felony murder if their car crashes into and kills an innocent motorist. Even though no one in the gang intended to get into a high-speed chase, and certainly didn't intend to kill the innocent motorist, the law considers each member of the gang responsible for felony murder.

A number of states place one or both of two limitations on the felony-murder rule. The first is that the felony must be dangerous, either inherently or under the facts of a particular case. Examples of inherently dangerous felonies are armed robbery and assault with a deadly weapon—the very nature of these felonies makes them dangerous. In contrast, a court could hold that a person who commits the felony of grand theft by stealing $5,000 worth of jewelry from a purse left on the ground was not engaging in a dangerous felony, and so is not responsible for felony murder when a bystander is later killed while the suspect was fleeing from the police.

The second limitation some states apply is the independent felony rule, meaning that the felony must be independent of the killing. In the previous example of the gang robbing the bank, the robbery felony was independent of the killing of the innocent motorist during the subsequent chase. Here's another example: suppose the gang threatens the customers in the bank with their guns, making them lie on the floor.

The bank guard tries to draw his gun and is fatally shot. One of the customers lying on the floor has a heart attack due to the stress and dies. The killing of the guard was part of the armed robbery and so cannot support a felony murder charge; the death of the customer from a heart attack was not a part of the robbery felony and so can support a charge of felony murder.

For the Record

Think my heart attack example is farfetched? It's based on a 1969 California case, *People* v. *Stamp*. You might ask why it matters whether the perpetrators are charged with committing murder during the felony, or felony murder. In some jurisdictions, felony murder can elevate a second-degree murder to first-degree murder. And it might matter a lot to the rest of the gang: if killing the guard were felony murder, they would all be liable; if it were not felony murder, only the shooter would be liable for the guard's murder.

Voluntary, Involuntary, and Vehicular Manslaughter

Manslaughter is the killing of another person without malice aforethought. Manslaughter is a different *crime* from murder, not merely a different degree or category of murder. Manslaughter is not broken up into degrees like first- and second-degree murder. Instead, it is usually divided among voluntary, involuntary, and vehicular manslaughter.

Voluntary Manslaughter

The best way to view voluntary manslaughter is to think of it as a killing that would be first-degree murder except that it was committed in response to some sort of provocation on the part of the victim—in other words, an in *the heat of passion* killing. To prove provocation, the defendant must show that his emotional state was provoked or caused by the person killed, and that there was no cooling-off period between the time he was provoked and the time he killed the person.

def•i•ni•tion

A killing in which the victim provokes or pushes the killer into an uncontrollable rage is legally referred to as a killing done under **the heat of passion.**

A person who gets in a brawl with another person and suddenly swings at his adversary after being punched, causing the other person to die from head injuries, commits the killing in the heat of passion. Perhaps the most classic example of heat of passion is a husband who walks in on his wife having sex with another man. If the husband immediately reacts by shooting and killing the wife and/or the lover, he is probably acting under the heat of passion.

The key in concluding that these scenarios are voluntary manslaughter instead of first-degree murder is that the there must be adequate provocation. Most states' criminal justice systems recognize adequate provocation only in certain circumstances:

◆ Mutual combat

◆ An illegal arrest

◆ Serious injury to a relative

◆ The discovery of infidelity

◆ Assault and battery

No matter how outraged or impassioned an individual is, if the provocation that caused that mental state is not one of the listed circumstances, the criminal justice system will not allow the killing to be reduced from murder to manslaughter as a killing committed under the heat of passion.

 Objection _____

Insulting words or gestures can often produce rage, but they are not enough by themselves to be substantial provocation. Similarly, road rage caused by offensive driving rarely, if ever, qualifies as "heat of passion" (and such incidents usually involve time to cool down as well). To qualify as provocation, there must be conduct so severe that a reasonable man would lose the ability to control his actions.

Adequate provocation is negated when a person has time to cool off before he actually kills another person. This cooling-off period is the time the law considers adequate for the passion clouding the person's thinking to clear enough to regain awareness of the consequences of killing another person. If there is adequate cooling-off time, the killing was a deliberate and conscious act, not one driven by mindless passion. It was murder, not manslaughter.

To illustrate this cooling-off factor, let's return to the example of the husband walking in on his wife in bed with another man. If the husband immediately grabs the bedside lamp and uses it as a club to commit the killing, there is no cooling-off period—the crime is manslaughter. However, if he goes back to his car, gets his gun, loads it, returns to the bedroom, and shoots the lovers, then the law is likely to deem he had adequate opportunity to cool down and to appreciate the consequences of his actions. The crime is murder in the first degree, not manslaughter.

Involuntary Manslaughter

Involuntary manslaughter is an unintentional killing that is the result of negligence so severe it is considered criminal. This is not the kind of negligence involved in civil law, which defines negligence as simply the failure to use reasonable care. Criminal

negligence is more. For instance, a person in a crowd of people at a New Year's Eve event who shoots a gun in the air may not intend to hurt anyone. But if someone is killed when the bullet falls back to Earth, the shooter is probably guilty of involuntary manslaughter. His careless disregard for the risk to others is more than mere negligence; it is sufficient to hold him responsible for the unintended killing of another person.

For the Record _____

A killing that occurs in the course of a misdemeanor is a misdemeanor manslaughter, under the same analysis that makes a killing in the course of a felony a felony murder.

Involuntary manslaughter charges usually come up in situations when the risk from carelessness is high, as with vicious animals, use of fire arms or explosives, and medical care. It also comes up when a public service creates a heightened duty of care, such as with buses, trains, and other public transportation services. Involuntary manslaughter is also frequently charged in cases that involve some sort of duty to act, and careless performance of that duty leads to a death. For example, a doctor has a duty to properly care for patient. If her failure to take necessary safety precautions causes the patient's death, she could properly be convicted of involuntary manslaughter.

Vehicular Manslaughter

We all know that driving a car carries the risk of an accident—and serious injury or even death—to ourselves and others. So when should a death caused by operating a motor vehicle be considered vehicular manslaughter? And since I described vehicular manslaughter in Chapter 2 as a "wobbler"—a crime that can be charged as either a misdemeanor or a felony—how is that question answered?

Two factors predominate in answering these questions: whether a driver was under the influence of alcohol or drugs, and whether he was driving with gross negligence, without caution or concern for the safety of others. If there is no DUI, or if the DUI driver was not responsible for causing the accident, it is usually charged as misdemeanor vehicular manslaughter. The result for the defendant is a shorter sentence and confinement in a county jail.

If the fatality was caused by a driver who was both driving under the influence and driving with gross negligence, it can be charged only as a felony. But driving under the influence alone cannot support a charge of felony vehicular manslaughter. Other factors must be present, such as reckless driving, drag racing or engaging in other speed contests, or ignoring the advice of others that one is too intoxicated to drive.

In addition to giving prosecutors discretion in charging, some state criminal justice systems give judges considerable discretion in sentencing when a violation of a vehicle code section has caused a death. A good example is the sentencing of Russell Weller, an 86-year-old man who lost control of his car and plowed into the crowded Santa Monica's Farmers Market in 2003, killing nine people. The jury convicted him of felony vehicular manslaughter. The judge said Weller deserved to go to prison, but at nearly 90 years of age and suffering from heart disease, he would simply be a burden to taxpayers. Instead, the judge sentenced him to five years' felony probation and ordered him to pay over $107,100 in fines and restitution.

Objection _____

A second DUI offense can subject the driver to second-degree murder charges if a death results. The reason: the "consciousness of guilt" theory. The first conviction, by plea or verdict, is deemed to have put the defendant driver on notice that driving under the influence can cause accidents in which people die.

The Definition of Life and Death

The issue of when life begins and when it ends involves political, ethical, and religious concerns—at least. These are extremely important issues—and they are well beyond the scope of this book. Yet, as part of defining when murder occurs, the criminal justice system must define when life begins and ends. So here we go. This subsection isn't about whether the criminal justice has done a good or bad job of defining life and death—it's just about what it has done, to date.

The issue that gets the criminal justice system involved in the question of when life begins is when a fetus is killed. Under most statutes, the homicide laws do not apply to a fetus. The criminal justice system adheres to the view that a fetus is not a human being who can be killed until it is born alive. Case law has routinely held that a woman's exercise of her constitutional right to abortion is not a violation of the state's criminal statutes.

However, the penal codes of some states recognize the fetus as a human being worthy of protection. California's Penal Code Section 187 is an example. It provides, "Murder is the unlawful killing of a human being, or a fetus, with malice aforethought." Section 187 then goes on to list several carefully worded exceptions, including if "[t]he act [of killing] was solicited, aided, abetted, or consented to by the mother of the fetus."

At the other end of the spectrum, all homicide crimes can hinge upon when death actually occurs. One of the biggest legal battles that occurs in courtrooms centers on what event causes a death. For example, if a stabbing victim survives the attack but dies a week later as a result of infection from the wound, is the person who stabbed the person guilty of murder or manslaughter?

When courts must analyze the actual cause of death, courts employ a test known as the "but for" test. The judge asks the jury to answer the following question: "Would the victim have lived but for the defendant's action(s)?" If the answer to that question is "yes," there is sufficient causation to hold the defendant responsible for murder or manslaughter.

Adding to the complexity of this question are modern medical devices and techniques that offer different means of analyzing when death occurs. More states are adopting the "brain dead" standard. Under this standard, death occurs when an electroencephalograph (EEG)—which measures the electrical activity in the brain—reads flat for a given period of time, even if the victim's heart and lungs are still active.

The Least You Need to Know

♦ The key difference between murder and manslaughter is whether there was malice aforethought.

♦ First-degree murder requires premeditation; second-degree murder doesn't.

◆ When an unintended death occurs during the commission of a felony, felony murder may be charged.

◆ Voluntary manslaughter is a killing that would be murder but for the fact the victim provoked extreme passion to kill in the perpetrator.

◆ Involuntary manslaughter involves a killing that results from a high level of carelessness or recklessness.

Chapter 4

Assault and Battery

In This Chapter

- ◆ The difference between assault and battery
- ◆ Simple assault and battery
- ◆ Aggravated assault and battery
- ◆ Hate crimes
- ◆ Gang crimes

We so often hear the terms *assault* and *battery* together in the news or on TV that they seem a single thing, like "rock and roll" or "here and now." Although assault and battery are closely related (and often are charged together), to really understand them, it is important to realize that they are separate and distinct crimes. Battery involves physical contact with the victim, but assault can occur with no contact at all. Battery can occur without assault, and assault without battery.

This chapter delves into the differences in and connections between these two crimes, in both their simple and aggravated forms. We then examine two special categories of crimes that often involve assault and/or battery: hate crimes and gang crimes.

Battery

Although the phrase is "assault and battery," let's begin with battery and then explain its relation to assault.

Historically, battery has been defined as the unlawful application of force to another person. But more recent statutes have expanded the scope of battery beyond the application of force causing bodily injury, to include any intentional, offensive touching of another person. Thus, today battery extends from clubbing someone with a baseball bat to surreptitiously fondling someone on a crowded subway.

Along with the expanded scope of battery in modern statutes has come refinement in the kinds of battery and their punishment. Traditional battery laws grouped together all kinds of batteries. But most state laws today separate batteries by the type of physical contact involved, such as the touching of a sexual battery or a force that causes physical injuries.

Modern statutes also separate batteries based on the relationship between the victim and the batterer. Examples include batteries on peace officers, domestic batteries, elder abuse, child abuse, and sexual assault.

Why draw such fine distinctions, you might ask? Because these separate categories of battery identify circumstances that the criminal justice system considers *aggravating factors*. These specific factors not only have different potential punishments—and can turn a misdemeanor battery into a felony—but also ensure that a defendant's rap sheet (the printout of his criminal history) indicates exactly the type of battery of which he was convicted or charged.

def•i•ni•tion

Aggravating factors are circumstances associated with a crime that increase its culpability under the law and, thus, justify increasing the severity of the punishment. Mitigating factors are the opposite of aggravating factors: they reduce the culpability and can warrant reducing the charge or lowering the sentence.

Batteries that do not have aggravating factors are known as "simple batteries" and are usually charged as misdemeanors. (Since the same aggravating factors apply to both batteries and assaults, we discuss those factors after we cover the two crimes separately.) For a simple battery, the defendant need not have actually intended to cause bodily injury or an offensive contact. If the defendant should have been aware that her actions would cause a battery, that is criminal negligence and is sufficient to commit the crime.

Some states find battery even without the required mental state if the defendant was engaged in an unlawful act at the time he applied force to the victim. For example, imagine that a burglar breaks into a residence intending to steal, is surprised by the occupant, and, without thinking, strikes out and harms the occupant. In addition to the burglary charge, the prosecutor could charge battery. She doesn't need to prove intent to commit a battery for that charge—the intent to commit the larceny is enough.

For the Record

Consent is a clear defense to battery. For example, if my friend tells me to punch him in the stomach to see how hard his abs are, then he has consented to any bodily injury the punch might cause. Implied consent is why football players are not charged with battery when they tackle an opponent during the game, or when a batter is hit by a pitch in a baseball game.

Assault

Two types of assault exist, both closely related to battery. One is an attempt to commit a battery that does not actually result in physical contact. The second is intentionally causing the victim to fear imminent bodily harm. Basically, assault is either trying to commit battery or making the victim think you are about to commit battery.

Both forms of assault require a very specific mental state. For the assault of attempted battery, the defendant must have intended to complete the battery—to illegally touch or apply physical force to the victim. For the assault of intentionally causing fear of imminent harm, the perpetrator must have intended to make the victim believe he was about to be battered—illegally touched or physically harmed.

So just intending to frighten the victim—say, by sneaking up behind him and yelling "Boo!"—does not qualify as an assault because no physical contact was threatened or intended. And unlike battery, criminal negligence or recklessness does not qualify, either; there must be actual intent.

But intent alone is not enough. The criminal justice system does not punish people for having violent thoughts. The offender must take some step toward carrying out the battery in order to be charged with assault. For example, sitting in your living room holding a baseball bat and fantasizing about clubbing the neighbor who cut down your tree is a very violent thought but would not qualify as an assault. However, going over to his yard, swinging the bat, and calling for him to come out and "Get what's coming to you" might very well be assault.

This form of assault—deliberately causing fear of imminent harm in the victim— also requires that the victim have a specific mental state. The victim must have had a reasonable fear of imminent harm. This means the victim must have been aware of the assault. For example, if the offender snuck up behind the victim, pointed a gun at her head, but was scared off by something before the victim knew he was there, there is no assault.

Similarly, there must be an actual and reasonable fear of harm. For example, if the victim sees the defendant grab a gun and point it at her, but the victim knows it's a toy gun, there is no assault because the victim does not fear imminent harm. The victim's apprehension is essential to this kind of assault.

Hearsay

What should the court or jury consider in deciding whether the victim was actually and reasonably apprehensive? Is it enough that the victim says so? Generally, no. The usual standard is whether the circumstances would likely have caused fear of imminent harm in a reasonable person. Mere words, without any action, will normally not suffice.

So as we conclude this tour of the separate crimes of assault and battery, you can see that the reason the two go together like peas and their pod is that a battery is basically a completed assault, and an assault is a not-completed battery.

Aggravated Assault and Battery

As I mentioned, simple assault and battery are treated as misdemeanors, with *simple* meaning that there was little or no injury and no aggravating factors that would warrant escalating the conduct to a felony.

With simple assault and battery, the criminal justice system recognizes that any invasion of one's personal space or threat to one's physical well-being is potentially a crime. But when more is at stake than mere contact, assault and battery can be felonies. Typically, felonious assaults and batteries involve a deadly weapon, the intent to use particularly violent force, or serious bodily injury to the victim.

In addition, misdemeanor battery may become the felony of aggravated battery when it is directed at certain people. For example, an attack on a child or police officer is considered aggravated battery; accordingly, the criminal justice system enforces more severe punishments.

Obviously, using a deadly weapon or violent force in a battery greatly increases the risk of *serious bodily injury* or death. Because of the heightened risk, such batteries are subject to much harsher punishments than your average scuffle between drinking buddies.

def•i•ni•tion

Federal statutes define **serious bodily injury** as involving a substantial risk of death, unconsciousness, extreme physical pain, disfigurement, or impairment. So small cuts, bruising, or other slight injuries would stay in the regular battery category, while more extreme injuries are aggravated battery.

Anything that could kill another person is considered a deadly weapon. This includes guns, knives, automobiles, clubs and other blunt instruments, and even rocks. I even had a case in which a lamp was considered a deadly weapon. How could a lamp be a deadly weapon, you might ask? Well, when the lamp actually causes a death, it qualifies.

Like battery, assault becomes a felony when more serious and violent harm is threatened. For example, if a defendant uses a deadly weapon to intentionally cause fear of harm in the victim, or has the intent to cause serious bodily harm, it is aggravated assault. The intent to rape the victim also raises the crime to aggravated assault.

Objection

Deadly weapons are not just aggravating factors in crimes such as assault and battery. Depending on individual state statutes, wrongful possession of a deadly weapon can be charged as a separate crime, even if the defendant never planned to use it to commit a crime.

Hate Crimes

The term *hate crime* is relatively new terminology for a type of crime that has been around for decades, if not centuries. The Holocaust, Armenian genocide, lynchings in America, ethnic cleansing in Africa, and suicide bombings in the Middle East are all examples of crimes motivated by hatred, and they demonstrate the level of personal and societal devastation that hate crimes can cause. Because of the heightened impact the motivation of hatred can have on the victim and society, all but four states have enacted criminal hate crime statutes.

For the Record _____

Some argue that special penalties for hate crimes are unnecessary because all crimes intend to harm the victim and that intent is already criminalized. Other opponents of hate crimes argue that the law punishes thought rather than conduct, which they argue is inappropriate in a free society.

Basically two forms of hate-crime statutes exist. One is categorized as a crime against civil rights. Any crime in which the offender is motivated by hatred or bias against a *protected class* of people is a hate crime. Federal laws and most states' laws consider race, religion, national origin, and color to be protected classes. About half the states have added sexual orientation and/or physical and mental disability as protected classes under their statutes. A few states also include political affiliation.

def•i•ni•tion _____

Protected classes are groups of people who, because they share a particular racial, cultural, religious, or other characteristic that has historically been the target of discrimination, receive specific protection under the law against such discrimination.

A recent case serves as a legal landmark for the occurrence of hate crimes based on sexual orientation. Matthew Shepard was a gay college student in Wyoming. He died in the hospital after being found beaten and left tied to a fence. In many ways, Shepard's case woke the country to the fact that hate crimes go beyond racial, religious, and gender issues.

The second type of hate crime is any crime that is motivated by hatred for a specific, identifiable group of people. Crimes against the person are all hate crimes when motivated by bias. Murder is a hate crime when the victim is killed merely because of her race. Assault is a hate crime when threats of violence are made because the offender dislikes homosexuals.

Crimes against property can also become hate crimes. Vandalism of a synagogue is a hate crime when perpetrated by an anti-Semite. Destruction of a woman's truck is a hate crime when motivated by misogynous intentions.

It is generally the prosecutor's burden to show that the defendant was motivated by bias or hatred to commit the crime. As with other instances in which the criminal justice system must prove intent (what was in the defendant's head at the time of the crime), such proof can be difficult.

Probably the easiest way to prove the motive behind a hate crime is to show the defendant's membership in a hate group such as the Ku Klux Klan. Motive can also be demonstrated if the defendant visited the websites of hate groups. Other evidence tending to show hate crime intent can include the defendant's own statements and written material found on his person, in his computer, or at his dwelling. Such bits of evidence are often not sufficient in themselves to conclusively show the required motive beyond a reasonable doubt, but each can assist the prosecutor substantially in meeting that burden.

Objection

Notice that the perpetrator's bias makes it a hate crime. Thus, it is still a hate crime even if it turns out that the victim was not actually a member of targeted class.

Some actions beyond typical criminal behavior can also qualify as hate crimes. One of the most quintessential symbols of bias and hatred is cross burning. In many states, the act of burning a cross on another's property is a hate crime. Also intimidating or terrorizing a victim by displaying a symbol like a Nazi swastika is often considered a hate crime. Notwithstanding the constitutional freedom of expression, expressions made with the intent to terrorize can be subject to criminal penalties.

Like crimes unrelated to bias, hate crimes can be either misdemeanors or felonies, depending on the seriousness of the action and the specific statute. For the most part, hate crimes result in enhanced sentences. For example, the sentence for vandalism in a particular state would tend to be greater if the prosecutor could prove that the vandalism was motivated by hatred or bias.

Gang Crimes

According to 2005 statistics, the United States is home to at least 21,500 gangs and more than 731,000 active gang members. Gang-related criminal activity occurs in all 50 states and all U.S. territories. Although most gang activity is concentrated in major urban areas, gangs also proliferate in rural and suburban areas of the country.

Gangs are nothing new—after all, there has always been power in numbers. Early gangs often came together based on nationality or cultural heritage, and some were known as powerful protectors of their neighborhoods. Gangs have historically also engaged in crime. Apart from mob crime, which often included murder, most gang crimes centered on theft and other street crimes.

The gangs we know today began developing about 40 years ago. During this time, larger gangs organized themselves, wearing official gang colors and claiming specific territory. These gangs surged in power and violence when drugs, specifically cocaine, became a valuable commodity. Gangs competed to control the lucrative drug trade, and its money raised the stakes of gang-on-gang violence, bought even deadlier weapons, and pushed gang crime to a whole new level—with an even greater impact on society.

For the Record _____

Even among those who study gang culture, there is little consensus on what distinguishes one kind of gang from another—what makes the Mafia different from an ethnic street gang, or taggers (those who "tag" territory by graffiti) different from bikers? Regardless of the possible psychological or sociological distinctions, the criminal justice system focuses on whether a group with some kind of commonality was involved in committing the crime.

As with hate crimes, the gang-crime classification enhances the sentence for the underlying crime committed. By its nature, a crime committed by a gang impacts not only the victim, but also the social order, so it warrants greater penalties.

But to get the enhanced crime status for a certain crime, the prosecutor must prove that the crime falls within gang activity. To show this, the prosecutor must prove the existence of the gang and prove that the actual perpetrator of the crime is an active participant in the gang.

Proving the existence of the gang is not always as easy as it might seem. Statutes generally define a gang as an ongoing group of three or more persons that uses a common name, sign, or symbol to identify itself, and whose primary activities are committing crimes. Gang experts often explain for the jury the significance of gang names and gang tattoos. They can also testify on the criminality of the gang's primary activities, which can range from burglary to drug trafficking, to murder, to vandalism.

Active participation in a gang means that the defendant knew of the gang's criminal activity and that the defendant promotes or assists other gang members in committing felonies. An interesting aspect of the gang crime category is that the actual crime for which the defendant is charged does not necessarily have to be gang related; it only needs to be committed by a gang member for it to be a gang crime. In other words, the crime can hold no benefit for the gang whatsoever, yet the defendant can still be tried for the enhanced crime.

The criminal justice system and other groups and agencies use things other than convictions and sentences to fight gang activity. Frequent police patrols in areas known for gang activity are used to discourage that activity. Some cities have passed ordinances indicating that they have no tolerance for gangs. And a number of organizations focus on keeping youth out of situations in which joining a gang may seem an attractive option.

The Least You Need to Know

- Assault and battery are separate crimes. Battery involves physical contact, whether violent or merely offensive. Assault usually means deliberately making a person fear for his physical safety.

- Certain aggravating factors can turn a misdemeanor assault or battery into a felony. These factors include using a deadly weapon, causing serious bodily injury, and targeting certain categories of victims, such as the police, children, or the elderly.

- A hate crime is any crime motivated by hatred or bias, usually the race, religion, sexual orientation, or other characteristic of the victim.

- A gang crime is any crime—gang related or not—committed by an active member of a gang. To support a gang-crime charge, the gang must have a name or other identifier and be engaged primarily in criminal activity.

- Conviction of a hate crime or gang crime charge results in an enhanced sentence for the underlying criminal conviction.

Sex Crimes

In This Chapter

- ◆ Sex crimes against adults
- ◆ Sex crimes against children

Few crimes can strike so deeply into a victim's psyche, or cause such lasting psychological damage, as sex crimes can. Yet while it might seem that a sex crime can be simply defined as any sex without consent, the criminal justice system draws many important distinctions in this area.

A sex act may be criminal even if consensual. It may or may not be criminal, based on the age of the victim (whether a child, a teen, or an adult). Furthermore, it may not be criminal at all, despite violating a long-established social taboo. This chapter unravels the web of sex crimes.

Sex Crimes Against Adults

Many people would agree that the most serious sexual crime against an adult is rape. Rape is categorized in two ways: forcible rape and statutory rape. Forcible rape is sexual intercourse that is forced onto a woman. In contrast, statutory rape is sexual intercourse with a female who has not reached the age of consent. Even if the underage female consents to the intercourse, it is statutory rape because of her age.

> ### Hearsay
>
> In most states, the legal definition of rape, read literally, does not apply to female-on-male forced sex. What do you think? If a woman uses force—say, a gun—to compel a man to consent to her sexual desires, should that be rape? In addition, male-on-male forced penetration isn't included in most states' definitions of "rape" either, but is instead classified as sodomy or forced penetration by something other than a penis.

For a rape to occur, there must have been sexual intercourse—an unwanted kiss or even a grope is not enough (although it may be another kind of sexual crime, as discussed shortly). The law is very liberal in how it defines penetration. Penetration can be slight, and the male does not have to emit any semen for it to be considered sexual intercourse.

Other forms of sexual assault—oral copulation, sodomy, and digital penetration—can be as traumatizing as rape. Many states punish these crimes just as seriously as rape. For example, in California, the sentence for forcible oral copulation is the same as for rape: three, six, or eight years in state prison.

Lack of *consent* is another necessary element to any rape charge. Sometimes this element is clear, such as when a woman is attacked at knife point, but the question of consent can also be difficult for a judge or jury to determine. What if a woman is silent? Is that consent or lack of consent? It depends on the circumstances: silence in the face of a threat, for example, satisfies the requirement for lack of consent.

def•i•ni•tion

Most states define **consent** as "the positive cooperation"—not influenced by fear, duress, or illegal substances—"by both parties, where both people can appreciate both the nature of the act and the consequences of the acts they are agreeing to."

Another related issue is whether the woman resisted the sexual attack. The law does not require resistance as evidence of lack of consent, however, if the threat of harm is overwhelming and forces the woman to choose between allowing the sexual intercourse and risking bodily harm.

In what may at first seem like a contradiction, a woman may consent to sexual intercourse, but the law still considers intercourse with her to be rape. These instances usually apply if some mental impairment prevents a woman from giving meaningful consent. For example, a woman who is too intoxicated to think clearly or is under the influence of drugs may be incapable of reaching any meaningful decision about consent. The woman may be responsible for putting herself in that condition, but a man who knows that she is not capable of giving meaningful consent will be liable for rape if he has sexual intercourse with her.

Consent obtained by deception is another area in which the criminal justice system draws a thin but clear line between what is rape and what is not. For example, a doctor may receive consent from a woman to examine her genital area, but he will be culpable for rape if he performs sexual intercourse with her. She has consented to the examination but not to the intercourse. In contrast, if a woman is deceived into consenting to intercourse—say by false promises of love, marriage, or compensation—her consent will be treated as legally effective because she in fact consented to the intercourse. She may have a legitimate civil action for breach of promise or fraud, but no criminal rape has occurred.

Besides rape and specific conduct charges like oral copulation, sodomy, or digital penetration, many states have less serious misdemeanor crimes known as sexual battery. A sexual battery can be charged if a person touches an intimate part of someone's body against that person's will or without consent.

Sex Crimes Against Children

According to FBI statistics in 2007, two out of three sexual abuses are perpetrated against children—teenagers or younger. One out of every five girls will be sexually molested before her 18th birthday, and one out of every six boys will be sexually molested before his 18th birthday. Many resources of the criminal justice system are devoted to combating the crimes of *child sexual offenders*.

Different kinds of "child sexual abuse" are recognized, but all have two basic elements: an adult, someone significantly older than the child, or someone who occupies a position of trust with the child uses the child for sexual stimulation or gratification.

def•i•ni•tion

The term **child sexual offender** refers to anyone who has been convicted of one or more of the child sexual offenses described in this chapter.

Exactly who is a "child" varies somewhat from state to state and from crime to crime, but the cutoff is usually 12 to 17 years of age.

The criminal justice system divides child sexual abuse into three categories: sexual assault, sexual molestation, and sexual exploitation. Let's examine them one by one.

Sexual Assault

Sexual assault involves physical contact—actual touching or other contact. Child sexual assault includes the following crimes when directed at children:

- ◆ **Lewd and lascivious acts**—this describes any sexual touching and is not limited to a child's private area. In fact, any touching that has an aura of "sexuality," regardless of location or the motivation behind it, can be considered lewd and lascivious acts.

- ◆ **Rape**—child rape occurs when a man penetrates a child's vagina.

- ◆ **Sodomy**—this refers to penetration—no matter how slight—of the anus by a penis.

- ◆ **Digital penetration by foreign object**—the vagina or anus are penetrated by something other than a penis.

- ◆ **Oral copulation**—this occurs when one person puts his or her mouth on another person's sexual organ.

- ◆ **Incest**—when there is a specific blood relationship between sexual partners, it is termed incest. In most states, incest is illegal between adults as well as with children.

Sexual Molestation

With sexual molestation, the focus is on the intent of the perpetrator to cause some sexually inappropriate behavior. This includes any act in which an adult engages in behavior that is not necessarily physical but that uses a child for sexual gratification.

One example of child sexual molestation is indecent exposure, in which a person exposes his genitals to others in public. Another example concerns *Peeping Tom statutes*, which involve a person who, while prowling, loitering, or wandering, "peeks" at someone without that person's knowledge to gratify sexual desires and lust.

Sexual molestation is further broken down into two categories: a *preferential child molester* is someone with a permanent fixation or desire to be with children. This is a person who either is *only* sexually attracted to children or is always attracted to children, with adults secondary in appeal. Preferential child molesters usually have many victims, probably more than are ever known or reported.

A *situational child molester* is someone who does not necessarily have a general sexual preference or attraction toward children, but who at some point engages in some sexual act with a child.

For the Record

Mary Kay Letourneau is an example of a situational child molester. Mary Kay—a sixth-grade teacher, married with children—had sex with a 13-year-old male student and served just over seven years in prison as a result. Upon release, she and her former student resumed the relationship, had two children, and ultimately married. Letourneau's unique attraction to the victim, not a general desire to be sexually gratified by children, led to her crime.

Sexual Exploitation

Sexual exploitation occurs when an adult victimizes a child for personal advancement, sexual gratification, or financial profit. Examples of this are creating and trafficking in child pornography, selling children into prostitution rings, exposing children to pornography, and so on.

The crime of "pimping and pandering" is another example of sexual exploitation when it involves children. Pimping and pandering refers to arranging the prostitution of another for money or other gain.

Another egregious form of sexual exploitation is human sex trafficking. Young women from a foreign country are enticed to come to the United States, often with promises of a better future and a chance at the American Dream. Once in the United States, they are physically imprisoned, often beaten or drugged, and otherwise forced to "pay" for their housing, transportation to the United States, and so on through prostitution.

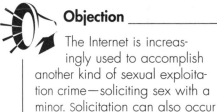

Objection

The Internet is increasingly used to accomplish another kind of sexual exploitation crime—soliciting sex with a minor. Solicitation can also occur on the phone or in person.

Estimates are that between 14,500 and 17,500 women are trafficked into the United States every year. With the passage of the Trafficking in Victims Protection Act in 2000, the federal criminal justice system has made reducing sex trafficking a national priority.

The Role of Consent in Child Sexual Assault

Every state has laws affirming that children under a certain age do not have the *legal capacity* to consent to any type of sexual contact. The laws setting a minimum age for effective sexual consent are similar to the laws setting the minimum age at which a child can make a legally binding contract.

def•i•ni•tion _____

Legal capacity means the ability to make a legally binding decision or act.

One reason these laws set minimum ages for legally binding decisions is that adults have historically taken advantage of the trust and reliance of children to exploit them. Another reason is that sometimes young people do not have the ability to make well-thought-out decisions. They may not truly appreciate the nature and the consequences of their actions.

As noted earlier, individual states set their own precise minimum age for valid consent. The median in the United States falls between 16 and 18 years old. Although actual birth age is one factor in the ability to consent, many states also have adopted "functional age" or "mental age" equivalents that can increase the age of consent. These statutes presume that people who are mentally or emotionally deficient lack the ability to make clear judgments about requests for sex, so predators can take advantage of them.

In cases dealing with children between ages 14 and 17, some states factor in the age difference between the alleged perpetrator and the victim to determine whether sexual abuse has occurred as defined by criminal codes.

Finally, some states have set absolute minimum ages below which a child cannot be considered capable of giving consent, regardless of circumstances or the age difference between the perpetrator and the victim. The cutoff for this type of statute in most states is age 14.

The Least You Need to Know

◆ Forcible rape is intercourse with a woman without her free and voluntary consent; statutory rape is intercourse with consent, but with a woman who is below the minimum legal age for giving consent.

◆ Sexual assault of a child involves actual physical contact of a sexual nature.

◆ Sexual molestation involves a perpetrator causing a child to engage in sexual conduct for the perpetrator's sexual gratification.

◆ Sexual exploitation involves taking advantage of children in sexual ways, such as through child pornography or prostitution.

◆ The minimum age for sexual consent varies by state but is usually between 14 and 16.

Chapter 6

Abuse and Beyond

In This Chapter

- ◆ Abuse between partners
- ◆ Abuse of children
- ◆ Abuse of the elderly
- ◆ Kidnapping, confining and transporting victims
- ◆ Stalking and other threatening behavior

What do the crimes of abuse, kidnapping, and stalking have in common, you might ask? Well, although they certainly have their differences, they and the other crimes we discuss in this chapter have a common element: the attempt to exert coercive control over another person. The control may take the form of neglecting someone who needs care, locking a person in a basement, or using stalking to intimidate someone. Physical force may be part of these crimes, but they primarily involve psychological and emotional coercion, manipulation, and ultimately control.

In many ways, abuse crimes pose special difficulties for the criminal justice system. They are often kept secret, carefully guarded behind closed doors. The intense emotions involved can suddenly and unpredictably explode into violence—even fatal violence. And the coercion that is part of the abuse often prevents the victim from calling the police or, if she does, from pressing charges.

These difficulties have resulted in legislation that gives the criminal justice system special tools for dealing with abuse crimes, including mandated reporting to ferret out abuse and emergency restraining orders in explosive situations.

Domestic Abuse

The term *domestic violence*, also known as intimate partner abuse, can mean different things to a psychologist, a lawyer, a victim, or a victim's advocate. But in the criminal justice systems of the states and the federal government—especially since the passage of the federal Violence Against Women Act in 1994—the crime of domestic abuse has a specific legal definition. The terms of that definition vary somewhat state-to-state, but they usually define domestic abuse as abuse committed against an adult by a spouse, a former spouse, a cohabitant, a former cohabitant, or a person the victim has been dating or engaged to.

For the Record

One example of differences in defining domestic abuse is that some states make any assault by a person who has one of the listed relationships with the victim a felony. Other states require that a visible injury result from the assault for the abuse to qualify as a felony.

One of the greatest difficulties the criminal justice system faces in dealing with domestic abuse is that the cycle of violence and reconciliation in such cases often leads the victim to change her mind about wanting to prosecute. Yet the cycle of violence will usually continue unless some form of intervention takes place, whether via the criminal justice system or through appropriate therapeutic remedies.

Dr. Lenore Walker first identified this cycle of violence and, in 1981, wrote of the three phases in abusive relationships: tension building, acute battering, and loving reconciliation.

In the tension-building phase, arguments and disagreements between the couple intensify, with the abuser increasing his belittling and insulting criticisms of the victim. The criticism may be that she is fat, a bad mother, unattractive, a sloppy housekeeper—whatever plays hardest on the victim's self-esteem. The victim strives harder and harder to become "perfect" for the abusive partner, and usually blames herself for failing. Feelings of shame from that failure and the continuing criticism may cause the victim to withdraw from other social relationships, making her increasingly isolated and more dependent on her abuser.

The growing tension leads to the acute battering phase. The victim may be slapped, shoved, punched, kicked, and so on. The abuser blames the victim for making his violent conduct necessary, often saying "it was her own fault" or "she wasn't living up to the proper expectations" or "she wasn't doing what she was told."

Victims are most likely to call law enforcement during the acute battering phase, and their reports of the abusive circumstances are at their most honest and forthright at that time. But this cooperation with law enforcement is usually short-lived.

During the third phase, loving reconciliation, the victim often changes her mind and decides she doesn't want to press charges against her abuser. In this phase, the abuser campaigns to get the victim back—maybe agreeing to counseling, promising to stop drinking, bringing her flowers and gifts, and apologizing. The more isolated the victim has become from family and friends, the more likely she is to take the abuser back.

As a prosecutor, I have seen abuse victims in the loving reconciliation phase recant, retract, minimize, and deny their statements, while blaming themselves for the abuse they reported while in the acute battering phase. When this happens in the courtroom, the jury is watching the cycle of violence unfold right before their eyes.

To break the cycle of violence, the criminal justice system often must disregard the victim's change of heart and prosecute the case anyway. In nonabuse cases, a prosecutor typically considers a victim's willingness to participate as a factor in deciding whether to pursue the case. But in domestic violence cases, the prosecution must consider that the victim's current reluctance may be due to the cycle of violence, and that the cycle will continue back into abuse unless intervention occurs.

For the Record

The victim's initial statements made to police officers can be used to contradict her later testimony in court if she denies or diminishes the abusive behavior. This is why the criminal justice system has well-trained police officers take the initial report when responding to domestic-violence cases.

Another tool that legislatures have given the criminal justice system for dealing with the potential explosiveness of intimate-partner abuse is the authority to issue emergency restraining orders. Normally, a restraining order (also known as a protective order) can be issued only after notice to the parties affected and a court hearing. But in most states, a police officer responding to a domestic violence call can get an emergency restraining order barring the alleged abuser from any contact with the victim for 24 to 72 hours, or until a permanent restraining order can be secured.

For the Record _____

Yet another tool that helps the criminal justice system combat domestic abuse is the federal Violence Against Women Act. Certain battered noncitizens can use special routes created through the act to gain legal immigration status.

Child Abuse

Child abuse is the physical, psychological, or sexual mistreatment of children. I discuss sexual abuse against children in Chapter 5, so I limit this section to physical and psychological abuse.

Physical abuse to a child is basically any nonaccidental physical injury to a child. This can include hitting, pushing, shoving, slapping, kicking, burning, and so on. Thirty-six states also include conduct that threatens the child's well-being or safety. One highly publicized example of this was Michael Jackson's dangling his infant child over a balcony rail for media photographers. Though no physical injury occurred, there was a substantial risk of harm to the child.

Neglect is probably the most prevalent form of child abuse in our country, making up approximately 55 percent of child abuse cases, according to recent FBI studies. Neglect includes the deprivation of adequate food, clothing, medical care, shelter, and supervision of a child. Seven states (Mississippi, North Dakota, Ohio, Oklahoma, Tennessee, Texas, and West Virginia) also include failure to provide necessary mental health care as a form of neglect.

Objection _____

Although emotional abuse is difficult to define, it is usually easy to prosecute. This is because the emotional abuse is often part of (or caused by) physical, sexual, or neglect abuse, and so is charged along with the accompanying abuse.

Emotional abuse of children is difficult for penal codes to define, yet all states except Georgia and Washington include it as a form of criminal child abuse. Typical language used to define emotional abuse includes "injury to the psychological capacity or emotional stability of the child as evidenced by an observable or substantial change in behavior, emotional response, or cognition," or as evidenced by "anxiety, depression, withdrawal, or aggressive behavior."

Two sets of courts deal with legal issues involving child abuse. The criminal court system tries defendants charged with child abuse and sentences those convicted. Family and dependency courts determine whether, when, and with what supervision a parent whom the court has found abusive can see or be with his child. Family courts can also terminate parental rights in appropriate cases.

Child Protective Services (CPS) is a typical name of the division within a state's or city's local social service agencies that deals most directly with child abuse. CPS is at the center of every community's child protection efforts. In most jurisdictions, CPS is the agency mandated by law to conduct an initial assessment or investigation of reports of child abuse or neglect.

CPS does not work alone. *Mandated reportage* helps CPS uncover and identify hidden abuse. Mandated reportage requires certain professionals to report abuse if they have reason to suspect it, if the victim or someone else tells them about abuse, or if they observe child abuse. The types of persons mandated to make such reports include doctors, teachers, counselors, police officers, and social workers.

> **Hearsay**
>
> Although many think that a patient's communications to his doctor or psychotherapist are absolutely confidential, even these confidential relationships give way to the mandatory reportage laws.

Elder Abuse

Elder citizens are given special protection under the criminal justice system due to their special vulnerability to not only physical and emotional abuse, but also to neglect and financial exploitation. This special vulnerability stems from two things:

- **Isolation**—Many elders live alone, with children who have moved away and contemporaries who are no longer physically able to visit or who have died.

- **Dependency**—Elders often become heavily reliant upon one or two family members, assisted-living services, or home care. This can leave them particularly vulnerable to caregivers, who may siphon off their money, neglect basic care duties, and take advantage of their physical and mental disabilities.

Prosecuting elder-abuse cases can pose particular difficulties for the criminal justice system. Like battered spouses, elders are often reluctant to testify against an accused family member or caregiver. Even more prevalent are the mental and physical problems that affect the ability of the victim to testify. For example, many victims are hearing impaired or blind. Some elders are stroke victims or have Alzheimer's or other medical afflictions that hinder their ability to remember or communicate, much less respond to tough cross-examination.

For the Record

All but eight states impose mandated reportage of elder abuse. As with laws mandating reportage of child abuse, these elder abuse reportage laws make certain professionals who provide services to the elderly criminally responsible if they fail to report an observation, disclosure, or reasonable belief of elder abuse.

Before we leave abuse crimes, let me mention one final tool in the criminal justice system's arsenal for dealing with abuse cases. This tool is based on the system's recognition that relationships with serious problems may need special help, not just jail time for the abuser. Additional forms of sentences, called enhanced sentencing, play a particularly important role in dealing with abuse crimes. Enhanced sentences may include mandatory parenting classes, marriage counseling, and anger-management classes.

Kidnapping and False Imprisonment

The historic kidnapping and murder of Charles Lindbergh's toddler son in the 1930s focused the country's attention and outrage on the crime of kidnapping. As a result, Congress enacted a federal kidnapping statute—popularly known as the Federal Kidnapping Act or sometimes as the Lindbergh Law.

The Lindbergh Law brought the full force of the federal criminal justice system to bear on the crime of kidnapping—whenever the kidnappers crossed a state border with their victim. No longer could the perpetrators evade the police of one state by fleeing to another. Federal law enforcement officers such as FBI agents have national enforcement authority.

While the precise definition of kidnapping varies in federal and state statutes, all contain the following elements: seizing, confining, and carrying away another by force, fear, or deception, or otherwise without their consent.

For the criminal justice system, the key element of kidnapping is generally the "taking away" part. But the system is concerned with more than just a person being taken somewhere he didn't want to go to. What makes the crime of kidnapping so dangerous, and thus worthy of extreme punishment in many states, is when the "taking away" moves the victim from a place of relative safety into danger. The risk created, not the distance of the "taking away," is the central issue in the crime of kidnap.

Consider an example. Suppose a person is dragged by his hand out of his house and down his front steps into his yard. He has been "taken away" against his will, but the difference in risk seems minimal—without more, kidnapping would not likely be charged. However, if a mob outside is screaming for vengeance against the man dragged out, the change in risk would be substantial—and kidnapping might well be charged.

> ### Hearsay
>
> Some people assume that for the crime to be *kid*-napping, a child or "kid" must be involved. While that may explain the origin of the term, kidnapping today applies to anyone taken against his or her will, adults as well as children.

Courts look at these factors to determine whether the necessary increased risk has occurred:

- How long the forced change in location continues

- Whether the "taking away" took place during the commission of another dangerous crime, such as when bank robbers take a hostage with them as they flee, or when a kidnapper rapes his victim

- Whether the "taking away" was an inherent part of another crime, such as when a thief forces someone at gunpoint to an ATM and makes him withdraw money to give to the thief

- Whether the "taking away" otherwise increased the risk to the victim's safety or well-being

 For the Record

Both kidnapping and false imprisonment often occur in the course of other serious crimes. But detaining, restraining, or moving someone at such times almost always greatly increases that person's risk of harm. Therefore, if kidnapping and/or false imprisonment are present, they are charged and prosecuted as separate, additional crimes.

False imprisonment is the act of confining someone to a particular area against her will. False imprisonment and kidnapping often fit together like peas fit into their pod. If something feels like a kidnapping but there is not enough movement to qualify as such, usually it qualifies as false imprisonment.

Basically, the criminal tells the victim by words or deeds, "You are not free to leave." A classic example is when a bank robber herds customers and bank employees to the back of the bank and makes them sit down and stay there until the robbery is over. There may not be enough "taking away" to qualify as kidnapping (the back of the bank might actually be a safer place to wait out the robbery), but there is definitely false imprisonment.

Although holding people against their will may feel wrong, it is not always a crime. In certain circumstances, someone may legally detain you. The police and law enforcement have the right to detain someone if they have probable cause to believe he committed a crime, or until a reasonable investigation can be done. An example of the latter is when the police are called to a crowded party where someone has been assaulted. The persons at the party may be detained until they have been interviewed about what they saw and heard.

For the Record

A person can be falsely imprisoned in his or her own home, such as when a rapist blocks the victim's bedroom door so she cannot leave.

Owners or employees at stores have a limited right to detain someone whom they believe is shoplifting, pending an investigation or the arrival of the police. Such "citizen's arrests" are covered in the discussion of warrantless arrests in Chapter 11.

Stalking

Stalking can be threatening, threats can be stalking, and (in some states) each can be neither. So let's talk about them separately.

Stalking is a term that, like *domestic abuse*, may mean different things to a psychologist, a victim's advocate, a lay person, and the criminal justice system. A woman who walks home from work and is followed every step of the way by a man who stares obsessively at her will likely feel that she has been stalked. But for the criminal justice system, that single instance of stalking behavior is not enough to constitute a crime.

To qualify as criminal stalking, a series (at least two) of such events or acts must take place. Many states also require some sort of credible (realistic) threat to the victim.

In some states, the threat can also be to someone the victim cares about, such as to a child or other loved one, a business associate, a relative, and so on.

Going back to my earlier example, if a man followed a woman home repeatedly, it would constitute stalking. Other kinds of obsessive behaviors and acts include these:

♦ Having unwanted (and often intimate or embarrassing) gifts and items delivered to the victim's home or office

♦ Asking the victim's family and friends about her, or digging into her personal files or other materials for such information

♦ Writing or posting cruel or untrue messages about the victim

♦ Photographing the victim without her consent

♦ Making harassing phone calls

♦ Following the victim or otherwise monitoring her whereabouts or actions

For the Record _____

In celebrity stalking or threat cases, it is not uncommon for the suspect to make threats against the celebrity's family, staff, agent, manager, or lawyer. The fact that these people are seen as obstacles or competitors for the celebrity's attention makes the threats terrifyingly credible.

Antistalking laws are relatively new to the criminal justice system—California adopted the first criminal stalking law in 1990. The law is still evolving as the criminal justice system, legislatures, and the public come to understand more about this special kind of abuse.

Hearsay
California's enactment of its antistalking law followed several high-profile cases that raised public awareness and outrage about stalking. These include the 1982 attempted murder of actress Theresa Saldana by a stalker who posed as Martin Scorsese's assistant to get Theresa's home address from her mother; the 1988 massacre by Richard Farley that followed an unsuccessful four-year stalking of a co-worker; the 1989 murder of actress Rebecca Shaeffer; and five Orange County stalking murders in 1989 that occurred even though each victim had obtained a restraining order against her stalker.

Threats

An individual threat or threatening act may not be enough for a stalking charge, but it may be a crime under the state's individual threat laws if it is sufficiently credible and potentially violent. A good example of such a threat is a man who shows a woman a gun he has just bought and says, "I'll kill you if you don't go out with me." The threat is violent; the purchase of the gun underlines the credibility of the threat.

Usually threats are part of the coercive behavior used in other types of abuse: a husband threatens punishment if a spouse doesn't "shape up" (or "put out"); a child abuser threatens to kill his young victim's mother if he tells her what is going on; a caregiver threatens to put an elderly person "out on the street" if he doesn't pay an exorbitant monthly "tip." In such cases, criminal threat charges can be brought as companion charges to the criminal abuse charges.

The Least You Need to Know

- ◆ Domestic abuse is abuse by one person in a marriage or other relationship against the other.

- ◆ Neglect is the most prevalent form of child abuse.

- ◆ Certain professionals dealing with elders or children are required to report signs of abuse.

- ◆ The isolation and dependence of many elders make them particularly vulnerable to abuse.

- ◆ False imprisonment is holding someone against his will; kidnapping is moving him to increase his risk of harm.

- ◆ Stalking is a pattern of two or more obsessive acts that threaten the victim or someone close to her.

7

Crimes Against Property: Larceny

In This Chapter

- ◆ The elements of the crime of larceny
- ◆ The different kinds of larceny
- ◆ The crime of receiving stolen property

We've all seen TV shows where an unsuspecting character returns to her home, finds all her belongings strewn about, sees her TV and stereo cabinet open and empty, and screams, "I've been robbed!" The reality is—she hasn't. She was a victim of burglary, which, although related, is a different crime than robbery.

That's what this and the next two chapters are about—the different kinds of crimes that can be committed "against property," as this group of crimes is known. These crimes are so closely related that some states group them together under the umbrella term "theft." They include larceny, embezzlement, false pretenses, receipt of stolen goods, extortion, and so on.

These are common crimes, and understanding the differences among them is important to understanding how the criminal justice system deals with them. Several factors distinguish these crimes, including how the theft occurred, its timing, and the intent of the defendant. That's what we'll be examining in these chapters. We start with larceny and receipt of stolen goods.

Larceny

Larceny is the legal term for what most people call stealing or *theft*. When the value of the stolen property is over a certain amount—in most states, $500—it is the felony of grand larceny. Less than that, the crime is a misdemeanor called petty larceny or petty theft.

def•i•ni•tion

Larceny and **theft** are often used interchangeably but mean the same thing—taking someone else's property with no intent to return it.

The elements of the crime of larceny—each of which must be proven for a conviction—are spelled out in its definition: it is the trespassory taking and carrying away of the valuable property of another, with the intent to permanently deprive the owner of possessing it. Let's examine those elements one by one so we know exactly what has to happen.

Trespassory

Can't you hear that word creak with old age? You probably recognize its root—*trespass*—which today is commonly taken to mean wrongfully going onto another's land. But before that, *trespass* had the more general meaning of simply being wrongful. (Which is how it is used in the Lord's Prayer: "Forgive us our trespasses, as we forgive those who trespass against us.")

For the Record

The best defense to a charge of larceny is that the defendant had the proper consent of the owner. If such consent can be demonstrated, then no larceny occurred.

So this element of larceny means that the taking of property was wrongful. A taking can be considered wrongful for two reasons: either it occurred without the consent of the owner, or the owner's consent was induced by the defendant's deception.

Taking and Carrying Away

The "taking and carrying away" element of larceny includes more than simply picking something up and making off with it. It means any form of acquiring dominion or exercising control over the property. The exercise of control does not even have to be done directly by the defendant—if the defendant uses an innocent third party to take the property, the defendant has committed larceny. For example, if I ask my unknowing friend to help me by carrying some books out of the library, claiming they are mine when they aren't, I have still committed larceny even though I never touched the books.

The "carrying away" part is a somewhat inconsequential requirement—moving the property even a matter of inches will suffice—and some states have deleted it from their statutes. Its real significance is that real property, land, cannot be subject to larceny since it cannot be carried away.

For the Record

One area where "carrying away" gets tricky is where the defendant sells property he does not own to a third party, but the defendant never moves the property. An example of this is when a computer repairman wrongfully sells a computer left in his shop for repair to an unsuspecting buyer, and the buyer "carries away" the computer. The states are split as to whether this qualifies as larceny. Some states attribute any movement of the property by the third party to the defendant—such as handing the computer to the buyer—and find that larceny has been committed.

Valuable Personal Property

The "valuable" part of this element had become largely insignificant—any value, no matter how small, will suffice. However, the computer age brought change here, as it has too many areas of the criminal justice system. Generally, it has not been considered larceny to use another person's computer without consent because of the inability to establish value. However, some states have expanded their larceny statutes to include the tangible and intangible data stored on and transmitted by computers.

An even trickier aspect of this "valuable personal property" element is that the property must be the kind of property the criminal justice system recognizes as subject to larceny. This means the property must be tangible, like a book or jewelry—something that can be carried away physically. The significance of this requirement is that, historically, services could not be stolen because they are not tangible. However, more recently, state statutes have added language to their statutes so that wrongfully acquiring the services of another is considered larceny as well. Usually, some tangible evidence is needed to support a claim that services were stolen, such as a check or deed.

Hearsay

You might think that if a defendant stole the title to a car, he has committed larceny by stealing ownership of the car. But larceny requires stealing possession of the thing stolen, not the title to it. Until the defendant takes possession of the car, he has not committed larceny.

Property of Another

This element seems straightforward, but did you know you can commit larceny by taking your own property? For example, if I take something into a shop to get it serviced, the service is completed, and I take my property back without paying for the service, then I have committed larceny. The criminal justice system recognizes that the repair shop has a superior interest in the property—payment for the service—at the time of my taking it back.

What if someone steals a TV, and I, in turn, steal it from the thief. Have I taken "property of another," even when the thief never owned the TV? Yes. This is another example of how larceny is about possession—I have taken possession of the TV without the thief's consent, so I have committed larceny. That the thief's possession of the TV was also wrong does not affect the larceny I have committed.

Another area in which the "of another" element becomes an issue is associations. For example, people who own property together—such as spouses in community property states—cannot commit larceny against each other, since both have a right to possession. However, most states will consider it larceny if one partner steals from a partnership. And some states have made their larceny statutes applicable when the spouses are separated or in the process of separation.

Objection _____

So can a condo owner commit larceny by taking a lamp from a common area, or is the lamp owned equally by all condo owners? Usually, the common areas are owned by the condominium association, not by the condo owners. The association agreement typically has a right-to-use provision that grants all owners equal rights to use the common areas. So what of the owner who takes the lamp? He's probably guilty of larceny.

Intent to Permanently Deprive

As we've seen, if a person takes someone else's property without their consent, it is a wrongful taking—a trespassory taking. But if the person intends only to borrow it, it is not larceny. Larceny requires the intent to permanently deprive the owner of the property. This is why a crime like joyriding does not qualify as larceny—the joyriders don't intend to permanently deprive the owner of the car.

This intent to permanently deprive must exist at the time of the taking for it to be larceny, with one important exception. If the taking is wrongful (without consent or if consent is gained by deceit), and the defendant later decides he's never going to give the property back, that is also larceny.

This exception to the requirement that the intent to permanently deprive be present at the time of taking is known as the "continuing trespass" exception. In such cases, the trespassory or wrongful taking is considered to continue until the time the intent to not return the property is formed.

For the Record _____

Remember that, first and foremost, larceny requires a _wrongful_ taking. Say you and I own identical watches, and I intentionally steal the one I think is yours, but I actually just took my own. There is no larceny, even though I intended to steal. This is what the criminal justice system calls a factual impossibility—one element of the crime cannot exist under the facts of the case.

The criminal justice system treats an intent to subject the property to a substantial risk of loss the same as an intent to permanently deprive. This makes sense, since if the property gets destroyed, it cannot be returned. A handful of states go further and provide that indifference to whether the property gets back to the owner is enough for larceny. In either case, the "continuing trespass" exception applies.

Let me illustrate with the joyriders I mentioned earlier. If the joyriders intend to use the car only to drive from point A to point B and leave it there, there would be no larceny because there is no intent to risk loss of the car and no intent to permanently deprive the owner of his car. (There might be, however, indifference to whether the car gets back to the owner, so this may be larceny in states where indifference is enough.)

However, if the joyriders decide to use the car in a street drag race or to drive through the surf on the beach, that would create a substantial risk of loss. Under the "continuing trespass" exception, that later-formed intent to drive dangerously is deemed to have been present at the time of first taking, so the joyriders are probably guilty of larceny.

For the Record

Sometimes a defendant will argue that although he took the property intending to keep it, he also intended to later pay for it. Although state laws vary on this, it is generally not enough that the defendant had a vague intent to pay the owner at some point. And the defendant must show that it was reasonable for him to believe the owner was willing to sell the property for the price the defendant intended to pay.

So we've covered the elements of larceny. Let's talk about the different kinds of larceny the criminal justice system has to deal with.

Larceny by stealth is the most traditional form of larceny—taking the property without the victim knowing it. Pickpockets are an example, as is a shoplifter who surreptitiously slips a bottle of perfume off a store counter into her purse.

Larceny by trick occurs when the theft occurs by deceit rather than by avoiding the owner's notice. For example, imagine that someone answers a sales ad for a car and says he'd like to take it for a test drive. The owner gives him the keys, but the "buyer" never comes back.

Larceny by an employee is pretty simple to understand—it occurs when an employee is given company property to use in his work, and the employee then takes it for his own use. But, as usual, variations from the basic pattern create difficult problems for the criminal justice system.

Objection _____

The exception of continuing trespass does not apply to larceny by deceit—the intent to trick must be present at the time possession is turned over. If a potential buyer actually intends to return the car at the time he is allowed to take it on a test drive, but he later changes his mind and decides to keep it, his taking is illegal (actually embezzlement—see Chapter 8) but is not larceny by deceit.

One variation is the level of authority given to the employee over the property. Remember, larceny is a crime of possession—there must be a taking without consent. For example, if a stock brokerage gives a broker authority to buy and sell stock for the brokerage's account and the broker does so but pockets the proceeds, that's probably embezzlement but not larceny. The stockbroker obtained complete possession of the stock, including the right to dispose of it, so his later selling it cannot be larceny.

In contrast, imagine an employee who is provided a laptop to use in his work, but she turns around and sells it—that's larceny. The difference is that the employer intended to keep possession of the laptop as a business asset and gave the employee only the right to use it. The stockbroker, on the other hand, was given the right to decide whether to keep possession of the stock.

Most states consider failure to report unidentified found property with the proper authorities, or to make some other public disclosure of finding it, to be larceny. What about if we find something valuable, like a wallet with money and credit cards in it? We all know we *should* try to return it to its rightful owner, but is it larceny if we don't? The answer is maybe yes, maybe no; when yes, the crime is known as larceny by finder. The property must first have been *lost* or *mislaid* by the owner rather than abandoned. If your neighbor intentionally puts out some old books for the trash truck, it isn't larceny for you to take one. However, if you find a $50 bill stuck in the pages of the book, you may be guilty of larceny by taking if you keep it. Your neighbor intended to abandon the book, but not the $50 bill—the bill was mislaid.

def•i•ni•tion _____

You might think using both **lost** and **mislaid** is redundant lawyer-ese. Actually, the two words mean different things, although the criminal justice system treats both the same for purposes of larceny. With lost property, the owner accidentally gave up possession, like unknowingly dropping your wallet on the sidewalk while rummaging in your purse. With mislaid property, the owner intentionally puts something somewhere but then forgets where.

Similarly, if I find one earring on the floor, I should know that it was more likely lost than abandoned. Most earrings come in pairs, so it's not likely that the owner of this one meant to abandon one earring and keep the other.

Second, even if the property is lost or mislaid rather than abandoned, it is still larceny by taking only if the following is true:

1. The defendant knew or could have discovered the owner's identity with reasonable efforts, and …

2. At the time of finding, the defendant intended to permanently deprive the owner of the property—to steal it.

For example, if a person takes mistaken delivery of property and thinks it is a gift, it may not be larceny. But if the package is addressed to someone else or otherwise is clearly a mistaken delivery, keeping it may be larceny. Taking the mistaken delivery and only later discovering the mistake is not larceny.

def•i•ni•tion

A **bailee,** also known as a custodian, is defined as a person with whom some article is left, usually pursuant to a contract, who is responsible for the safe return of the article to the owner when the contract is fulfilled. Related examples arise in parking garages and self-storage units.

To understand larceny by bailee, you have to understand who or what a bailee is. A *bailee* is someone with whom you leave your property for some reason, and who is supposed to return it to you undamaged. Examples include checking your coat at the theater and leaving your car at the repair shop.

Traditionally, larceny by bailee required that the bailee physically break into the property left in his care. More recently, some states will find a bailee guilty of larceny whether or not the property was broken into. Other states consider theft by a bailee to be a form of embezzlement, which the next chapter discusses.

Receiving Stolen Property

We've talked about accessories after the fact—people who help a person who has committed a crime avoid discovery or arrest—and said that the criminal justice system views such accessories to be just as responsible for the crime as the person who committed it. The concept you learned there applies here, too. A person who knowingly receives stolen property is helping the criminal who committed the theft and is an accessory to larceny.

The level of knowledge the recipient must have that the goods were stolen varies among states. Most require that he know that the goods are stolen at the time he receives them. This doesn't mean he had to witness the theft; it is enough for the recipient to know from the circumstances that the goods were stolen, such as from the thief's character, their past dealings, or the fact that the thief paid no money for the item.

Some states use a lesser level of knowledge, requiring only that the recipient had reason to believe the goods are stolen. This makes the crime easier to prosecute—it is easier to prove what the recipient should have realized from the factual circumstances than to prove what he actually knew. A small number of states have removed the knowledge requirement entirely, making anyone who receives stolen goods an accessory after the fact, even someone had no reason to believe the goods were stolen. Whether such statutes violate the Fifth Amendment's guarantee of due process is open to question:

> *No person shall be ... deprived of life, liberty, or property, without due process of law....*

Beyond knowing that the goods were stolen, the recipient must intend to deprive the victim of the property. This element is key because it acts as a safeguard for police and good Samaritans who receive stolen property for the express purpose of returning it to its owner. Some states word this exception differently, requiring an intent to return the goods to the owner rather than the absence of an intent to deprive the victim of the property. Since the testimony of intent in such circumstances is usually confirmed by actual attempts to return the property, the different wording has little practical effect.

For the Record _____

If a prosecutor feels it will be difficult to prove the wrongful taking element for larceny, she likely will file a receiving stolen property charge. That charge requires only knowing that the goods were stolen, plus intent to deprive of ownership.

Receiving stolen property does not require physical possession of the property—the stolen jewels need not be physically handed from the thief to the receiver. The stolen goods are considered received when the recipient directly or indirectly exercises control of the property. An example of this is when the receiver has a car thief deliver the car to specific garage—which is, in fact, a chop shop, a place where a car is disassembled so the individual parts can be sold without revealing that the source of the parts was a stolen car.

Another state-to-state difference in the crime of receiving stolen property is *how* the property must be stolen. In most states, property obtained by larceny, robbery, or burglary can be charged as receipt of stolen property. Other states have more narrow statutes that exclude property obtained by embezzlement or false pretenses. Other states have broader statutes that include any of the crimes against property.

For the Record

As you might expect, a thief cannot be convicted of receiving stolen goods from himself. However, states vary on whether other participants in the theft can be charged with receiving stolen goods, such as if the driver of the get-away car is paid off with part of the stolen goods. Most states say that an active participant in the theft cannot be charged with receiving goods stolen in the theft.

The Least You Need to Know

- ◆ In most states, grand larceny is the theft of property worth more than $500; theft of property worth less is petty larceny.

- ◆ Larceny requires both the taking of another's property without his consent and the intent to not return it.

- ◆ A person who finds lost property can be charged with larceny only if he could find the owner with reasonable effort and he kept the property with the intent to permanently deprive the owner of it.

- ◆ A person who receives stolen property with knowledge that it was stolen is an accessory after the fact and is as responsible for the theft as the person who committed it.

Crimes Against Property: Deceit

In This Chapter

- ◆ Embezzlement, and how it differs from larceny
- ◆ The crime of false pretenses, and how it differs from both embezzlement and larceny
- ◆ Mail and wire fraud
- ◆ Fraud in the purchase or sale of securities
- ◆ The burgeoning crime of identity theft

A trusted bookkeeper creates a fictional supplier, writes thousands of dollars' worth of checks to the fake supplier for materials never delivered to her employer, and pockets those checks herself.

An investment advisor confesses to something called a Ponzi scheme, and his clients wake up the next morning to find they have lost their life's savings.

A mass mailing offers shares in a newly discovered diamond mine whose assay reports paint a glowing—and false—picture of diamonds littering the mine floor.

These are all crimes against property that involve some kind of fraud. Like larceny by trickery, they all involve the use of deception to take something of value from its rightful owner. But fraud crimes like embezzlement, securities fraud, and identity theft are different from larceny and have key differences among themselves.

Embezzlement

Remember how we talked about larceny being a crime of stealing possession of another's property? Well, embezzlement is the crime of stealing *ownership* of property, not merely possession of it. This may seem like a distinction without much of a difference. After all, if a thief makes off with my bicycle, the fact that he has stolen only possession, not ownership, of my bike is little consolation to me.

But sometimes this distinction matters a lot. Let's return to the stockbroker example I used in the last chapter. The brokerage firm gave the broker full possession of stocks owned by the firm so he could buy and sell stocks for the brokerage's account. Because the broker had rightful possession of the stocks, he could not wrongfully take possession of them and so could not be charged with larceny if he sold them and pocketed the proceeds. He could, however, be charged with embezzlement: while he had lawful possession of the stocks, he wrongfully took ownership of them by selling them as his own.

Let's break embezzlement down into its elements so we can take a look at each. While the precise definition of the crime varies from state to state, most generally provide that the crime of embezzlement requires that a defendant …

1. With lawful possession

2. Of the property of another

3. Converts ownership of it

4. With the intent to defraud the rightful owner

Lawful Possession

The earliest embezzlement statutes were passed to fill the "rightful possession" gap in the crime of larceny, one of those crime elements that appears simple on its face but can turn tricky in practice. As a result, many state statutes take the approach of specifically listing certain categories of people who have lawful possession of another's property. These include agents like the broker employee in our example, who is an agent of his employer for purposes of buying and selling the brokerage's stock. Another category is fiduciaries, such as trustees who administer a trust for the benefit of its beneficiaries or a lawyer who receives a client's funds to use in closing a transaction being handled by the lawyer.

Another not-so-obvious category of persons who have lawful possession of another's property is public officials. Public officials have possession of public funds, or money paid to a governmental entity (like a county or state) by its taxpayers. If an official uses those public funds to pay a contractor for putting in a new swimming pool in his backyard, he may well have committed the crime of embezzlement.

Objection _____

Because a list of specific categories of people potentially subject to an embezzlement charge may inadvertently leave a loophole or two, some state statutes take a broader and more general approach. They say that anyone entrusted with the property of another may be charged with the offense.

Conversion

Conversion, when used as an element of embezzlement, is basically a fancy way of saying "making something your own." It occurs when I convert something you own into something I own. Returning to our embezzling stockbroker, conversion occurred when he sold the stocks for his own benefit.

In more specific legal terms, conversion is seriously interfering with the owner's rights in the property, or doing something with it that goes beyond the terms under which the owner gave the defendant possession of the property. Many states have taken embezzlement a step further so that hiding property can satisfy the conversion element if it is done with the intent to embezzle the property.

def•i•ni•tion _____

Conversion is taking ownership of property that legally belongs to someone else.

Objection

Another way that embezzlement differs from larceny is that the "carrying away" element on larceny is of no consequence for embezzlement. Since the defendant has the right to possess the property, he may move it at will without consequence. Conversion is necessary to demonstrate the intent to deprive the owner of the property.

Property of Another

Generally, embezzlement statutes define "property" more broadly than larceny so that it includes intangible as well as tangible property. The most significant, practical difference of this broader definition, however, is that real property—land, houses, buildings—can be embezzled.

The "of another" requirement plays out a little differently from larceny as well, again because we are dealing with ownership and not just possession. For that reason, it's just not possible to embezzle your own property, and there isn't that "superior interest" scenario as there was for larceny. (Remember the example of a person who committed larceny by taking back something he owned from a repair shop without paying for the repair? The repair shop had a "superior interest" in the repaired item until the shop got paid for its work.)

But co-owners both have rights to own the property, so it is hard to show conversion when one takes ownership from the other. But even if it is difficult to show that one co-owner's taking full ownership interest is embezzlement, it may be possible to show that it is fraud.

For the Record

Some more recent state statutes treat embezzlement as just one form of larceny rather than a separate crime. In these states, the larceny elements also have to be proven, such as that the offender intended to permanently deprive the owner of possession of the property as well as ownership of it.

Another way the "property of another" element can get tricky is when the alleged embezzler converts the amount she is owed as a commission. For example, say a building owner agrees to pay a real estate broker a 4 percent commission if she sells his building. She sells it, but instead of turning over all the sale proceeds to the owner, she deposits 4 percent in her own banking account. Is it embezzlement? Generally, no—unless a state's embezzlement statute says differently. The manager is usually considered to be a co-owner of the money, since she is entitled to her portion of it, and she cannot embezzle property she owns.

Intent to Defraud

Embezzlement requires an intent to defraud, which basically means that the defendant must knowingly use fraud to accomplish the conversion. Do you remember the book-keeper example I used at the start of this chapter, the one who paid the phony supplier and pocketed the checks herself? It was fraud for her to set up a supplier she knew was fake, and fraud to write checks for supplies she knew were never delivered. Since she clearly did both intentionally, she knowingly used fraud to convert her employer's money to her own.

The fraudulent intent must exist at the time of the conversion. Let's use the dishonest stockbroker to illustrate this bit. Suppose the broker sold a block of Megabucks, Inc., stock for his employer, fully intending to deposit the proceeds in his employer's account. Minutes after his sale went through, however, Megabucks announced a steep drop in sales, and as a result, the value of its stock immediately plummeted 30 percent. The broker then falsely records his sale of Megabucks stock as having been made after the fall in the stock price rather than before, and pockets the 30 percent difference himself. There was no fraudulent intent at the time he sold the stock, but there was fraudulent intent at the time he converted 30 percent of the proceeds to his own use.

Because there must be a specific intent to defraud, a person who honestly believes she is entitled to the property cannot commit embezzlement. This is called the "claim of right" defense, and it applies to embezzlement just like it does to larceny.

Another situation in which larceny and embezzlement may overlap is when a person intends to convert another's property from the very first moment she is entrusted with it. Some states consider this larceny by trick, and others say the defendant may be convicted of either larceny by trick or embezzlement.

Objection

The owner of the embezzled property is generally not required to make a demand that it be returned. However, such a demand and refusal by the defendant is often helpful to prove the element of conversion.

False Pretenses

The crime of false pretenses, also known as fraud, is another crime created to fill a gap in the law of larceny. As with embezzlement, the specific definitions of false pretenses vary. But the basic requirements are that the defendant obtains ownership of someone else's property by knowingly or recklessly telling a falsehood to induce the victim to turn over ownership to him. This sounds a lot like both embezzlement and larceny by trick, so let's start by pointing out the differences.

The key difference between false pretense and larceny by trick is the same as that between embezzlement and larceny: larceny is about possession of the property, while false pretenses and embezzlement are about ownership of the property. Often possession and ownership go together, but not always. In fact, it is possible to commit the crime of false pretense without ever taking possession of or even seeing the property.

For example, let's say I lie to you by saying your house was left to me in your father's will, but that you can stay living there if you sign the title over to me. If you do, I have acquired ownership of the house by false pretenses, even though I never took possession of the house or even stepped through the front door. In contrast, suppose I lie and say that your father's will said you got title to the house but also provided that I was to be allowed to live there rent free, so you let me move in. That is larceny by trick because I have gained possession but not ownership of the house.

For the Record

Like embezzlement, "property" includes a broader range of things than larceny. Property can be land, securities, and, in some states, even services.

The key difference between false pretenses and embezzlement is, believe it or not, also possession. With embezzlement, possession of the property is entrusted to the embezzler, who then converts ownership to himself. With false pretenses, the defendant is not entrusted with possession of the property. He may acquire possession along with ownership as a result of his false statements, but possession is not required as an element of the crime of false pretenses.

So that's how to tell these three related but different crimes apart. Now let's take a look at a couple of important aspects of the crime of false pretenses.

Knowing or Reckless

There has to be a certain level of dishonesty involved for a false pretenses crime to occur. It can't just be a mistake or the innocent passing on of incorrect information. The defrauding party has to either know he is lying, or be reckless about whether the information is a lie.

The "know he is lying" part is easy to understand. We all know when we're flat-out lying. The harder part is defining reckless misrepresentation and separating it from negligent misrepresentation. Basically, being negligent means being careless about whether one's statement is true or false; being reckless means not giving a hoot one way or the other, and doing little or nothing to find out. So if the defrauder doesn't know whether the statement is true, or does not have any information that would make her believe it's true, it's probably reckless misrepresentation to assert that the fact is true.

Misrepresentation of Fact

Three important aspects of a misrepresentation must be proven to establish the crime of false pretenses. First, the misrepresentation must be about a past or present fact, not a false promise to do something in the future and not a false statement that something will happen in the future. This applies even if the defrauder knew at the time he made the statement that there was no chance it would ever be true.

For example, if a mechanic lies about my car needing a whole new brake system when it needs only a new set of disks, that is a false statement of a present fact and may constitute the crime of false pretenses. However, if the mechanic promises that if I get a full brake job, he'll give me free tune-ups for as long as I own my car, that is a representation of future facts and cannot support a false pretenses charge. Even if the mechanic knows he's going to use the money from my brake job to retire next week to Florida, he hasn't committed the crime of false pretenses.

For the Record _____

Just because the mechanic's misrepresentation doesn't meet the elements of the crime of false pretenses, he won't necessarily get away with it. I could sue him in civil court for the value of what was promised, and some states have recently started allowing prosecution for a false promise if it can be proven the defendant had no intention of fulfilling the promise when he made it.

In addition, the misrepresentation must be an affirmative statement. If the defendant knows the victim is mistaken about a key fact and does nothing to correct the mistake, for example, his silence is generally not the misrepresentation of fact required for a charge of false pretenses. However, failure to speak up and correct a mistaken impression held by the victim can constitute the necessary misrepresentation of fact if the defendant helped to create the false impression in the first place.

Second, the misrepresentation must be made with the intent to defraud the victim—to cause the victim to transfer ownership of the property.

Third, the misrepresentation must cause the victim to transfer ownership of the property, or at least be a material or significant reason for the victim's decision to make the transfer. The misrepresentation does not have to be the only reason for the victim's decision, but it must play a meaningful role in that decision.

Objection

The defrauder may be charged with attempted false pretenses if the misrepresentation was meant to cause the transfer of title but the victim didn't fall for it.

False-pretense cases can turn into a swearing contest between the alleged defrauder and his victim. As a result, some states require more evidence to prove the crime. For example, states may require witnesses to the misrepresentation and/or require that the misrepresentation be in writing.

Mail Fraud/Wire Fraud

Any chapter on fraud crimes would be incomplete without a discussion of the favorite catch-all charge of federal prosecutors—mail or wire fraud. Nearly every federal prosecution of a "white-collar" crime includes a charge of wire or mail fraud. Why? Because mail or wire fraud basically must only have one element for the prosecutor to prove: that mail or wire communications were used as part of an attempted scheme to defraud.

The "mail" may be any kind of mail, whether the U.S. Postal Service or private postal carriers like FedEx or UPS. Similarly, the "wires" may be telephone, telegraph, or Internet cable wires. Because of the breadth of the mail or wire fraud statutes and the relative ease of proving them, federal prosecutors routinely include these charges in everything from your run-of-the-mill fraud case to crimes dealing with public corruption, Internet sex rings, and complex security fraud cases.

Similarly, the *scheme to defraud* is relatively easy to prove, requiring only the following proof:

def•i•ni•tion

The key phrase used repeatedly in both wire and mail fraud prosecutions is **scheme to defraud.** This phrase has been given a very broad interpretation by the courts.

♦ The defendant participated in the scheme.

♦ The scheme involved material misstatements or omissions.

♦ The defendant acted with specific intent (or purpose) to defraud.

♦ The scheme resulted in (or would have resulted in, upon completion) the loss of money, property, or lawful services.

Securities Fraud

When people think of white-collar crime, securities fraud often comes to mind. Securities fraud cases often involve scoundrels tricking innocent people out of large sums of money and tend to capture the interest of pundits and citizens alike. The recent exposure of Bernard Madoff's *Ponzi scheme* is a good example.

But what is a "security," anyway? Most people know the term includes things like shares of Microsoft stock, but security statutes and the courts that interpret them have given the term a very broad meaning. Basically, a "security" is anything that gives an investor a piece of a company, whether that is a piece of a company's assets (such as stock) or a piece of its liabilities (such as a bond).

def•i•ni•tion

A **Ponzi scheme** is a form of fraud in which artificially high rates of return are paid to early investors in order to attract new investors. The capital invested by the new investors funds the high rates of return paid to earlier investors.

Both states and the federal government have securities fraud statutes, and, of course, they differ somewhat. But most criminal enforcement of securities fraud is based on a federal law commonly referred to as 10b-5, or a state law equivalent. To obtain a 10b-5 conviction, the prosecutor must prove the following:

◆ The defendant engaged in a fraudulent scheme, made a material misstatement, or failed to provide material information to someone he owed a duty to provide it to.

◆ The scheme, misstatement, or omission occurred in connection with the purchase or sale of a security.

◆ The defendant acted "willfully," or intentionally.

One of the most publicized forms of securities fraud is insider trading. Insider trading occurs when a person buys or sells securities based on information not available to the public. The ideological reason this is a crime is that a fair market requires that everyone have equal access to material information. Because of some very highly publicized cases, the government has cracked down on insider trading by amending the federal sentencing guidelines to allow for stiffer penalties, including increased jail time and higher fines.

For the Record

The congressional materials leading up to the 1988 Insiders Trading Sanctions Act quote a speech by Ivan Boesky to business students in its explanation of the policy behind the act: "Greed is all right, by the way. I want you to know that. I think greed is healthy. You can be greedy and still feel good about yourself." Ivan Boesky pled guilty to insider trading, was sentenced to three years in prison, and was banned from the securities industry for life.

Some criminal fraud statutes provide for additional penalties when the fraud affects a financial institution, insurance company, or governmental entity because of the public interest in protecting these entities. For example, some statutes provide enhanced penalties when the fraud is used to extort, conceal, or affect bankruptcy; when health services are fraudulently used or billed by either providers or consumers; and when government benefits such as welfare have been fraudulently obtained.

Identity Theft

Identity theft is a huge and growing problem for people in the United States and around the world. In 2007, it accounted for approximately 37 percent of the consumer fraud complaints filed with the Federal Trade Commission.

It's not hard to see why. Stealing an identity and using it to obtain money and pricey goods offers great potential profit at very low risk. After all, there is no victim contact and so no risk of eyewitness identification; there is no weapon; the theft and use of identity information can be done in complete anonymity and at any time of day or night; and, best of all, the stolen loot is delivered!

In addition, the labor involved in investigating these crimes is high, law-enforcement agencies are overworked and under-resourced already, and so the risk of apprehension is not as high as it should be. Even if an offender is caught, the fact that no physical violence was involved and the monetary losses were (usually) relatively small means that sentences are typically low. Okay, enough of my grousing. Let's go over the different kinds of identity theft and then move on to some things you can do about it.

Four distinct kinds of identity theft are currently recognized; unfortunately, future advances in technology will likely bring more:

♦ In financial identity theft, the thief gets loans or credit cards by pretending to be someone else.

- In identity cloning, a person uses someone else's identity to conceal his own, perhaps to avoid paying his debts, to enable him to work in the country illegally, or for some other reason.

- In criminal identity theft, a person charged with a crime provides someone else's name instead of his own to the authorities. While this doesn't necessarily avoid punishment, it keeps the person's criminal record under his own name clean.

- Finally, in synthetic identity theft, when the identity thief uses a partially or entirely made-up identity.

Stealing mail or rummaging through trash cans may once have been the best way for identity thieves to get the personal information needed to steal an identity, but modern identity thieves have developed many more advanced techniques. In this computer age, more people are losing their identities because of hacked computer databases; information lifted from networking websites such as MySpace, Facebook, and YouTube; and fraudulent use of the Internet such as phishing (setting up websites that mimic those of reputable companies).

Identity theft impacts not only adults, but children as well. One new form targets children's Social Security numbers and personal information. As if parents didn't have enough to worry about with the risks of sexual abuse and abduction! Identity thieves use the child's identity to get credit cards, apply for loans, and purchase expensive goods. The results for children can be even more devastating than for adult victims, since an unsuspecting child may not discover the misuse of his identity for years or even decades.

 **For the Record** _____

Concerns over identity theft led Congress to pass the Identity Theft and Assumption Deterrence Act in the late 1990s. The act makes the knowing and unlawful transfer or even possession of identification documents a federal crime, and allows the Federal Trade Commission to track incidents of financial identity theft.

Here's a checklist of ways parents can help protect their children from identity theft—most apply to adults as well.

- ❏ Monitor your children's postal mail.

- ❏ Shred any unwanted credit-card offers or other documents that contain your child's personal information.

❏ Contact the police if you receive any bills, statements, or similar documents in your child's name.

❏ Keep necessary documents that contain your child's personal information, especially his or her Social Security number, in a safe place.

❏ Regularly request credit reports on your child's behalf from each of the three major credit bureaus (Experian, Equifax, TRW)—preferably quarterly or at least twice a year.

❏ Request a report from the Social Security Administration on your child's behalf at least once a year and compare the reported income to your child's actual income.

❏ Never put personal information about your children on the Internet, and make sure they understand why they should not, either.

❏ Advise older children not to put their full names, dates of birth, or other personal information on social-networking sites such as Facebook and MySpace.

❏ Conduct regular Internet searches with tools like Yahoo! and Google for information on your children or indications someone else is using their identities.

❏ If a legitimate company requests your child's Social Security number, ask why and try to avoid disclosing it unless absolutely essential.

❏ Consider commercial services that will monitor your child's credit and alert you of any misuse.

❏ Remember that even people you know can be identity thieves, as can be employees of legitimate companies without their employer's knowledge.

❏ Talk to other parents, get their ideas, and spread these tips around.

If you become a victim of identity fraud, here are some steps you can take to help reduce the expense and damage to your credit:

◆ Place a fraud alert with all three major credit bureaus.

◆ File a formal police report.

◆ Call all your creditors, credit card issuers, and banks and other places where you maintain financial accounts immediately.

◆ Send identity theft affidavits (use certified mail, return receipt so you will have a record) to the places listed above notifying them that you are victim of fraud, explaining the circumstances, and providing a copy of the police report or its identifying number to substantiate your report.

◆ Make a report with the FTC.

Being proactive and initiating the contact with your creditors may give you a better chance they will work with you. And remember, many credit card issuers cap their customer's liability for fraudulent use of their cards to the first $50—provided the customer gives them timely notice as required in the cardholder agreement.

The Least You Need to Know

◆ Embezzlement occurs when a person entrusted with something of value by its rightful owner uses fraud to take ownership of the property for himself.

◆ A person who obtains ownership of someone else's property by knowingly or recklessly telling a falsehood to induce the victim to turn over ownership commits the crime of false pretenses.

◆ Mail or wire fraud is often charged along with other fraud-based charges because it is relatively easy to prove that mail or wire communications were used in the course of committing the fraud.

◆ Identity thieves no longer rely solely on stealing mail or rummaging through trash cans to get the personal information they need. Nowadays, they glean the information they need to steal an identity from hacked computer databases; information lifted from networking websites such as MySpace, Facebook, and YouTube; and fraudulent use of the Internet, such as phishing.

◆ The best way to protect yourself and your children from identity theft is to protect your personal information, especially your full name, date of birth, and Social Security number.

Crimes Against Property: Using Force

In This Chapter

- ◆ Burglary, and how it differs from theft
- ◆ Criminal trespass
- ◆ Arson
- ◆ Disorderly conduct and rioting
- ◆ Criminal vandalism

Some crimes against property go further then just stealing money or jewelry—they invade our homes, our safe sanctuaries. Burglary, arson, and vandalism are crimes that shake our sense of security. Anyone who has had their home burglarized, vandalized, or burned down knows the feeling of vulnerability these crimes can create. For this reason, the criminal justice system metes out harsh sentences against defendants convicted of burglary, arson, and even some kinds of vandalism. But like with other crimes, the system lays down specific elements for each crime, each of which must be proven before the accused is convicted and sentenced.

Burglary

The traditional definition of burglary is the breaking and entering of the dwelling place of another at night with the intent to commit a felony inside. Again, individual states have altered one or more elements of this definition. For example, some expand on the "dwelling place" element to include other places, such as offices, garages, or barns. Another common change is to expand the "at night" element to any time, day or night. Some states eliminate the "entering" element. Others change the felony element, making the intent to commit a misdemeanor inside sufficient for burglary.

But under all these definitions, burglary is ultimately the crime of preparing to commit another crime—it is fully completed once the offender breaks in and enters someone else's house in order to commit another crime inside, whether it be theft, rape, arson—anything.

While the person breaking and entering must intend to commit a crime inside, he doesn't need to actually commit it. It is still burglary if the offender changes his mind after breaking and entering, or if he is prevented from committing the crime he intends.

Hearsay

Note that burglary is not theft, contrary to what many people think when they hear the word *burglary*. Indeed, *burglar* and *thief* are often considered synonymous. As we saw in the last chapter, however, theft is larceny; burglary is the act of breaking in and entering with the intent to commit theft (or some other felony).

Breaking

The "breaking" element does not require jimmying open a door or smashing through a window. All the criminal justice requires is that some amount of actual or constructive force be used to accomplish entry. The actual force used can be as little as nudging a slightly ajar door far enough open to enter, or sliding open an unlocked window. Any physical force used to remove some barrier to entry will suffice. The slightly ajar door would prevent entry if it weren't opened more, so physically moving it out of the way is "breaking in"—even though it takes minimal effort and doesn't "break" anything to do so.

Hearsay
While most people know it is breaking and entering to bust through a locked door, many people think it is not breaking and entering if the door is unlocked. This is simply wrong. The criminal justice system makes no such distinction. In fact, most modern statutes have eliminated the "breaking" element entirely, or deem breaking the "plane of air" by entering enough. What matters is that an intruder has entered another's dwelling without their consent.

"Constructive" breaking occurs when a barrier to entry is removed in some nonphysical way. Threatening someone to let you in is one example of constructive breaking. Another is having a co-conspirator already inside the home who lets you in.

Entering

Entering the home can also be actual or constructive. Actual entry occurs when any part of the intruder's body enters the home. In most cases, entering an instrument in the home rather than a body part will not satisfy the requirement. Constructive entry occurs when the intruder uses a child or a mentally incompetent person to enter the home. The criminal justice system does not consider children or mentally incompetent people to have the intellectual capacity and judgment to be considered responsible for committing a crime, but that does not save the defendant who uses them to accomplish his crime from being charge

Note that if the only breaking occurs while exiting, the crime is not burglary. Suppose, for example, a thief enters through an open window (i.e., no breaking), but has to open the back door (a breaking) to carry out his loot, the thief has committed larceny but has not committed the additional crime of burglary.

Note also that "breaking" alone—removing a barrier to entry—is not enough for burglary; there must also be entry. For example, if a thief jimmies a window open, setting off an alarm, and then immediately flees, there has been a "breaking" but not the "breaking and entering" required for burglary.

Dwelling Place of Another

A dwelling place is a place that is used for sleeping on a regular basis. There can be other uses for the building without taking away its status as a dwelling place. For example, if the first floor of a house is used as a store and the upstairs as a dwelling, a thief who breaks into the first floor has broken into a dwelling—even if he never goes upstairs. And it doesn't matter if the person living upstairs is temporarily absent—the multiuse building is still a dwelling.

Similarly, structures or buildings that are either contiguous with or in the area immediately surrounding a dwelling are considered part of the dwelling for purposes of burglary, whether or not they are used for sleeping. This might include such structures as a garden shed or garage.

For the Record _____

Most states have added the crime of commercial burglary to supplement their residential burglary statutes. While the elements of commercial burglary are essentially the same (except that the dwelling need not be a home), the punishment is not usually the same. For example, in California, residential burglary is considered to be first-degree burglary, which qualifies it as a strike under the Three Strikes Law. The higher sentencing schemes for residential burglary reflect the serious emotional and mental damage that can result when one's home has been invaded.

For burglary, the dwelling must be "of another"—you can't commit burglary by breaking into your own home. So if one spouse locks the other out and the one locked out forces his way back in, it cannot be burglary. Similarly, if you break into your own apartment, your roommate cannot call the police claiming you burglarized it.

For purposes of the "of another" element, the criminal justice system looks to the person living in the dwelling, not the person who owns it. So a landlord can commit burglary on her own building if she breaks into an apartment inhabited by a tenant. Similarly, the law recognizes that there can be multiple dwelling places within one structure, such as an apartment building or condominium. A person living in one apartment in a building who breaks into the apartment of another cannot defend against a burglary charge by claiming he broke into his own dwelling.

"At Night"

Historically, the fact that darkness can disguise people's identity and activities had a lot to do with why burglary was originally just a "nighttime" crime. As I mentioned, many states have done away with this limitation, redrafting their statutes so that burglary can be committed any time of the day or night.

For the Record _____

For the "at night" element, in those states that still have it, it doesn't matter whether parts of the burglary occur on different nights—say, if a thief breaks a basement window in a house one night and returns the next night to enter through that broken window. As long as both the breaking and the entering occurred at night, it is burglary.

Intent to Commit a Felony in the Dwelling

Because burglary is a crime of preparing to commit another crime, the intent to commit the felony within the dwelling must be present at the time of breaking and entering. So a thief who opens and crawls through a garage window with the intent of stealing the car inside commits burglary. In contrast, an intruder who enters the same way but did so to gain shelter from a rainstorm, but decides to steal the car after he's inside, does not commit burglary.

Doing the Time for a Burglary Crime

Like murder, burglary is categorized by some states into different degrees according to the seriousness of the crime. Shorter and longer sentences are handed down accordingly. First-degree burglary, also called aggravated burglary, receives the harshest punishment. Typical aggravating circumstances recognized by the criminal justice systems of the various states include being armed during the burglary, burglarizing an inhabited dwelling (even if the inhabitants are temporarily absent), or assaulting a person as part of the breaking and entering.

Did I mention that burglary is the crime of preparing to commit another crime? This is the last time, I promise. But I want to point out that if the defendant commits both the burglary—the crime of preparation—and the crime he's planning, then the defendant can be charged with both the crimes. And two crimes mean two sentences.

Trespass

Criminal trespass is similar to burglary, but without the element of intending to commit another crime once inside the dwelling; it also usually applies to any structure, not just dwellings. All that is required is that a person enter the home, apartment, business, or other establishment of another without their consent.

An example of when criminal trespass might be charged instead of burglary is if the intruder is scared off by an alarm after entering a home but before committing a separate crime inside. In such cases, it may be difficult to prove the intent to commit the separate crime necessary for burglary. Criminal trespass, however, can be charged based merely on the wrongful entering. There is no requirement that the person intended to steal anything or to commit any additional crime.

Trespasses are generally filed as misdemeanors, but certain circumstances can aggravate a trespass to a felony:

- Trespass after or while making a credible threat

- Trespass to interfere with a business

- Trespass on a school's grounds by a sex offender

- Trespass with certain prior convictions (like residential burglary)

As can be seen, these aggravating circumstances elevate the possible risk of harm from the trespass, warranting higher sentences.

Arson

The traditional definition for arson is the malicious burning of the dwelling place of another. Just like burglary, arson is a crime concerned with possession, not ownership. So everything we discussed in the burglary section about the "dwelling place of another" applies here to arson. You can't commit arson by burning down your own home, and a landlord can commit arson by burning his own building if a tenant lives in it.

Objection

Don't go burning your house down just because I said it's not arson. It is often another crime, one that can carry a stiff sentence because of the risk it creates for adjacent structures and the people in them.

The rest of the arson definition is a bit trickier. Let's start with the "malicious burning" element, which is a throw-back to the "malice aforethought" element of homicide. Like homicide, the malice required for arson can be one of three mental states:

- Specific intent to burn

- Knowledge that the dwelling will burn as a result of one's actions

- Gross indifference to creating a risk of burning the dwelling

Proving specific intent to burn, like proving specific intent to murder, is easier when there is a strong motive. For arson, this is often the property damage insurance covering the inventory of a business that is failing, or covering the contents of a home for which the owner can no longer afford the lease.

Hearsay

A common plot in TV dramas involves a failing business burning down its own building for the insurance proceeds. But if the building is not also a residence, this is not arson—at least, in states which have not expanded the "dwelling" element to include business structures. It is also not arson if, as is presumably the case, the defendant occupied the building to run his business. The burning would not be to the structure "of another." Some states have added insurance fraud to their arson statutes to cover circumstances such as these.

It is often hard to prove what is in the defendant's head—the specific intent. It is usually easier to prove the factual circumstances that show the defendant knew that his actions would result in the burning of the dwelling. It is also often easier to prove gross indifference to the risk of burning someone else's home. For example, setting fire to your own house often creates an obvious fire hazard to a close neighbor's house, so it qualifies as the gross indifference element of arson.

In addition to the "malice" element of arson, there has to be some actual burning going on. But as with the minimal force required for the "breaking in" element, the burning element doesn't require open flames or an inferno. While smoke damage or discoloration is not enough, charring is. The burning has to be done to the actual structure of the dwelling, such as the walls or framing—not, for example, just the drapes or a piece of furniture. But the whole thing doesn't have to burn down—it's enough for the structure to be damaged, even if the damage isn't serious or the structure hasn't been completely destroyed.

As with the crime of burglary, some states have modified the elements of arson, usually in ways that make it more broadly applicable. Some of the changes consist of including structures other than dwellings, disregarding ownership and occupancy, making explosions arson even when there is no burning, providing that the damage

Hearsay

Boom! You might be surprised to hear that blowing up a dwelling is not arson. However, it becomes arson if the explosion causes a fire that damages the structure. As I said, there has to be burning going on for it to be arson.

may be to personal property as well as to the structure, and stating that burning as part of insurance fraud is arson.

Disorderly Conduct and Rioting

Conduct that qualifies as disorderly is basically anything that creates a public nuisance or disturbs the peace. Examples include excessively loud noise, public drunkenness, and brawls. Disorderly conduct falls pretty low on the totem pole of serious crime. Some states classify it below a misdemeanor level offense, treating it as an infraction for which the offender is ticketed and released.

Objection

Peaceful and well-intentioned political demonstrations or protests can constitute disorderly conduct if, for example, they disrupt a lawful assembly or obstruct traffic flow.

def•i•ni•tion

Rioting is an unlawful assembly of three or more people (some states require only two) who have gathered to carry out an unlawful purpose in an unlawful way.

The common understanding of *rioting* is essentially that it is disorderly conduct on a grander scale, with many more people. But the crime of rioting under the criminal justice system is much more serious than mere disorderly conduct. It occurs when people gather together in order to commit unlawful acts in unlawful ways.

Many of us remember watching on TV the riots in Los Angeles that erupted after the videotaped beating of Rodney King. It was clear from the participants' actions that they had come together to ransack, vandalize, and steal from the stores in the area. This was an example of people coming together to carry out an unlawful purpose by unlawful means. Participants could be charged with both unlawful assembly and rioting, plus any separate crime they committed, such as theft, vandalism, and so on.

The risk of injury and damage from rioting is so severe that the criminal justice system treats inciting a riot or even attempting to incite a riot as crimes, even if no riot results and even if the inciter does not participate in the rioting. It is enough for a person to deliberately provoke or inflame others so that a clear danger of rioting is present.

Vandalism

The crime of *vandalism* consists of purposefully defacing or damaging property, public or private. It encompasses a wide range of actions done for a wide range of reasons. The defacement or damage may be to buildings or other real property, or may be to personal or public property like a car, a fence, or a subway train.

You are probably most familiar with vandalism in the form of graffiti, which is certainly vandalism but is also considered by many to be a form of artistic expression. Other more violent types of vandalism can involve breaking windows, salting lawns, cutting down trees, and knocking down traffic signs. Paul Newman's character in *Cool Hand Luke* committed vandalism when he went through town one night cutting the heads off all the parking meters.

Vandalism is generally filed as a misdemeanor crime when the damage is minor, like paint that can be cleaned off. But if there is serious property damage or large financial loss, vandalism may be charged as a felony. This is another example of a "wobbler," an offense that may be charged as either a misdemeanor or a felony, with the choice usually based on the financial cost to fix the damage.

def•i•ni•tion

While **vandalism** is the intentional damaging of another's property, the property need not be physical. Deliberately spreading a computer virus, for example, can be vandalism. Specific statutes also deal with this and other forms of cybercrime.

For the Record

In some cities, it is considered misdemeanor vandalism to even possess the means by which to commit vandalism, if the intent to use them as such can be proven. Glass cutters, cans of aerosol paint, and a handful of felt-tip markers qualify as the means to commit vandalism.

Vandalism that is directed toward a legally protected class of people, such as a particular racial or religious group, may qualify as a hate crime (discussed in Chapter 4). If so, it, too, can elevate the misdemeanor to a felony.

Different state statutes sometimes refer to vandalism as criminal mischief, malicious mischief, or criminal trespass. Whatever the name, they all criminalize behavior that purposefully damages the property of another. While total destruction of the property is not required, there must be some diminished use or functionality of the property or other damage to it.

The Least You Need to Know

◆ Burglary is not theft. Traditionally, it is the acts of breaking and entering a dwelling place of another, at night and with the intent to commit a felony inside.

◆ If the intruder commits the intended felony once inside, he has committed both burglary and the second felony. He can be charged, convicted, and sentenced for each of the two separate crimes.

◆ The traditional definition for arson is the malicious burning of the dwelling place of another.

◆ The crime of rioting occurs when three or more people come together to carry out an unlawful purpose by unlawful means.

◆ Vandalism is the purposeful damaging or defacement of another's property, and it carries sentences that vary according to the seriousness and cost of the damage caused.

Crimes Against Society and Justice

In This Chapter

- Car accidents caused by alcohol or drugs are crimes against not just the immediate victims, but against all of us who depend upon an ordered society

- Drug trafficking and terrorism undermine the safety and security of our society

- Using bribes or extortion to influence a judge or other government official is a crime against justice

- Other crimes against justice include perjury, obstructing police investigations, and failing to comply with court orders

Crimes against society and justice are often called victimless crimes, since no particular individual is the intended victim. Personally, I think that's a misnomer. These kinds of crimes have many victims and can cause extensive and serious harm. Drunk driving, drug trafficking, bribing a judge or politician, lying under oath, and destroying evidence are crimes that hurt all of us who count on a safe, organized society and a fair, effective justice system. These crimes strike at the heart of our social order.

In this chapter, we examine these crimes and how the criminal justice system deals with them, starting with crimes against society and moving on to crimes against justice.

Crimes Against Society

Crimes against society are often harmful to the person engaging in the crime as well as to society. For example, a drunk driver is often injured or killed, and also endangers everyone else on the road. Likewise, many drug users have their lives destroyed by their addiction, and few drug traffickers live to ripe old ages.

But these crimes also take a serious toll on society. Some states, such as California, refer to crimes against society as crimes against public health, since they affect the overall health of the population.

Many of us have friends or family members who have been touched by the tragic ripple effects of drunk-driving accidents. A drunk running a red light who kills someone leaves not one victim, but many. Maybe a family will be left to struggle for years with the loss of a parent's love and support. Maybe a business will fail after its founder is killed, putting the company's employees out of work. Accidents like these put new burdens on the community as it struggles to assist those affected by the accident and to provide continuing medical and rehabilitation care to those injured.

Driving Under the Influence

A motor vehicle is a deadly weapon, especially at high speeds. So when a person chooses to operate that deadly weapon on the public highways, among all the other motorists, with his motor skills, reaction times, judgment, and attention impaired by drugs or alcohol, the penalties are appropriately severe.

You do not have to be "drunk" or even intoxicated to be guilty of drunk driving. The crime isn't "drunk driving," but rather "driving under the influence." Whether or not a driver is under the influence is often determined by the blood drug level. The federal government mandates that states treat .08 percent blood alcohol level and higher as being "under the influence," regardless of how sober the driver may appear.

But a driver with a blood alcohol level of less than .08 won't necessarily escape a charge and conviction of driving under the influence. Many states, such as California, also allow drivers' appearance and behavior to factor into whether they are considered "under the influence." The wordings of individual state statutes vary, but the basic question is usually whether alcohol or drugs have impaired the driver's ability to drive with the ordinary caution of a prudent person. Impairment can be shown by such things as erratic driving, slurred speech, failure to pass roadside sobriety tests, and so on.

For the Record _____

Driving under the influence and driving while under the influence are often referred to by their initials, DUI and DWI. Both mean the same.

A less serious crime, known as "wet reckless," is alternative to the crime of driving under the influence. (*Wet* is a reference to liquor, and *reckless* refers to how the driver was driving.) Prosecutors may allow a defendant to plead to this lesser crime if there are mitigating circumstances, such as that the defendant's blood alcohol was low, no evidence of impairment was presented, no accident occurred, and so on. Pleading to or being convicted of this lesser crime functions much like a driving under the influence conviction and counts as a prior DUI offense if the defendant has subsequent convictions, but it has less stigma and less stringent probationary terms.

Driving under the influence can be charged as either a misdemeanor or a felony, depending on a number of factors. Examples of factors that may result in the offense being charged as a felony include these:

- An extremely high blood alcohol ratio (in California, .20 percent or higher)

- A prior conviction of driving under the influence

- An accident causing injury to another person

Some drivers think that they can avoid or reduce the chance of a DUI conviction if they refuse to take the blood alcohol test. This can be risky. First, as I mentioned earlier, "under the influence" can be proven by other, physical signs of impairment. Second, many states allow the refusal to take the test to be used as evidence against the driver. Third, in many states, a person who refuses to submit to a blood alcohol test automatically loses his driver's license for a year—even if he ultimately wins his case.

Hearsay

But doesn't the Fifth Amendment protect a defendant from being forced to give evidence against himself, like a blood test?

No person ... shall be compelled in any criminal case to be a witness against himself ....

The answer is that, under the law, a license to drive is considered a privilege, not a right. By accepting a state-issued driver's license, a person agrees to submit to a blood alcohol test (whether by blood, breath, or urine) when asked by a police officer.

A defendant's prior convictions for driving under the influence play a huge role in both charging and sentencing his subsequent DUI arrests. In California, for example, after three DUI convictions within 10 years, the fourth offense automatically becomes a felony.

Even a single conviction can have a big effect—it can lead to being charged and convicted of murder. Normally, second-degree murder is not charged in DUI cases involving a death because it's hard to prove the necessary element of implied malice, which means that the defendant acted with conscious disregard for life. But if a defendant had a prior DUI conviction, the prosecution has a better chance to show that the defendant actually knew the potentially fatal dangers of drunk driving.

 Objection

Many people find that a single conviction of driving under the influence can lead to a string of offenses. This is because their sentence may include various restrictions on the use of their driver's license imposed by both the court and the state's Department of Motor of Vehicles. Besides dealing with fines, jail time, and community service consequences of driving under the influence, the defendant must deal with the punitive aspects of the DMV.

In some states, the judge sentencing a DUI defendant must warn the defendant that driving under the influence of alcohol and/or drugs is unsafe and that "if you continue to drive while under the influence of alcohol, drugs, or both, and, as a result of that driving, someone is killed, you can be charged with murder."

Possession of Drugs

Crack cocaine, meth, heroin, nonprescribed OxyContin—it is a harsh reality that illegal drugs are a growing problem in our society. We take a look at the elements and aggravating circumstances of drug-possession crimes, and then take a quick tour through the main drugs the criminal justice system deals with.

Generally, the crime of drug possession requires a certain mental state—the possession must be willful, meaning that the defendant must know that drugs are in his possession. Unwittingly or mistakenly acquiring drugs does not qualify. But a defendant cannot "play dumb." If he has reason to believe that something he receives contains drugs, he can be charged with possession.

State and federal laws provide different penalties for violating drug-possession laws, depending on the type and amount of the controlled substance the person has. A good example is cocaine, which we get to in a minute. Generally, the more drugs are in the defendant's possession and the more potent and addictive the kind of drug is, the higher the sentence. Plus, the greater the amount of drugs, the more likely the defendant will be charged with not just possession, but intent to sell—an aggravating factor we discuss next.

For the Record

To successfully prosecute any drug-possession case, the prosecutor must show that the amount confiscated was a "usable quantity" of the drug. Not much is required for a "usable quantity," however. In most states, just 0.02 or 0.05 grams of cocaine, heroin, or methamphetamine is enough.

In addition to the amount and kind of drugs involved, prosecutors and judges look at why the defendant has the drugs in his possession, or what he intends to do with them. For example, selling drugs is considered much more serious than simply possessing them. The rationale is that people who have drugs for their own personal use are primarily harming themselves, but people who have them to distribute and sell are spreading drug addiction and harm to many, and damaging society as a whole.

Objection

Even a nonusable quantity (such as residue) can support a selling charge if other components are present that are associated with drug sales, such as a scale, baggies, or a payment and sales list.

Cocaine is a highly addictive stimulant (or "upper") drug that is second only to marijuana in its popularity. It comes in two forms: powder cocaine and crack cocaine. Powder cocaine is snorted through the nose—a relatively less effective method of introducing it into the blood stream. Far more effective is converting powder cocaine into the solid crack cocaine and then smoking it.

Crack is cocaine in its most potent and addictive form. For this reason, federal sentencing guidelines provide severe sentences for possession of even small amounts of crack cocaine. For example, the sentence for trafficking just 5 grams of crack cocaine is the same as for trafficking 500 grams of powder cocaine. This disparity has drawn much criticism, but the sentencing guidelines remain in place.

Heroin is another highly addictive, illegal drug, but unlike cocaine, heroin is a depressant. It creates a relaxed, euphoric state in its users. It is usually injected into the vein with a needle and syringe. The active ingredient in heroin is derived from the opium poppy flower and is also used for the natural painkillers morphine and codeine. Since heroin has relaxing tendencies, it is sometimes mixed with cocaine. This combination of relaxant and stimulant creates a much greater risk of seizure or overdose than either drug alone.

Yet another illegal drug with legitimate medical uses is methamphetamine. More commonly referred to as "meth," this stimulant drug is extremely addictive. It can be taken in a number of ways, including smoking, swallowing, snorting, or injecting. Fighting meth possession is particularly difficult for the criminal justice system because it can be made from ingredients commonly available in household products or cold medicine. Federal regulations placing strict limits on the quantity of meth ingredients that can be purchased at a time are helping.

For the Record

Besides possession of particular drugs, prosecutors can file charges for possession of drug paraphernalia, meaning items associated with the use of drugs. These include things such as crack cocaine–smoking devices, hypodermic needles, or syringes, even if no drugs are present. The nature of the item, its proximity to drugs, and other situational factors determine the criminality of the possession.

Marijuana is derived from the cannabis plant, which is dried and then smoked in a pipe or hand-rolled cigarette, or "joint." It is referred to as a "gateway drug" because it is often a first step toward the use of other, more dangerous drugs.

As with other drugs, how a marijuana possession case is charged is based on the quantity of drugs and the purpose of the possession. Many states have reduced the punishment for possessing small amounts of marijuana to mere confiscation or a fine. While merely possessing a small amount of marijuana for personal use can be an infraction, possessing large amounts for the purpose of distribution and sale is often prosecuted as a felony.

Beginning around 1996, some states moved to add a "compassionate use" defense to their marijuana possession laws for medicinal use of marijuana. These include Alaska, California, Colorado, Hawaii, Maine, Montana, Nevada, Oregon, Vermont, and Washington. Such compassionate use defenses usually apply only to the patient or the patient's primary caregiver.

Prescription drugs are treated like illegal drugs when the person in possession of them does not have a prescription for them. Possession of prescription drugs is often used to show intent or serves as the basis for other drug- or alcohol-related crimes. For example, a person arrested for driving under the influence of drugs may also be charged with the illegal possession of prescription drugs, to help prove that the impaired driving was a result of the prescription drugs.

Terrorism

Terrorism has taken on new definitions and levels of criminality, due to the tragic events of the last decade. While the focus of many of our laws and our anti-terrorism efforts is on international terrorism, terrorism can be a domestic crime as well. The 1995 bombing of the Alfred P. Murrah Federal Building in Oklahoma City is one tragic example of domestic terrorism. And while most of the terrorists we hear about today are carrying out the commands of a larger terrorist group, terrorism can also be an individual crime.

Terrorism is generally defined as a violent or dangerous action meant to intimidate or devastate a society or government. Current statutes, such as the USA Patriot Act, specifically identify actions, weapons, targets, and locations in defining criminal terrorist activities. The statutes also describe the available punishments, including the death sentence, if anyone is killed by the terrorist activity. And although it has received a great deal of criticism, the government has expanded the level of surveillance and searches that can be used to hunt down terrorists and their activities.

Crimes Against Justice

Again, crimes against justice do not have a "victim" in the usual sense, but they none-theless cause serious harm. When someone bribes a judge, lies in court, or resists arrest, the victim is really the criminal justice system itself. These crimes undermine the integrity and effectiveness of the system and prevent justice from being served.

Bribery

Many of us tend to use the word *bribery* rather loosely, like when someone jokingly says a mother "bribes" her child to eat her vegetables by promising her dessert. But in the criminal justice system, bribery has a very specific and narrow definition: offering or requesting something of value with the intent to influence some action done by a public official as part of his office or duties. The target of the bribe must be a public official or someone with a public or legal duty to the community. In other words, offering a maitre d' $50 if he can get you a good table is not bribery—unless, perhaps, he is working a state dinner at the White House!

Bribery occurs in two directions. Both the person offering the bribe and the public official who requests or accepts the bribe are guilty of bribery. Both can be charged, or each can be charged independently.

The attempt to bribe doesn't have to succeed for the crime to be committed; the crime is complete as soon as an offer or demand is made with the intent to influence official action. The government official might refuse the bribe, but the person offering the bribe is nonetheless guilty. In the same way, if a judge indicates to an attorney that a favorable ruling can be bought, the judge is guilty of bribery even if the attorney ignores the offer. Contrary to what you may have seen on TV, there is no need for money to actually change hands.

Bribery requires that the bribe be made with the intent to influence the actions of a public official in the performance of his official duties. Usually, this means that the bribe must be made before the act sought to be influenced. For example, if a judge decides something in your favor, and afterward you reward the judge with a million dollars, that is not bribery because it was not made with the intent to get the favorable ruling. On the other hand, if you promised the million-dollar payment with the intent to influence the judge's decision, that is bribery even if the actual payment is made after the ruling.

Although money is probably the most obvious and common form of a bribe, anything of value can suffice. For example, it could be a new car or a piece of property. The bribe could also involve something intangible, such as gaining favor or casting an official vote a certain way.

For the Record

Some federal laws relating to bribery are known as the "anti-kickback statutes." The Foreign Corrupt Practices Act, one example, makes it a crime to offer a bribe to a foreign official to get or retain business. The Medicare and Medicaid Patient Protection Act, known as the Anti-kickback Statute, imposes criminal penalties on persons who offer anything of value in order to obtain any business paid for by Medicare, Medicaid, or any other federally funded program.

Extortion

Extortion is another way of getting what you want in a criminal way. It's like *bribery*, in that it involves an attempt to influence the behavior of another, but it is a different crime. First, the person targeted need not be a public official—any use of one's position or power to take money, property, or services from someone else is extortion. Second, extortion usually involves the threat of harm rather than the offer of benefit. For example, if a public official threatens some harm unless he is "paid off," such as a health inspector threatening to close a restaurant unless he is paid, the charge would probably be extortion rather than bribery.

Extortion can also be compared to larceny, in that it is a form of stealing. With larceny, however, the threat of harm is usually immediate, like a thief pointing a knife at you and demanding your wallet. With extortion, the threat is usually of future harm or danger. The harm threatened may be to someone other than the person who has the property, such as when harm to a child is threatened in order to extort payment by the parent. The threat also does not need to be physical harm. For example,

def•i•ni•tion

The threat of harm vs. the promise of benefit is the primary distinction between **extortion** and **bribery**. For example, offering to buy a favorable ruling from a judge is bribery, while threatening physical harm to the judge unless she rules in your favor is extortion.

a threat of embarrassment, ridicule, or public exposure of something private could be enough to qualify as extortion.

The quintessential example of extortion is when organized crime demands "protection" payments from local store owners, threatening to bust up or torch the store if the payments aren't made. At its most extreme, organized crime and drug cartels attempt to coerce entire governments—police officers, judges, and politicians—to ignore their illegal acts by threatening violent retaliation.

Perjury

Just like on TV, every time someone testifies in court, they first take an oath to tell the truth, the whole truth, and nothing but the truth. Giving false testimony is, in essence, an attempt to cause a miscarriage of justice—to cause the criminal justice system to reach a wrong result. Accordingly, lying or giving false testimony under oath is a very serious crime called perjury.

At one time, the crime of perjury applied only to false testimony in court or in some other judicial proceeding. But more recent statutes have extended it to false statements in any proceeding where an oath has been administered. This means that lying in a congressional hearing or even signing a false affidavit qualifies as perjury.

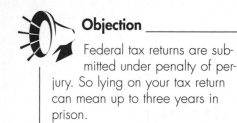

Objection

Federal tax returns are submitted under penalty of perjury. So lying on your tax return can mean up to three years in prison.

The good news is that not every misstatement under oath will lead to criminal charges for perjury. Like most crimes, there is a mental state required; for perjury, it is the intent to make a false statement. So unintentional or careless misstatements will not qualify for the crime.

Also even if intentional, the false statement must be regarding a material fact. "Material" means that the fact lied about could affect the outcome of the case or hearing. Testifying in court that you are 28 years old when you are actually 31 probably isn't perjury unless your age is relevant to the crime at issue. But providing a false alibi by saying the defendant was with you on the night of the crime could greatly influence the outcome of the case and would be perjury.

Perjury is taken very seriously as a criminal action. State and federal statutes provide for very harsh punishments for anyone found guilty. Still, the reality is that prosecution for perjury is more often threatened than filed. One reason is the difficulty of proving the specific intent to lie. Another is that the conviction that was the main point of the prosecution was obtained despite the perjury.

However, in some high-profile cases, a perjury or obstruction of justice charge may be the charge most likely to produce a conviction. A recent well-known example was the trial of Vice President Cheney's chief of staff, Lewis "Scooter" Libby, who was convicted on one charge of obstructing justice, two counts of perjury, and one count of lying to federal investigators regarding the leak of the secret CIA status of Valerie Plame.

For the Record _____

It is also a crime to cause another person to commit perjury. This is called subornation of perjury. One example is an attorney who encourages her client to give false testimony in court. It is also subornation of perjury to pay a witness to give false testimony, or to coerce false testimony by threats of harm.

Resisting Arrest

Resisting arrest is a misdemeanor that subverts the justice system by preventing a suspect from being charged, tried, and punished if guilty. This crime immediately conjures up images of a high-speed chase, with suspect fleeing the police. But evading police is not the only means of resisting arrest. Fighting or threatening a police officer during an arrest also qualifies, as does giving police a fake identification card. Anything that prevents law enforcement from properly arresting a suspect meets the requirement for resisting arrest. The exception to this crime is that a suspect may use reasonable force to defend himself from excessive force used by the arresting officer.

Objection _____

Historically, you could resist arrest when the arrest was illegal. Not so anymore. In almost all states, it is a crime to resist any arrest by what appears to be a police officer.

Failure to Comply with Court Order

Failing to comply with a court order is generally known as contempt, or contempt of court. A common example popular with TV shows is when an attorney, witness, or member of the audience becomes unruly and the judge pounds her gavel and yells, "Sit down and be quiet, or I'll find you in contempt!"

Contempt can certainly happen within the courtroom when anyone defies the authority of the judge. Another more common example in real life occurs when an attorney continues to press a line of questioning even after the judge has ruled the evidence inadmissible. Another example occurred in a Washington, D.C., drug case when the defendant made threatening gestures to intimidate a witness during testimony. Even people watching in the courtroom can be held in contempt for defying a judge's order to stay quiet during the trial.

But contempt of court isn't limited to the courtroom. It also applies when someone disobeys a court order to do or refrain from doing something outside the courtroom. For example, jurors are routinely ordered not to discuss the case with outside people. A juror who responds to a newscaster's question about the case or discusses it privately with a spouse could be held in contempt.

Restraining orders, which require a person to stay away from another person or place, are another kind of court order that has an effect outside the courtroom. For example, in domestic violence cases, a restraining order is often issued against the violent spouse, parent, or partner, requiring him to stay away from the victim. Contacting the victim would be a violation of the court's restraining order and, therefore, contempt.

Obstructing Justice

Obstruction of justice is a broad crime that encompasses any attempt to interfere with virtually any part of the criminal justice system. A witness at the scene of a crime who gives false information about what she saw could be charged with obstructing justice. Destroying evidence and jury tampering are other examples of obstructing justice. Generally, obstruction is any kind of interference with the work of police officers, investigators, prosecutors, or other officials working in the criminal justice system.

Obstruction of justice is a particularly useful charge for prosecutors because it often applies even when more serious charges cannot be proven. For example, lying to police during an investigation would not qualify as perjury because it was not under oath. But this would be considered obstruction of justice.

A recent and well-known example of this use of an obstructing justice charge occurred in the Martha Stewart case. After Ms. Stewart sold her stock in a friend's company, that friend was investigated for insider trading. To make her sale of the stock look more legitimate, Ms. Stewart falsified her own trading records. As it turned out, her stock sale didn't qualify as insider trying, but she ended up in jail for obstructing the investigation.

The Least You Need to Know

- Driving under the influence means driving with a blood alcohol level of .08 percent or above, or driving when one's ability to operate the vehicle with ordinary caution has been impaired by alcohol or drugs.

- Possessing any usable amount of illegal drugs, like crack cocaine and heroin, is a crime, but the harshest penalties are for possessing large amounts and/or possessing with the intent to sell them.

- Terrorism is the use or threat of violence to influence or devastate a government. It can be domestic as well as international, and it can be committed by individuals as well as members of a group or movement.

- Bribery is offering or requesting something of value with the intent to affect the official actions of some government employee. The thing of value does not have to actually change hands; just the offer or request is enough.

- Perjury isn't just lying in a courtroom; it applies to any statement known to be false that is made under oath or "under penalty of perjury."

- It is a crime to obstruct or interfere with any part of the criminal justice system, including the investigation of a crime, the collection of evidence, the arrest, and the trial itself.

Part 3

From Crime to Trial

Part 3 outlines the steps that occur between the crime and the first day of trial. We talk about how the system learns about a crime and then about what goes on in the police investigation. As you'll see, the U.S. Constitution plays a big part in how these questions and many others in the criminal justice system are answered.

After an investigation and arrest, the next step is the prosecutor or grand jury's decision of what specific crime or crimes should be charged against the defendant. Through all of this, one of the most important aspects of the criminal justice system is in play—the rights of the accused. These rights affect not only the investigation and arrest, but also how and when the trial is conducted, the evidence that may be used, the sentence, and even if and when a case may be retried.

How a Case Gets Into the System

In This Chapter

- ◆ Learning a crime has been committed
- ◆ Investigating the crime
- ◆ Understanding the rights of the suspect
- ◆ Arresting the suspect
- ◆ Deciding what crime to charge

"The night was still and peaceful, until its silence was shattered by the unmistakable sound of gunfire, then sirens ...."

Of course, a crime kicks off the involvement of our criminal justice system. But how? And what's the process from the crime to the arrest, to the filing of formal court charges? That's what we cover in this chapter.

How the Criminal Justice System Learns of a Crime

The police are the front line of the criminal justice system. They learn that a crime has been committed in a number of different ways. The main ones are these:

◆ A 911 call from a concerned citizen

◆ A burglar alarm or other automated alert

◆ A report made by an individual, often the victim

◆ A report from another government agency

◆ Officers on patrol observing a crime in progress

However the word of a crime comes in, the police are the first part of the criminal justice system to respond—often with sirens wailing and red and blue lights flashing.

For the Record _____

All 911 calls are recorded. Because these tapes often record a witness or victim while they are under high levels of stress, they can be an excellent source of statements for use at trial, since they convey the emotion as well as the facts of an event.

The Investigation of the Crime

If the report gives the location of the crime, the first responding officers (normally called patrol officers) go straight there. They secure the crime scene to prevent curious onlookers from disturbing any evidence, and they conduct a preliminary investigation. If the location is unknown, the officers typically interview the caller or other person who reported the crime. In either case, the goal of the preliminary investigation is threefold:

◆ Decide whether a crime was committed.

◆ Gather the basic facts—who did what to whom, where, when, and who saw it?

◆ Decide whether to bring in the forensics team to lift fingerprints, take photographs, analyze DNA, and so on.

If the preliminary investigation indicates that a crime has been committed, a senior police officer called a detective is assigned to conduct further investigations. Sometimes it isn't clear what category of crime occurred, so assigning a detective must wait until the proper police unit—Homicide, Burglary, Vice, and so on—is determined.

When the type of crime is clear, however, the assignment is often made so quickly that the detective arrives at the crime scene while the preliminary investigation is still going on. One of the first responding officers briefs the detective on what they have learned so far, and then the detective takes charge. The transfer from preliminary investigation to primary investigation has been made.

During the detective's primary investigation, she tries to determine exactly what happened and who is responsible, and also gathers and preserves the evidence that will be needed to prove the case in court. This investigation often includes interviewing witnesses, ordering laboratory examination of physical evidence, obtaining court-issued warrants to search specific locations such as a residence or a vehicle, checking alibis, and so on.

The Suspect's Rights During Investigation

The U.S. Constitution protects the civil liberties of suspects in a way that makes our criminal justice system different from any other in the world.

Search and Seizure

Perhaps the single most important of these liberties is the Fourth Amendment's protection against unreasonable searches and seizures: the right to be secure in our person, our homes, and our belongings. This is the right that is often summarized as "the right to be left alone."

> *The right of the people to be secure in their persons, houses, papers, and effects, against unreasonable searches and seizures, shall not be violated ....*

So what makes a search or seizure unreasonable? That turns on the concept of an expectation of privacy. When the police want to search someplace where a citizen has an expectation of privacy, they must first get a search warrant. If there is no expectation of privacy, they may search without a warrant. A warrant is a document issued by a court authorizing law enforcement to take action.

A judge can issue two types of warrants: an arrest warrant and a search warrant. An arrest warrant authorizes a suspect's arrest, while a search warrant authorizes the search of a place, such as the suspect's residence or place of work. One key difference between the two is that search warrants expire, usually in 10 days, whereas arrest warrants do not.

As you might expect, the question of when and where a person has an expectation of privacy has produced much litigation. Even regarding a person's home, where courts say we have our greatest expectation of privacy, the issue is not always clear. A house or apartment is clearly covered, but what about a motel room? Yes, it is treated like a home. What about a camper's tent in a public park? Yes, there, too. What about other places where people live, like cardboard boxes, make-shift homes under bridges, cars, and so on? These may *not* be protected.

Hearsay

While the Fourth Amendment bars police from searching your apartment or motel room without a warrant, it does not bar your landlord from doing so. Many people think the Constitution protects them from *all* unreasonable searches, but it applies only to "state action," or searches by a government agency.

To obtain a search warrant from a court, the police must show there is *probable cause* to believe that necessary evidence is at the place to be searched. The warrant must also meet three criteria:

◆ Describe the place or person to be searched.

◆ Describe the property to be seized.

◆ Be signed and dated by a judge or magistrate.

Thus, a search warrant to search a home would not permit the search of a detached garage, and a search warrant to seize illegal drugs would not permit searching the hard drive of a computer.

> *[N]o warrants shall issue, but upon probable cause, supported by oath or affirmation, and particularly describing the place to be searched, and the persons or things to be seized.*

Probable cause is a critical term in the arrest phase of the criminal justice process. It means something more than a mere suspicion, and something less than "beyond a reasonable doubt"—exactly where between the two depends on the facts. However, probable cause must be based on objective, demonstrable facts, not on an officer's or witness's personal hunch, belief, or intuition.

A number of exceptions arise for the requirement to get a warrant before conducting a search. If the person consents to the search or if the evidence of the crime is in plain view—such as when it is visible through a window—no warrant is necessary. Other exceptions are emergency circumstances, hot pursuit, search incident to an arrest, stop and frisk, administrative searches, and automobile searches.

> **Objection**
>
> Anyone served with a search warrant should carefully read the definitions of where the police may search and what they may search for, as well as confirm that the search warrant is signed by a judge and dated.

Miranda Rights

The Fifth Amendment grants anyone charged with a crime the right against self-incrimination:

> *No person shall be ... compelled in any criminal case to be a witness against himself ....*

One of the most famous Supreme Court cases—*Miranda* v. *Arizona*—provided guidance on what this means. The Court found that when a suspect is in custody, he cannot be questioned before being "read his rights." Those rights are...

♦ The right to remain silent, to not answer questions.

♦ The right to know that anything the suspect says can be used against him in a court of law.

♦ The right to speak to a lawyer.

♦ The right to a court-appointed lawyer if the suspect cannot afford to pay for one.

In certain circumstances, the Miranda warning is not required. The most obvious is when a suspect is not in custody, meaning he is free to leave. Other exceptions are traffic stops, general questioning at the scene of a crime to gather initial facts, and questioning by a private party. Miranda rights also do not apply if there is no questioning, such as when the suspect voluntarily or spontaneously confesses or provides other information.

The Arrest of a Suspect

As a result of the police investigation, suspicion often centers on one particular person—the prime suspect or "person of interest," as she is often called. Before that person can be arrested, however, there must be enough evidence to establish probable cause to believe that she has committed the crime.

Hearsay

"Police—open up!" is not just an expression used on TV and in movies. It is actually derived from the legal requirement that police officers announce their presence before executing a search warrant. This is known as the "knock and notice" rule.

Once the police have probable cause, they do not have to wait until they have finished their investigation before making the arrest. Indeed, one reason for making an arrest as early as possible is to prevent a suspect from fleeing while the investigation continues.

For felonies, the police have a choice of two avenues for making an arrest. First, they may ask a judge to review the evidence and decide whether there is probable cause for the arrest. If so, the judge issues an arrest warrant authorizing the arrest.

Alternatively, the police may choose to make the arrest based on their own assessment that probable cause for arrest exists; this is called a warrantless arrest. For misdemeanors, the police may make a warrantless arrest only if they witness the crime.

So why would a detective or police officer choose to get a warrant if he doesn't have to? The most common reason for getting a warrant is that the police cannot find the suspect. Warrants are entered into a national system, so any detention of the suspect anywhere in the country, such as if she is pulled over for a traffic infraction, will result in her arrest for the crime charged in the warrant.

Another reason for getting an arrest warrant is to prevent a later legal challenge to the arrest on the grounds there was no probable cause to support it. By applying for a warrant and getting a pre-arrest ruling from the court that probable cause exists, the police avoid the risk that the arrest and any evidence obtained as a result of it will be thrown out later.

Sometimes the police do not have the time to seek a warrant, such as when an officer witnesses a crime in progress. The officer is free to decide, upon the evidence right then, whether there is probable cause to make a warrantless arrest.

Another kind of warrantless arrest is a *citizen's arrest*. Different states have different rules for these. The most common kinds of citizen's arrests involve misdemeanors (less serious than felonies), for which most states require that the citizen making the arrest have personally observed the offense, that the citizen sign a document confirming the arrest and that the offense occurred in his presence, and that he then turn the suspect and the document over to the police. There is no requirement that the citizen actually handcuff the suspect, though, to qualify as a citizen's arrest.

For the Record

Citizen's arrests are most common these days in retail stores where private security guards are employed to catch shoplifters. Although the security guard's uniform may make him look like a police officer, he is not one. A security guard has no more authority to make an arrest than any other private individual.

Use of Force During an Arrest

The controversy over the use of force in making an arrest is not over *whether* force is allowed—it is—but rather *how much* force can be used. Generally, police officers may use the level of nondeadly force that is necessary to make an arrest.

For example, using any significant force on an unarmed, nonresisting suspect would probably not be necessary or reasonable. However, if a suspect resisted arrest by punching the police officer, more force, such as using a nightstick, might appropriately be used to make the arrest. Handcuffs are generally accepted as not being excessive force, and most police departments recommend their use to ensure that a suspect doesn't flee or cause harm.

The law makes a distinction for the use of *deadly force*—such as a gun—in making an arrest. Each state has its own rules for when deadly force may be used, but most look to the following factors:

◆ Whether it is apparent that the police officer is official law enforcement, such as from the police uniform, badge, presence in a police car, and so on.

◆ Whether the officer has told the suspect the reason for the arrest.

◆ Whether the officer personally believes deadly force is necessary to prevent death or great bodily injury to himself or other persons.

def•i•ni•tion

Deadly force is force that poses a high risk of death or serious injury to the human target. It does not matter whether death or injury actually results.

- The number of persons who are at risk of being hurt by the suspect.

- What the officer knows about the criminal history of the suspect.

Deciding What Crimes Will Be Charged

It is usually the police who bring a case, along with its investigation file, to the district attorney's office. Every now and then, it will be the victim or a victim's advocate who calls the DA's office, usually about the same time as the police do. Once the arrest is made, the *prosecutor* has only a short time to decide what formal charges to bring against the suspect. The laws of many states require that charges be brought within 72 hours after the arrest—California allows only 48 hours. These are called speedy-trial laws.

def•i•ni•tion

The **prosecutor** is the lawyer who presents the case to the court on behalf of the government. Prosecutors go by a number of different titles, depending on which part of the government they work for: for example, district attorneys (also called state's attorneys) prosecute cases on behalf of their states, United States Attorneys do so on behalf of the federal government, city attorneys do so on behalf of their city and so on.

What charges a prosecutor decides to bring—in other words, the crime with which the defendant will be formally charged—can play a huge role in the outcome of the case. For example, the first decision the prosecutor makes is whether to charge the suspect at all. No matter how guilty the police think a suspect is, unless the prosecutor decides there is enough evidence to support a conviction, the case will not go to trial. If the prosecutor decides to bring charges, she must decide what crime to charge. Different crimes carry different potential penalties. As I discussed in Chapter 2, crimes fall into three basic categories: felonies, misdemeanors, and infractions. Which category of crime the prosecutor charges can have a big impact on the potential penalties.

- Felonies, the most serious category of crimes, usually carry penalties of one year or more in a state prison. Examples of felonies are rape, kidnapping, and grand theft (theft of property exceeding a certain value).

- Misdemeanors carry less serious penalties for conviction, usually no more than a year in county jail. Shoplifting and driving under the influence are examples of common misdemeanors.

◆ Infractions are minor offenses, such as a traffic ticket, and usually carry only a monetary fine.

In addition to the different categories of crimes, certain charges carry mandatory sentences upon conviction. For example, California law requires a 10-year sentencing enhancement if a person is convicted of using a gun in the commission of an offense. Unless the prosecutor includes the use of a gun in the charge, the defendant cannot be convicted of it—no matter how convinced the jury or judge is that he actually used a gun.

> **Hearsay**
>
> Many people think the police decide what crime a suspect will be tried for, since the police charge a suspect with a specific crime at the time of arrest. However, the prosecutor decides what—if any—crime will be charged.

The Formal Charging Process

In some (but not all) states, the prosecutor may bring the charges by way of grand jury indictment. The prosecutor convenes an assembly of members of the community, called a grand jury. The prosecutor presents the charges and the evidence to support them to the grand jury, which then assesses whether enough evidence exists to support bringing charges against the suspect. If so, the grand jury indicts the suspect on the charges.

Only about half the states still use grand juries, often limiting their use to the most serious crimes. The federal government uses grand juries only for "capital, or otherwise infamous crime[s]," as required by the Fifth Amendment:

> *No person shall be held to answer for a capital, or otherwise infamous crime, unless on a presentment or indictment of a grand jury, except in cases arising in the land or naval forces, or in the militia, when in actual service in time of war or public danger ....*

The effectiveness of the grand jury process as a check on the prosecutor's charging discretion has been questioned, since the prosecutor selects the members of the grand jury, its proceedings are secret, and the suspect cannot attend or present evidence.

If the prosecutor proceeds without a grand jury, a document called a complaint formally charges the accused. Both a complaint and an indictment put the defendant on notice for what charges are being brought, whether they are misdemeanors or felonies, who the alleged victim is, and when the alleged offenses occurred.

The Least You Need to Know

- ◆ The police investigate reports of crimes and gather the evidence to support arrest and trial of a suspect.

- ◆ The U.S. Constitution protects against unreasonable searches and seizures by the police or other government agents.

- ◆ An arrest is made if and when there is probable cause to believe the suspect committed the crime.

- ◆ The prosecutor decides what formal charges should be brought against the suspect and sets out those charges in either a grand jury indictment or a complaint.

Chapter 12

Defenses, Justification, and Excuses

In This Chapter

- ◆ Defending yourself, others, or property
- ◆ Incapacity defenses: insanity, infancy, and intoxication
- ◆ Mistakes of fact or law
- ◆ Duress
- ◆ Entrapment
- ◆ Other defenses

Until now, we've focused a lot on the elements of different crimes and on the prosecution's job of proving them. We've been sitting at the prosecutor's table in the courtroom, so to speak. In this chapter, we take a stroll over to the defense counsel's table and look at things from their perspective: what tools does the criminal justice system give defense counsel to try to get a not-guilty verdict for a client?

The Defense of Challenging the Prosecution's Case

Probably the most common defense technique is to attack the prosecution's evidence. Remember that for a prosecutor to convict a defendant, she must present enough evidence to prove each element of the crime beyond a reasonable doubt. And she must convince all 12 jurors that she has met that burden.

If the accused can raise a reasonable doubt about one element of the crime in the mind of just one juror, she wins. So you can see why attacking the prosecution's evidence is so popular. That can be done a number of ways:

♦ **Was a witness biased?** For example, did the witness get a favorable plea bargain in return for his testimony? Does he bear a grudge against the defendant? Is there a civil suit pending?

♦ **Were proper police procedures followed?** A famous example of this defense was Johnny Cochran's challenges to the forensic lab procedures of the Los Angeles Police Department in the O. J. Simpson trial.

♦ **Did a witness really see what he thinks he saw?** Was the witness too far away to reliably make out the defendant's features? Was it too dark? Did everything happen too fast to get a good look?

♦ **Are there other explanations for the evidence against the defendant?** Is it possible that the accused was carrying an axe because he was chopping wood, not because he intended to commit assault and battery? Were the defendant's fingerprints in the victim's home because she attended a party there the previous week?

♦ **Does the defendant have an alibi?** Can a defense witness place the defendant away from the crime scene at the time of the crime? Unless there is an eye witnesses to the crime who can positively place the defendant at the scene, the prosecution will probably lose.

def•i•ni•tion

In the criminal justice system, to **impeach** means to raise doubts about the credibility or believability of a witness's testimony.

These defense techniques seek to raise a reasonable doubt about the believability or credibility of some part of the prosecutor's case. This is called *impeaching* the prosecutor's evidence. One of the most effective ways to impeach is by close cross-examination of a witness. If the defense can expose some weakness in the witness's and get the witness to admit it while on the stand, that can be very persuasive to a jury.

Challenges to the prosecutor's evidence can also be made by offering new evidence, such as a witness who describes how dark it was at the time an eyewitness claims to have seen the defendant. Or a witness might testify that she saw the defendant in another town at the time of the crime.

In a rape case, a common challenge to the prosecution's evidence is for a defendant to concede the sexual activity, but to claim it was consensual. This calls into question the sufficiency of the prosecutor's proof of an essential element of the rape charge—that the sex be without consent.

Another common way to attack the prosecutor's evidence is known as SODDI, which stands for "some other dude did it." In this scenario, the accused argues, "I didn't do it—you've got the wrong guy." Cases in which a group of people are involved in some sort of melee are particularly prone to a SODDI defense.

In addition to defending by challenging the prosecutor's evidence, a defendant can raise an independent defense, often called an affirmative defense. When the defendant has the evidence to raise such an affirmative defense, it can be one of the strongest legal tools the defense has.

Affirmative defenses fall into two different categories: justifications and excuses. Justification defenses basically say, "What I did may usually be wrong, but the special circumstances in my case made it okay this time." Killing in self-defense is an example of a justification defense. Excuse defenses, on the other hand, say, "Okay, what I did was wrong, but something special about me means I shouldn't be blamed for it." Excuse defenses include things like insanity and intoxication. We look at both kinds of affirmative defenses next.

For the Record

Skilled police officers always try to get some sort of statement from the defendant or the suspect. Even if the statement does not amount to a full confession, it may be an admission that places the defendant at the scene of the crime, thus lessening the effectiveness of a SODDI defense.

Self-Defense

For most of us, the concept of self-defense is nothing new. I remember fighting with my sister as a child and feeling vindicated when I explained to my mom, "She hit me first!" It seems innate that we have the right to protect ourselves. And for the most part, we legally do have that right.

Hearsay

My mother wasn't much impressed by my "justification," of course—and neither would the criminal justice system be. What I engaged in was retaliation, not self-defense. The system gives us the right to prevent someone from hitting us, not to retaliate by hitting back. Only if hitting back is necessary to defend against further attack would it be self-defense.

Generally, you can use reasonable force to protect yourself as long as you reasonably believe it is necessary because of an imminent threat of harm (that is, harm that is about happen right away). Does such a multipart definition sound familiar? Just as crimes have multiple elements that must be proven before a defendant may be convicted of one, affirmative defenses have multiple elements that must all be present for one to apply.

What all those words in the self-defense definition really add up to is this:

1. You can't retaliate.

2. You can't go overboard.

Self-defense is about protection, not getting even. So if someone throws a rock at you and runs away, you can't chase after him, throwing rocks as you go. As soon as he ran off, the threat was gone and you no longer had anything to defend yourself against.

Similarly, self-defense is doing just what is necessary to protect yourself. If that same guy threw a spit wad at you and instead of running away made like he was about to throw another, you can't pull out a gun and shoot him. That's going overboard. The bottom line is that you must be reasonable in your belief that you're threatened, and reasonable in what you do to defend yourself.

Objection

Reasonably believing that force is necessary to defend yourself does not mean that you have to be certain, or right. The question the criminal justice system asks is whether a reasonable person confronted with the same circumstances would have thought force was necessary. For example, if an attacker threatens you with what a reasonable person would think was a real gun, it doesn't matter if it later turns out to be a toy gun.

Speaking of guns, that brings us to another technicality of self-defense. Using deadly force in self-defense is reasonable only if the attacker is about to kill or seriously injure you, and if deadly force is the only way to prevent that harm. This is really just part of not going overboard. If there's a reasonable way to defend yourself with less-than-deadly force, then using deadly force is excessive and does not qualify as self-defense.

Historically, the criminal justice system has required a person in fear of attack to retreat to safety, if possible, rather than use deadly force in defense. While this is still the rule in some states, most states no longer place such a heavy burden on the defender. For the most part, if there is another nondeadly means of defense, it should be used, but there is no retreat requirement under most states' laws. Even states that have the retreat requirement do not require you to retreat from your home.

What about a wife whose husband has repeatedly battered her for years who kills her abusive husband in his sleep? Because the abuser was asleep, the imminent harm part of self-defense is not present. But if she waits until the abuse is imminent, she may be unable to defend herself.

Called the Battered Spouse Syndrome, this is obviously a special circumstance. Whether and when it is justified, self-defense is an evolving issue in the criminal justice system. Some states consider evidence of the repetitive history of the abuse when deciding whether the harm was imminent. But most states still require immediate risk of harm, without considering the abusive past.

 Objection _____

Self-defense is never an optional claim for someone who initiates the fight or physical confrontation. Even if the initiator uses mild force, such as pushing another person, and that other person comes back with a deadly weapon, the initiator must retreat. However, mere words are not enough to make someone the initiator; the person must use physical force of some kind.

Defense of Others

Generally, our criminal justice systems treats defending others from harm the same as it does self-defense. In other words, if Ted reasonably believes Alice is in imminent danger of being harmed, Ted may use reasonable force to protect her. Again, Ted is not justified to retaliate or to go overboard in the force he uses.

There is one significant difference among the states regarding defense of others: whether the defender steps into the shoes of the person he's defending or stays in his own shoes. Let's go back to Ted and his defense of Alice. In states that treat Ted as stepping into the shoes of Alice (okay, okay, just imagine Alice has big feet), he has only as much right to defend her as Alice has to defend herself. If Alice was the initial aggressor, she would lose the right of self-defense. So if Ted steps in to defend her, he could be criminally responsible if he causes harm—even if Ted didn't know Alice was the initial aggressor.

If you think that seems a bit unfair on Good Samaritan Ted, you'll find a number of states agreeing with you. They treat Ted as staying in his own shoes. It doesn't matter whether Alice could claim self-defense. Those states treat Ted as justified in stepping in to defend Alice if he reasonably believed Alice was under attack and used only force that was reasonable under the circumstances.

Defense of Property

Just as with self-defense, defense of property allows you to use reasonable force if it's necessary to protect your property or prevent a crime involving your property. However, this defense will never permit the use of deadly force to protect only property, with one exception—your home.

Historically, defense of property has allowed the use of deadly force to keep someone from entering your home. Such a broad rule had obvious drawbacks—it could cover such things as shooting a neighbor who comes home drunk one night and mistakenly enters the wrong apartment.

Nowadays, the law values human life a bit more and uses a rule more like self-defense. You can use deadly force to protect your home only if you reasonably believe the person is about to enter your home, that he intends to commit a dangerous felony or cause you injury, and that deadly force is necessary to stop him.

All states agree that deadly force may be used to keep an intruder from entering the home. But the states have come to different conclusions about whether protecting the home permits the use of deadly force against an intruder already inside the home. However, even in states that do not permit deadly force to be used once the intruder gains entry, other defenses may apply and may justify the use of deadly force, such as self-defense or defense of others.

To illustrate, let's imagine that Alice married her hero, Ted, and they are upstairs one night watching TV when they hear a breaking window downstairs. Ted grabs a gun from his bedside table and goes to investigate. Ted finds a burglar with Alice's prize sterling silver tea set already in his sack. The burglar turns to flee. The only way to stop him is to shoot. Would Ted be justified in shooting the burglar?

In a state that does not permit deadly force to be used to protect the dwelling once the intruder is inside, the answer would be no. For one thing, the thief is already in the house—Ted would not be protecting his home by preventing his entry. For another thing, the thief's attempt to flee shows Ted is no longer at risk of a dangerous felony or personal injury.

Suppose, however, that Ted gets downstairs and finds the burglar about to enter the window he broke. Seeing Ted, the burglar pulls a knife and tells Ted to lie face down on the floor "if he knows what's good for him." In all states, these circumstances would probably justify Ted's use of deadly force to prevent the thief's entry or in self-defense.

Still, the states are split on whether deadly force can be used when the burglar only intends to steal without causing any harm to the inhabitants of the house. For example, if an unarmed burglar breaks in to steal your TV, it is unlikely that he wants to hurt you or commit a dangerous felony because he has no weapon. Some states would still allow the use of deadly force to prevent him from entering your house, but others would not.

For the Record _____

Although you can sometimes use deadly force to protect the home, you cannot set up death traps. For example, rigging a shotgun to fire if the garage door is opened at night would not qualify as defense of property. Deadly force can be used only when it is necessary, and that means you need to be there to make that decision.

Remember that this defense of property in the home rests on reasonableness. So even if the burglar says he came in only to steal the TV, his actions or other circumstances may nonetheless make it reasonable for the homeowner to feel endangered. At trial, it will be the burglar's word about what he intended against the homeowner's word about why she was afraid he was going to hurt her. If the jury finds it was reasonable for her to be afraid, the defense of property would probably apply.

Insanity

The insanity defense is an excuse defense rather than a justification defense, like self-defense and defense of property. Everyone has heard of the insanity defense—it seems a favorite for novels and TV shows. To many, it might seem like an easy way for criminals avoid conviction, but in reality, the insanity defense is rarely used and almost never successful. Why?

 ◆ As in other areas of the law, the defense has very specific and detailed requirements—and those required for the insanity defense are particularly difficult to prove.

 ◆ Every case begins with a presumption of sanity. This means the burden is on the defendant to prove insanity.

 ◆ Most states require that the defendant prove insanity by clear and convincing evidence. A few, like California, require only proof by a preponderance of the evidence.

The insanity defense actually involves four different tests—it's an issue the criminal justice system has struggled with for a long time. One old test, known as the Durham Rule, said that a defendant could not be convicted of a crime if it was the product of mental disease or defect. The vagueness of this rule was its downfall—it's not used anymore.

For the Record

Some states don't like any of these four insanity tests as they are, so they pick and choose parts from them to come up with their own tests for insanity.

Today the most popular insanity test among state and federal courts is called the M'Naghten Rule—a funny name, but a better test. This test finds insanity when, because of mental illness, the defendant either did not know what he was doing or did not know it was wrong. Because this test focuses on the defendant's ability to know right from wrong, it's also known as the right–wrong test. After his attempted murder of President Reagan, John Hinckley was found not guilty by reason of insanity under this test.

Critics of the M'Naghten Rule say it doesn't consider the possibility that mentally ill defendants may know right from wrong but be incapable of controlling their actions. For this reason, some states use the Irresistible Impulse test in combination with M'Naghten, finding the insanity defense made out when an insane impulse controlled the defendant's actions. But this rule has its critics, too, who point out that it's hard to know how strong the "impulse" has to be to qualify as "irresistible."

The last test, called the Substantial Capacity Test, is also widely used. It states that a defendant cannot be convicted of a crime if, because of mental disease or defect, he lacked the substantial capacity to appreciate the criminality of his conduct, or lacked the substantial capacity to conform his actions to the requirements of law.

The complexity of the Substantial Capacity Test leaves much room for interpretation. Where the M'Naghten Rule asks simply whether the defendant knew right from wrong, the Substantial Capacity Test asks whether he had "substantial capacity" to "appreciate" at some level the "criminality" of his conduct. What qualifies as "substantial capacity" and how much awareness it takes to "appreciate" criminality are just some of the very gray areas associated with the Substantial Capacity Test. Still, many federal circuit courts and several state courts favor this test.

Hearsay

The popularity of the recent film *Milk* has focused attention on Dan White's conviction of voluntary manslaughter rather than first-degree murder. White's lawyer used the so-called "Twinkie defense" to convince the jury that White's mental depression diminished his mental capacity to the point that he was incapable of premeditation or forming the specific intent to kill that are required for first-degree murder.

So what happens if a defendant succeeds with an insanity defense? Does he get away with murder? Not quite. In a couple states, the jury is given the option of finding the defendant guilty but mentally ill. This finding makes the defendant serve the time for the crime committed, but recognizes the mental illness.

Usually, however, the jury returns a verdict of not guilty by reason of insanity. Instead of jail, legally insane defendants are committed to a mental hospital. They are required to stay in the facility until they can show beyond a reasonable doubt that they have become sane or no longer pose a threat to society.

Objection

Four states—Kansas, Idaho, Utah, and Montana—have eliminated the insanity defense altogether. These states feel that, since all crimes require a certain mental state, the need for an insanity defense can be met by the defendant showing that he lacked the required mental state because of his mental illness.

Infancy

Infancy is an excuse defense that means that the defendant is incapable of committing a crime because he is a child. Historically, only children under the age of 7 years have had infancy as a complete defense. A presumption of incapacity was added for children between the ages of 7 and 14. This meant the law assumed that the child lacked capacity, but the prosecutor could prove otherwise. For example, the fact that a 13-year-old hid a weapon probably means he had the capacity to understand the consequences of his actions.

Hearsay

Although the infancy defense is still good law, it's rarely used. Now most children are tried as delinquents in juvenile court rather than in criminal court. The juvenile court system is designed with children's ages in mind and regularly deals with issues of the relative capacity of young minds to understand the consequences of their actions.

Intoxication

It's not unusual for people to blame their behavior on intoxication, whether by alcohol, illegal drugs, or legally prescribed drugs. Loads of people do dumb things when they're drunk and later say they didn't know what they were doing. Most of the time, the only consequences are embarrassing stories. But when the result is a crime, claiming you were drunk or high usually won't do you any good.

To provide a complete defense, the intoxication must be involuntary. Involuntary intoxication happens when the defendant is forced to take drugs or alcohol when he doesn't know he's been slipped drugs or alcohol, or when he doesn't know the intoxicating effects of what he's taking.

Slipping LSD into the punch at a party, for example, might well result in the involuntary intoxication of some guests. On the other hand, if someone slips a fifth of vodka into the punch, most people would soon become aware that the punch has been spiked. If they continue to drink the punch, they're probably getting voluntarily intoxicated.

Voluntary intoxication is a whole different story—it provides only a limited defense, if any. Think back to when we talked about murder in Chapter 3: first-degree murder requires the specific intent to kill another person, with premeditation, while second-degree murder requires only the general intent of malice. Voluntary intoxication can be a defense to the specific intent and premeditation elements of first-degree murder, reducing it to second-degree murder. Also if a murder defendant can show that voluntary intoxication caused her to be completely unaware that she was killing a human being, because of either a hallucination or a black-out, murder can be reduced to manslaughter.

For the Record

Most states treat involuntary intoxication the same as insanity, so it's a complete defense to the crime. At the opposite end of the spectrum is Montana, which is the only state that does not allow any evidence of intoxication to be admitted into court.

Let's consider a couple examples. Larceny requires the specific intent of permanently depriving the owner of property. If I get drunk at a tailgating party and decide to use my buddy's tickets to the game to start the barbeque, I didn't have the specific intent to deprive him of his property. Without that specific intent, I could not be convicted of larceny.

In contrast, battery requires only the general intent to offensively touch another person. If, after using drugs, I hallucinate and think my neighbor is a troll, and I punch him, intoxication is not a defense for me. I had the general intent to hit the troll, which just happened to be my neighbor. And the only reason I thought my neighbor was a troll was because I had voluntarily used hallucinatory drugs.

Voluntary intoxication can have a special role as a defense to a rape charge. Rape is a general-intent crime, so for the most part, voluntary intoxication is no defense. But a few states will consider evidence that the defendant was so intoxicated that he could not even have formed the general intent for intercourse.

Mistake of Fact or Law

We all make mistakes. We're only human. But don't count on that as a defense to a criminal charge. The criminal justice system recognizes mistake as a defense in only a few limited circumstances.

In criminal law, mistakes fall into one of two categories: mistakes of fact and mistakes of law. Mistakes of fact can make a difference in the level of intent for a crime. If I aim a gun at a friend and pull the trigger, mistakenly believing the gun is unloaded and intending only to scare him, the mistake means I did not have the specific intent to kill required for first-degree murder. I could, however, probably be charged with second-degree murder or manslaughter.

Usually, a mistake of fact can have this limited defensive effect only when the mistake is honest and reasonable. For example, with self-defense, you might mistakenly but reasonably believe that someone following you down an alley swinging a baseball bat is about to attack you. However, if the guy with the bat is decked out in a baseball uniform, is walking with teammates similarly attired, and is heading toward a public softball field down the street, mistaking him as an attacker probably would not be reasonable.

Objection

Remember that strict-liability crimes do not have any mental state or intent requirement, so mistake of fact is not a defense. Thus, a defendant's mistaken belief that his lover is over 18 is not a defense to a statutory rape charge, a groom's mistaken belief that the divorce from his prior wife is final is not a defense to a bigamy charge, and a bartender's mistaken belief that a customer is old enough to buy a drink is not a defense to a charge of serving alcohol to a minor.

Even an honest and reasonable mistake of fact will not provide an excuse for a defendant who still meant to commit a crime. For example, I may have honestly and reasonably thought the watch I was stealing was just a cheap Rolex knock-off, worth no more than $50. But if the watch turns out to be a genuine Rolex, my mistake won't be a defense. And the fact that I intended to commit only petty larceny (a misdemeanor) won't prevent me from being charged with grand larceny (a felony).

An honest but unreasonable mistake can be a defense, but only to the specific-intent element of a crime. If I honestly but unreasonably believe a gun is unloaded and shoot someone with it, my mistake means I did not have the specific intent to kill with premeditation required for first-degree murder. I probably would, however, be charged with second-degree murder.

Unlike mistakes of fact, mistakes of law will almost never be a defense. If the criminal justice system let off every defendant who claimed he or she didn't know something was against the law, few could be convicted. It would open the gates for a flood of defendants who suddenly didn't know that killing, for example, was illegal.

To avoid the easy out of claiming not to know the law, mistakes of law aren't a defense. It is the citizen's job to know the law, not the criminal justice system's job to teach it. The only real exception is if the defendant was relying on a law or a ruling that was changed after she acted. In that circumstance, the defendant was actually complying with the law as it was at the time of the crime—and it is unfair to convict her for an unforeseen change in the law.

Objection

Even if your attorney gives you mistaken advice about the law and you rely on it, your mistake about the law is not a defense. You might, however, have grounds for a civil malpractice action against your lawyer.

Duress

It's the ultimate "what if" question. What if someone said he'd kill you if you didn't burn down your neighbor's house? That's what the law calls *duress.* Would you do it? Should the criminal justice system treat you the same as an arsonist who doesn't act under duress?

Most states recognize duress or coercion as a complete defense, but only in these cases:

1. There was an immediate threat of harm or death.

2. The defendant reasonably believed that the threat would be carried out.

3. The defendant had no reasonable means of escape.

This definition means that there's no duress defense if someone says they'll kill you next week if you don't steal a million dollars this weekend. There's a threat of death, but it's not an immediate threat. Without an immediate threat, there is time to notify the police or other authorities.

The only crime that can't be defended with duress is murder. Most states are not willing to allow you to end one human life just because your own is threatened.

Entrapment

The entrapment defense protects defendants who are tricked by the police into committing a crime. An obvious example is when police go undercover to offer a public official a bribe. The point of the defense is to help people who would not have engaged in the crime if the conduct of the police hadn't led them into it.

Ultimately, the key issue for the entrapment defense comes down to predisposition. Was the defendant predisposed to commit the crime, or did he decide to break the law only after excessive pressure from the police? If it can be shown that the defendant was predisposed to commit this crime before police entered the picture, the entrapment defense will fail.

For the Record

To show a defendant's predisposition to commit a crime, most states allow evidence of the defendant's past criminal record to be considered. Normally, that past record is inadmissible, because the criminal justice system does not consider the fact that you offended in the past to be proof that you offended this time.

The Least You Need to Know

- A common defense is to try to raise a reasonable doubt about some critical element of the prosecutor's case.

- Self-defense justifies self-protection, not retaliation. The defensive force used must be reasonable.

- Using deadly force solely to protect property is almost always considered unreasonable.

- The insanity defense basically requires that the defendant's mental illness rendered him incapable of appreciating what he was doing was wrong.

- Voluntary intoxication and a factual mistake are never complete defenses, but they may reduce the level of a crime.

- Entrapment occurs when the police trick or talk a person into committing a crime she wouldn't otherwise commit.

Chapter 13

The Rights of the Accused After Arrest

In This Chapter

- ◆ Why and when perfectly good evidence is kept out of the trial under the exclusionary rule

- ◆ Making sure we have the right guy through lineups and other identification methods

- ◆ The defendant's right not to take the stand, and to make his accusers come to the trial and be examined

- ◆ The fair trial rights: a speedy and public trial with an attorney representing the defendant

- ◆ The defendant's ultimate safeguard: a fair and impartial jury

Defendants are afforded a number of constitutional rights before and during trial. Specifically, the Fourth, Fifth, and Sixth Amendments to the Constitution provide persons accused of a crime with a number of significant rights. Some of these rights—like the right to not be subjected to unreasonable searches or seizures, and the right to a Miranda warning—apply before a defendant is charged. We talked about these rights in

Chapter 11. Another right applies after the trial—the right not to be tried twice for the same crime. The Fourth Amendment says:

> *All persons born or naturalized in the United States, and subject to the jurisdiction thereof, are citizens of the United States and of the state wherein they reside. No state shall make or enforce any law which shall abridge the privileges or immunities of citizens of the United States; nor shall any state deprive any person of life, liberty, or property, without due process of law; nor deny to any person within its jurisdiction the equal protection of the laws.*

In this chapter, we look at the defendant's constitutional rights during the trial process. All of these rights are aimed at protecting individuals from unreasonable police actions, preserving the fairness of the criminal justice process, and ensuring correct results. Defendants are presumed innocent until proven guilty by the prosecutor, and the prosecutor must meet the burden of proof without violating any of the defendant's rights. This chapter looks at those rights in detail.

Exclusionary Rule

Have you ever heard someone say that a defendant "got off on a technicality"? More often than not, the "technicality" was some application of the exclusionary rule. Stripped of its legal mumbo-jumbo, the exclusionary rule basically says that improperly gained evidence cannot be used at trial—it is excluded from evidence. The exclusionary rule is probably the most powerful tool in the defense counsel's arsenal, and it is one of the most frequently used.

However, you won't find the exclusionary rule in the Bill of Rights, or the Fourteenth Amendment, or anywhere else in the Constitution. It is a court-made rule designed to deter police from gathering evidence illegally. If illegally obtained evidence can't be used, the argument goes, the police won't use illegal methods to gather it in the first place.

Hearsay
Although it is common to speak of these constitutional amendments as applying to each state's criminal justice system, the Supreme Court has held that the entire Bill of Rights— Amendments 1 through 10—apply only to the federal criminal justice system. The Due Process and Equal Protection Clauses of the Fourteenth Amendment, passed shortly after the Civil War, extended many of the accused's rights in the Bill of Rights to the states.

So the exclusionary rule isn't so much a right as it is a way to enforce other rights. Its most common application is to enforce the right to be free from unreasonable searches and seizures. For example, if a search were conducted without a warrant or probable cause, any evidence found during the search would be excluded from trial.

Similarly, if a suspect isn't read his Miranda rights when he should be, including the right to remain silent and to have a lawyer present while being questioned, then anything the suspect says after that point will be excluded from evidence—even a flat-out confession.

The application of the exclusionary rule can be harsh. As often depicted on TV and in the movies, the extreme example of letting a clearly guilty defendant free simply because the evidence against him must be officially ignored under the exclusionary rule does not, to many, seem like "justice."

Critics of the exclusionary rule argue that it has no real deterrent effect on police misconduct, and that there are better ways to prevent police officers from overstepping the law. Some of these other possible ways include fining police officers, prosecuting them, and using formal disciplinary reviews.

Proponents of the rule counter that the rights involved are key to protecting individual liberties, as well as vital to a fair criminal justice system, and that the exclusionary rule does a better job of protecting those rights than anything else currently in practice. No doubt this debate will continue, but for now, the exclusionary rule is an important part of the criminal justice system and is being applied every day.

The exclusionary rule has only one exception: the "good faith exception." This exception is narrower than it sounds. It applies only if a search warrant has been issued and, unbeknownst to the police officer, there is some problem with the warrant. If the officer relied on the warrant honestly and in good faith, the evidence obtained using it won't be excluded.

The effects of the exclusionary rule can extend beyond the evidence gathered during the illegal search. This is as a result of a corollary to the exclusionary rule known as "fruit from the poisonous tree." Under this corollary rule, if the evidence gained during the search leads the police to other evidence, that other evidence is also excluded as "fruit from the poisonous tree." Say that while investigating a bank robbery, the police illegally enter a suspect's house. There they find evidence indicating that the stolen money was buried under a tree stump on a neighbor's farm. With the permission of the neighbor, the police search his farm and find the stolen money; a shovel under a bush nearby has the suspect's fingerprints on it. Although the search of the farm for the stolen money was with the property owner's consent and thus was legal, the evidence found would still be excluded as "fruit" of the earlier, illegal search of the suspect's house. Note, however, that if the police had other, legally obtained evidence leading them to the stolen money, it would not be excluded as fruit of the illegal search.

For the Record

One common—and, for many, difficult-to-accept—application of the fruit of the poisonous tree rule is when a police interrogation leads the detectives to the scene of the crime, or perhaps a murder victim's body, and the interrogation is later found to have been in violation of Miranda. The evidence gained as a result of the information obtained in the interrogation would probably have to be excluded as fruit from the poisonous tree—even when it is conclusive proof of the defendant's guilt.

Lineups and Identification

Of course, to get a conviction, the prosecutor must prove not only that a crime occurred, but that the defendant committed it. Prosecutors often rely on eye witnesses, who may be civilians or police officers, to identify the defendant as the perpetrator. "If the man you saw running from the Capital Savings and Loan with a gun on the night of April 17, 2005, is in the courtroom today, would you please point to him?" is a typical identification question, familiar to anyone who watches courtroom dramas on TV or at the movies.

However, the first time a witness is asked to identify the perpetrator usually doesn't take place in the courtroom. Whether a witness can make that identification is usually tested well before the court date. Such a test, called a "pretrial confrontation," generally takes place one of three ways: by photographs, a live lineup, or a field *show-up*.

def•i•ni•tion

In a **show-up**, a police officer shows an eyewitness a single suspect and asks, "Is this the person who committed the crime?" A show-up is considered the form of identification most open to suggestibility, or the most susceptible to improper influence by the police. It is generally used only immediately after a crime has occurred, while the victim and police are still out in the field.

Defense motions challenging a pretrial identification usually focus on claims that the way the identification was conducted suggested to the witness who she should pick, or otherwise affected the accuracy of the identification. The police officers who were present often are called to testify about the circumstances of the pretrial identification. When determining whether to admit or exclude an out-of-court identification, judges weigh several factors:

♦ The witness's opportunity to see the criminal at the time of the crime

♦ The witness's attentiveness

♦ The witness's ability to accurately describe the defendant

♦ The witness's degree of certainty

♦ The time that has passed between the crime and the identification

Against Self-Incrimination

"I take the Fifth!" has become a common phrase in our society. I remember using it as a high-schooler when my parents asked me if I'd finished my homework. The Fifth Amendment bestows a right most people are familiar with—the right against self-incrimination. But not everyone knows just what "self-incrimination" is, or that this right applies outside as well as inside the courtroom.

> *No person … shall be compelled in any criminal case to be a witness against himself ….*

As we discussed in Chapter 11, as soon as an individual is suspected of a crime, he may refuse to speak to police, prosecutors, or anyone else. This is where the phrase "you have the right to remain silent" comes from in the Miranda warnings a police officer gives during an arrest.

The right to remain silent continues throughout the investigation, into the grand jury hearing (if there is one), and into the trial itself. The defendant has the right to completely refuse to testify at trial, and the prosecutor cannot compel him to take the stand as she can other witnesses.

Of course, if the defendant chooses to testify on his behalf, the prosecutor may then cross-examine him—but only on the subjects about which the defendant testified. We discuss examination and cross-examination more thoroughly in Chapter 15, but here it is important to note that the defendant can waive the right to remain silent. If the defendant "opens the door," as lawyers call it, by voluntarily testifying on a subject, he loses the ability to assert the Fifth Amendment for all questions on that subject. The right can be used as a shield, but not as a sword to give a one-sided version of the facts.

Objection

This risk of opening the door is why most defense attorneys keep their clients off the stand. It not only allows full cross-examination on the subject to which the defendant testified, but it also puts his credibility at issue. This means evidence that might otherwise be inadmissible may be allowed in for the purpose of impeachment, such as evidence of the defendant's prior bad acts, certain prior convictions, and so on. The admissibility of such evidence is discussed in more detail in Chapter 15.

Almost as important as the right to remain silent is the right to not have that silence used against you. It may seem a natural inference that if someone "takes the Fifth," he must have something to hide. But this is an inference our criminal justice system rejects. The right to remain silent would be rendered almost useless if one's silence could be taken as evidence of guilt.

As a result, a prosecutor may not argue to the jury or even suggest that a defendant's refusal to testify is evidence of his guilt. And in virtually every trial where the defendant chooses not to testify, the judge specifically instructs the jury that his silence cannot be used against him.

Against Double Jeopardy

In addition to providing the right against self-incrimination, the Fifth Amendment guarantees that no defendant may be tried twice for the same crime.

> *…nor shall any person be subject for the same offense to be twice put in jeopardy of life or limb ….*

This right, known as the right against *double jeopardy*, applies any time there is a final judgment entered after trial. Well, not "any time"—there are some important exceptions, which we get to in a minute.

Why would a prosecutor even want to try a defendant twice, you may ask? Imagine that a defendant is acquitted of a crime and, months later, the police find irrefutable new evidence that the acquitted defendant did commit the crime. If the prosecutor tries to charge the defendant again based on this new evidence, the case will be dismissed on the basis of double jeopardy. Even if the new evidence was not available at the time of the first trial, still the Fifth Amendment would bar a second trial.

def•i•ni•tion

Double jeopardy means being tried twice for the same crime. The term comes from the fact that the second trial exposes the defendant a second time to the "jeopardy" of being convicted and sentenced.

Double jeopardy, however, applies only when the second trial would be for the same crime. A good illustration of how this can be misunderstood is the movie *Double Jeopardy*. It's one of my favorites, but the movie gets the double jeopardy rule wrong. In the film, Ashley Judd's husband fakes his own death and frames her as his murderer. She is charged with his "murder" and is tried and convicted. Later, after she is released from prison, she finds her husband and tells him that she can shoot him in full view of the public and not be charged with any crime. Since she has already been tried for his murder, she claims, she'll be protected by the double jeopardy rule from being tried a second time.

It makes a great story, but it just ain't so. The first charge was for a murder that occurred on a different day, at a different place, by different means. Double jeopardy applies only to a second trial for the same crime, on the same facts. Killing her husband in public years after the first "murder" would be a different crime, and she could be charged and tried again.

Okay, now that we understand what double jeopardy is, let's look at the exceptions—where there is a second trial but the double jeopardy rule doesn't apply. The most common is when a defendant appeals his conviction, and the conviction is overturned by the court of appeals. The basis for overturning it would be that the first trial was not fair for some reason—for example, evidence was admitted that should have been excluded, so the defendant gets a new trial. This is not double jeopardy.

Another exception arises when both the state and federal governments criminalize the defendant's actions. In such cases, the defendant can be tried for the federal crime in federal court and then in state court for the state crime. Since the trials are not for the same crimes, it's not double jeopardy. As I write this, I am dealing with a case in which the federal assistant attorney general has filed child pornography charges against a defendant arrested here in Los Angeles, since the federal AAG has all the interstate commerce evidence and can get stiffer sentences based on that evidence. I am prosecuting the state law charge of lewd act on a minor against the same defendant.

The last exception is when a judge declares a mistrial, which means the trial is stopped for some reason before there is a verdict. Because double jeopardy requires both a trial and the entry of a final judgment, redoing the first trial is not double jeopardy.

Because of double jeopardy, a prosecutor generally cannot appeal if she loses and the jury acquits the defendant. However, in two situations an appeal of an acquittal is possible. In the first, the prosecutor can prove that the first trial was a sham. For example, if the defendant bribed the judge or jury to get acquitted, the prosecutor can appeal for a new trial.

In the second situation, a prosecutor may appeal when the jury convicts the defendant but the judge exercises her discretion to set aside the verdict (more about this in Chapter 15) and enters a judgment of acquittal. Neither of these two situations occurs frequently, so the double jeopardy rule generally means that an acquittal is final.

> **Hearsay**
>
> Everyone knows that the jury acquitted O. J. Simpson in his criminal case, but some may not know that he was later tried in civil court for the murders and found liable. This may seem like double jeopardy, but it is not because the criminal and civil charges were different.

> **For the Record**
>
> A mistrial can be declared for a number of reasons. Examples include a deadlocked jury that cannot reach a verdict; juror misconduct, such as a juror reading newspaper accounts of the trial; improper admission of evidence; and a discovery that the court does not have jurisdiction over the case.

To a Speedy and Public Trial

One of the rights that the Sixth Amendment guarantees to accused persons is the right to a speedy and public trial. Now, I know that, for some people, using *speedy* in any sentence about the judicial system may seem an oxymoron. And it's true that some cases can take more than a year to come to trial in our overburdened system.

> *In all criminal prosecutions, the accused shall enjoy the right to a speedy and public trial ....*

But the point of this part of the Sixth Amendment is not to make sure that the trial happens in two weeks rather than two months. Nothing in the amendment defines the amount of time that qualifies as "speedy." The purpose is to prevent a defendant from being locked away indefinitely while the government claims a trial is on the way.

When a defendant challenges the time it takes to bring his case to trial, the courts look at several factors to see if the right to speedy trial has been violated. These factors include the length of the delay, the reasons for it, and what harm the defendant has suffered as a result of the delay. Frequent causes of delay are the time it takes to gather all the necessary evidence; conflicts in scheduling the availability of the court, counsel, and witnesses; and the defendant's own motions or other actions that cause delay. For these reasons, courts decide whether the right to a speedy trial has been violated based on the specific circumstances of each case, without any hard-and-fast rules.

The accused's trial must also be public, which means anyone who wants to can come in and observe what is happening. This is in the Sixth Amendment not to humiliate the defendant or subject him to public scrutiny, but to keep the government from secretly manipulating the system to its own ends. By barring closed-door judicial proceedings, the criminal justice system makes sure its activities are transparent and open to review and challenge by the general public.

For the Record _____

In extreme cases, the judge may restrict or even bar public attendance. For example, the number of press correspondents and other persons in the gallery may be limited if both sides request it and the judge agrees that the restriction is necessary to avoid publicity from interfering with the fairness of the trial.

To an Attorney

Another vital component to a fair trial is knowing how to prepare and present an effective defense. The Sixth Amendment promotes this by requiring that the defendant be provided an attorney to assist him in doing so. As you may have gathered by now, the criminal justice system can get pretty complicated, and it has many rules that must be followed before trial and at trial. For a trial to be fair, the defendant needs someone who knows the ropes and can advise and represent him.

In all criminal prosecutions, the accused shall enjoy the right … to have the assistance of counsel for his defense.

But as you may also know, attorneys are expensive. The criminal justice system does not allow expense to defeat the right to counsel, however. If the defendant cannot afford an attorney, the court will appoint one—often called a public defender—to defend him. This right is so important that it is part of the Miranda warning, which advises the accused, "You have the right to an attorney; if you cannot afford one, one will be appointed for you."

Objection

A defendant who gets an appointed attorney does not have the right to pick which public defender she wants to represent her. The public defender agencies have their own rotation, workload balancing, and other procedures for allocating assigned cases. Some unhappy defendants bring motions to "fire" their appointed lawyer, but these are rarely granted because the court's definition and the defendant's definition of competent representation are often different.

Like most other rights benefiting the defendant, the right to an attorney can be waived. After all, this is a free country, and no one can force a lawyer on you. A defendant who chooses to represent herself is called a "pro se" defendant. When a defendant refuses a lawyer and requests to represent herself, the judge makes sure that the defendant understands the risk she is taking. Once the judge is satisfied that the defendant understands the repercussions of self-representation, the trial commences. Of course, a defendant who chooses to proceed pro se cannot later appeal a guilty verdict based on her lack of counsel at trial.

The Supreme Court has made clear that the right to counsel means the right to *effective* counsel. It is not uncommon for a defendant who loses at trial to claim that his attorney—whether private or a public defender—did such a poor job that he didn't get a fair trial.

Objection

Even lawyers recognize the dangers of self-representation. A long-standing adage in the profession is "A lawyer who represents himself has a fool for a client."

The 1984 Supreme Court case *Strickland* v. *Washington* established a two-part test for deciding whether an attorney's representation was defective enough require reversal of a conviction or death sentence. First, the defendant must show that the errors or omissions in the attorney's performance were "so serious that counsel was not functioning as the 'counsel' guaranteed the defendant by the Sixth Amendment."

Such errors might include failing to object to damaging evidence that would have drawn an objection from reasonably competent counsel; not advising the defendant of certain rights, including plea bargains offered by the prosecution; and failing to conduct a proper investigation into the facts of the case, such as ignoring possible circumstances that might mitigate a death sentence, or accepting the prosecution's DNA evidence without reviewing the credentials or methodology of the DNA expert.

To an Impartial Jury

One of the most important rights provided to a defendant is the right to have a jury of his peers determine the issue of guilt or innocence. Historically, this right has protected accused persons from having their fate determined by a judge appointed by—and beholden to—the king. In other words, it is another example of protecting the individual from a justice system manipulated by the government.

> *In all criminal prosecutions, the accused shall enjoy the right to a speedy and public trial, by an impartial jury of the state and district wherein the crime shall have been committed, which district shall have been previously ascertained by law ....*

As you can see, the expression "a jury of one's peers" doesn't actually appear in the Sixth Amendment. And the meaning of what it does say—"an impartial jury of the State and district where in the crime shall have been committed"—as interpreted by the Supreme Court, has changed a great deal since the Sixth Amendment was drafted, as we discuss in more detail in Chapter 14. For now, I just note that currently this requires a random selection of jurors from the area where the crime occurred, without excluding anyone based on race, gender, or any other identifiable trait.

 For the Record _____

The right to a jury does not apply for offenses that will result in six months or less in jail, called petty offenses.

To Confront Accusers

The Sixth Amendment also gives accused persons the right to confront their accusers. This means that someone who will offer evidence against the defendant must do it in open court, in front of the defendant, and be subject to cross-examination by defense counsel.

> *In all criminal prosecutions, the accused shall enjoy the right ... to be confronted with the witnesses against him ....*

An "accuser" is not just the victim of the alleged crime. Any witness the prosecution uses to show the defendant's guilt must present the testimony in court and be cross-examined. Cross-examination is a powerful tool for ferreting out weaknesses in a witness's testimony, as well as possible bias, contradictions, and other reasons to question the believability of the testimony of these accusers. Therefore, the right to confront accusers in open court is a vital part of a fair trial for the defense.

The right of confrontation also means the defendant can require people with relevant information to testify at trial. If they do not come willingly, the defendant can *subpoena* them, which is essentially using a court order to compel them to appear.

The right to confront accusers can create proof problems for the prosecution. For example, the prosecutor might want the jury to hear the tape of a 911 call during which the caller described a man running from a liquor store right after a hold-up—a description that matches the defendant to a T. But if the prosecutor cannot find the identity of that 911 caller and bring her to the trial, the defendant will not be able to question the witness. Therefore, using the tape at trial to help prove the guilt of the defendant would violate the right of the defendant to confront his accusers.

Objection

Failure to obey a subpoena's demand to appear and testify can result in a warrant being issued for the witness's arrest, admonishment, and/or punishment for contempt of court.

The Least You Need to Know

- The Fourth, Fifth, and Sixth Amendments to the Constitution, most of which the Fourteenth Amendment were made applicable to the states, give an accused person a number of significant rights designed to protect him from improper prosecution and to provide him with a fair trial.

- The exclusionary rule prevents the prosecutor from using illegally obtained evidence, as well as any additional evidence that illegally obtained evidence leads to.

◆ The Fifth Amendment's right against self-incrimination means the defendant cannot be compelled to take the stand. But if the defendant chooses to testify, that opens the door to full cross-examination on the subject of the defendant's testimony.

◆ The Fifth Amendment bars double jeopardy, or being tried twice for the same crime. However, a second trial can occur if a conviction is reversed on appeal, if a judge declares a mistrial, or if different state and federal laws criminalize the conduct.

◆ The accused has the right to a fair trial, which means a public trial that is not unreasonably delayed, with an attorney (paid for by the state, if she can't afford one), in front of an impartial jury of her peers.

◆ The right to confront one's accusers, guaranteed by the Sixth Amendment, gives the defendant the right to cross-examine anyone offering evidence against him, and to compel witnesses to come to trial and testify on his behalf.

Part 4

The Trial Process

Part 4 is the real bail-to-jail portion of this book. We start with the main players in the courtroom cast—not just the judge and the lawyers, but the bailiff, the clerk, and the court reporter. We walk through setting and making bail, and the process of deciding who will sit on the jury.

Then the trial starts. We examine not only exclusionary rule and its "fruit of the poisonous tree" counterpart, but also what "hearsay" is and why a defendant's record of past crimes is almost never admissible. The decision of guilty or not guilty is up to the jury, but the Constitution, laws, and the judge decide what evidence the jury gets to work with.

Chapter 14

The Court Is in Session

In This Chapter

- Who's who in the courtroom
- The defendant's first appearance: reading the charges, taking his plea and setting bail
- How the judge decides if the prosecutor's case is strong enough to go to trial
- Resolving key legal issues by motions before trial
- Selecting the jurors

Ah, our journey through the criminal justice system has finally reached the courtroom! The suspect is no longer merely "a person of interest"; he is now a defendant, formally accused of a crime. In movies and TV shows, the courtroom trial often seems to come immediately after the arrest—the defendant has his "day in court," the jury reads its verdict, and we're done.

But are these impressions correct? Not really. Many people don't realize that the defendant's "day in court" is really made up of many days in court, often spread out over weeks, months, and even years. This chapter takes you through the first steps in that process, from the day the defendant first walks into a courtroom to the day the jurors take their seats in the jury box, ready for the trial to begin.

The Courtroom Cast

Most people would rather slip into a dentist's chair than step into a courtroom—even if they aren't the defendant! Why? Apart from the image of a sharp-tongued Judge Judy slamming a gavel and glowering at us, the courtroom can be a scary place. The judge sits behind a raised desk, garbed in a severe black robe. The lawyers spar, the witness sits all alone in the witness box, and a number of other people scurry about following rules and procedures they all seem to know like the backs of their hands—but which are a complex and mysterious maze to most normal people. Let's demystify it, starting with the cast of characters.

Judges

Most people don't have any difficulty identifying the judge. The judge sits at the front of the courtroom, usually dressed in a black robe. Judges are like umpires in baseball, or referees in football or basketball. Their role is to see that both sides follow the laws, rules, and procedures that ensure a fair trial

The judge doesn't have a role in either proving or disproving that the defendant is guilty. Nor does the judge have a role in reaching a verdict of guilty or not guilty (unless the defendant chooses not to have a jury). The judge is an impartial figure in the courtroom, making sure the constitution and criminal laws and procedures are properly applied.

The judges, often referred to as magistrates or commissioners, decide all the legal issues in a case and instruct the jury on the law it is to apply. The jury decides all the factual issues—who did what to whom and where?—and then applies the law as the judge has explained it. If the defendant chooses not to have a jury trial, the judge takes on the jury's job of deciding the facts, applying the law, and reaching a verdict.

Sometimes, especially in high-profile cases, judges have to take some extreme actions to ensure that the defendant receives a fair trial. For example, the judge may close the courtroom, barring all spectators and media from the proceedings. Or, as happened in the O. J. Simpson murder trial, the judge may go even further and sequester the jury, which means to separate them 24/7 from all outside contacts—even their families.

Objection _____

The judge has the power to enforce the rules of her court by holding in contempt anyone who violates them, and fining or even jailing someone on the spot. Even if you are only an observer, avoid anything that may disturb the proceedings—such as talking or taking a cell phone call. Otherwise, you may hear the judge order the bailiff to remove you from the courtroom.

In addition to controlling the rules and procedures of the courtroom, the judge controls what evidence the jury will hear. When one side objects to some bit of evidence or testimony offered by the other side, the judge *sustains* or *overrules* the objection.

I talk much more about what evidence gets admitted or excluded, and why, in Chapters 15 and 16. For our purposes here, it is important to note that although usually the jury decides whether there is enough evidence to convict the defendant, the judge decides what evidence the jury will hear.

def•i•ni•tion _____

To **sustain** an objection means to grant it, resulting in the evidence being excluded; to **overrule** the objection means to deny it, resulting in the evidence being admitted.

So how does a judge get to be a judge? It varies by state and between the federal and state justice systems. Federal judges are appointed by the President of the United States and confirmed by the Senate—the same process followed to seat justices on the Supreme Court. Article III of the U.S. Constitution mandates that all federal judges be appointed for life, a measure intended to protect their impartiality:

> *The judicial Power of the United States, shall be vested in one supreme Court, and in such inferior Courts as the Congress may from time to time ordain and establish. The Judges, both of the supreme and inferior Courts, shall hold their Offices during good Behaviour ....*

A federal judge may be removed only by impeachment for treason, bribery, or other high crimes—just like the President.

Hearsay

Many think "to impeach" means to remove from office. However, impeachment is the bringing of formal charges, which is followed by a trial on those charges in the Senate. In the history of the United States, 14 federal judges have been impeached, but only 7 were convicted by the Senate and removed from office.

In most states, the governor appoints state court judges, often from a list of candidates that a judicial commission provides. Once appointed, state judges serve for a term set by statute, usually 6 years for a trial court judge and 12 years for an appellate court judge. After one term, judges in most states are subjected to a retention election. Retention elections basically let the people vote on whether the appointed judge should keep his seat.

> **For the Record** _____
>
> A minority of states have judges elected by public vote in general elections rather than by governor appointment. One criticism of such systems is the possible appearance of impropriety that may arise from judges raising campaign funds from attorneys and others who may appear before them in court.

Attorneys

The other major players in the courtroom scene are the attorneys. In criminal court, the attorneys are either prosecutors or defense attorneys. Both are legally trained and both are *officers of the court*, but their objectives in the courtroom are very different.

def•i•ni•tion _____

As **officers of the court,** attorneys have obligations to the court as well as to their clients, including the duty to not offer evidence the lawyer knows is false, to refrain from giving personal opinions about the guilt or innocence of the defendant during trial, and so on.

Prosecutors are government employees who represent the government—federal or state—at trial. In the state criminal court system, prosecutors are generally known as district attorneys, or DAs. In the federal criminal court system, prosecutors are usually called federal prosecutors.

In smaller prosecution offices, individual prosecutors must be ready to prosecute all different types of criminal cases. In larger offices, prosecutors are organized into specialized units that focus on particular types of crimes, much like police departments. Homicide units and Gang Crimes units are examples of typical prosecution units.

As we saw in the last chapter, prosecutors are largely responsible for deciding whether to bring criminal charges against a suspect, and what charges to bring. Then, at trial, the prosecutor has the job of proving the charge beyond a reasonable doubt. Knowing how high a standard this is, many suspects are not charged because the prosecutor concludes there is not enough evidence to convict.

On the other side of the courtroom are the defense attorneys. Unlike prosecutors, who are always government employees, defense attorneys are hired and paid by the defendant. A defendant may choose any private criminal defense attorney he wants and can afford. Private defense attorneys cost money—usually a lot of money, given the many hours involved in the pretrial and trial proceedings. So in practice, only defendants with significant resources can choose any lawyer they want.

But no defendant goes to trial without a lawyer to defend her, unless she insists on representing herself. As we'll see in the next chapter, the Supreme Court has held that an accused's right to counsel is part of the legal due process guarantee in the Sixth Amendment to the Constitution:

> *In all criminal prosecutions, the accused shall enjoy the right ... to have the assistance of counsel for his defense.*

Even if a defendant insists on representing himself at trial, the judge may appoint an attorney anyway to act as "standby counsel," especially when the potential sentence is severe.

A defendant who cannot afford an attorney is appointed one, usually a public defender but sometimes one from the private sector. Private-sector attorneys may have a contract with the government or may have volunteered to be available for appointment. But most of the time, a public defender is appointed to represent the defendant. Like prosecutors, public defenders are government employees. Although they are paid by the government, they are professionally and ethically obligated to provide their clients with diligent, competent representation.

Unlike the high "beyond a reasonable doubt" burden of proof prosecutors face, defense attorneys face a much lighter burden of proof. If the defense can raise a reasonable doubt in just one juror's mind, the jury will not be able to reach the unanimous vote necessary to convict the defendant. The first chapter discussed the differences in these burdens of proof in more detail.

For the Record _____

A unanimous vote is required for both a guilty verdict and a not-guilty verdict. A jury that cannot reach a unanimous vote is called a hung jury, which results in a mistrial and possible retrial. Note that juries never decide that a defendant is "innocent"—only that he is "not guilty," meaning only that the prosecutor has not proven the defendant guilty.

The Other Courtroom Players

The judge and the lawyers play the lead roles in the courtroom, but many other people assist in the administration of justice. One critical person is the court clerk. Each judge has a court clerk who keeps the court's schedule and also makes sure every order or judgment is properly recorded. The clerk also administers the oath to tell the truth to each witness, and is in charge of all the exhibits that become part of the evidence at a criminal trial.

The clerk has direct access to the judge and often has had long experience with him. This makes the clerk a wonderful source of information for the lawyers and can make one's trial experience far smoother. Each judge runs his courtroom slightly differently, and the clerk can give the attorneys insight on particular procedures the judge follows, any pet peeves, what time court starts and ends, and so on.

Like the judge in his distinctive black robe, it is not hard to recognize the court bailiff—he's the one in a police uniform, often carrying a gun, and wearing a badge. The bailiff calls the court to order and announces the judge when she enters the courtroom. The bailiff's responsibilities also include maintaining order while court is in session.

For the Record

Some courts have full-time bailiffs, while others use marshals or sheriff's deputies. Their functions are the same, but a sheriff or marshal may work court detail for a period of time and then be transferred to patrol or some other assignment.

The bailiff is often the only person who has contact with a jury outside of the courtroom. He escorts the jury between the courtroom and the jury room if, for example, the judge asks for jurors to be excused while the lawyers argue an issue of law that has come up during the trial. If the jurors have any special requests, questions, or needs, the bailiff talks directly with them and then reports to the judge—who then consults with the attorney on each side and gives the bailiff a response to take to the jury.

The court reporter is responsible for taking down a verbatim record of everything said during court proceedings. This includes every lawyer's question, every witness's answer, every objection, and every ruling from the judge. The only exception is if the judge—and only the judge can do this—instructs the court reporter that something is "off the record."

The court reporter is responsible for transcribing the verbatim record made during the trial into a permanent, typewritten transcript, and certifying it as an accurate record of the proceedings. This is an especially important function, since the record of exactly what was said at trial is often the basis for an appeal.

Arraignment

In all criminal prosecutions, the accused shall enjoy the right ... to be informed of the nature and cause of the accusation ....

The first appearance that a defendant makes in the courtroom is called the arraignment. At the arraignment, the accused is formally put on notice of two essential things:

♦ The charges made against him, including any aggravating factors that could increase his sentence (called "enhancements").

♦ The constitutional rights that apply during a criminal proceeding, such as the right to remain silent, to be represented by an attorney, to have a jury trial, and to confront witnesses against him. We go over these rights in the next chapter.

Upon knowing the charges against him and the rights he has as an accused person, the defendant then makes an initial plea of either guilty or not guilty.

Hearsay
One of the most-watched arraignments was in 1993, when O. J. Simpson was arraigned for the double murders of his ex-wife, Nicole Brown Simpson, and her friend Ron Goldman. When asked how he wanted to plead at the initial arraignment, Simpson said "Absolutely, positively, 100 percent not guilty." Whatever effect that may have had on the press and public, in the criminal justice system, it had no greater effect than a simple "not guilty" plea.

In about 95 percent of felony cases, the defendant pleads not guilty at the first appearance. This is because the defendant doesn't yet know what evidence the prosecution has against him. At the arraignment, the defendant first learns the specific charges against him and gets his first *discovery* of the evidence gathered against him, including the police report. Only after the arraignment and discovery can the defendant and his attorney properly evaluate the prosecutor's case, look into possible defenses, and make an investigation plan of their own to prepare his defense.

def•i•ni•tion

Every accused person has the right to **discovery,** meaning the right to see and review before trial the documents, witnesses, and other evidence that will be offered against him at trial. At the arraignment, it is the prosecutor's duty to turn over the police reports, criminal records, and any available evidence to the defense for examination.

Setting and Making Bail

As you might imagine, if the defendant were simply released after the arraignment and asked to please return for his trial, some might not show up. Bail is how the criminal justice system makes sure the defendant shows up for trial. According to the Eighth Amendment:

> *Excessive bail shall not be required, nor excessive fines imposed, nor cruel and unusual punishments inflicted."*

The defendant must put up a certain amount of money, called bail, before he will be released pending trial. Then if he doesn't show up at trial, that money is forfeited. The magistrate judge officially sets the amount of bail at the arraignment. The appropriate dollar amount of bail for each type of criminal charge is set by statute, but judges have discretion to deviate from the schedule, deny bail entirely, or change the amount of bail after it has been set if circumstances change. Before doing so, the judge asks the prosecutor and defense attorney to address two questions:

- ◆ Is the defendant a flight risk? In other words, do any special factors about this defendant make it more or less likely that she will show up at trial? For example, a defendant with additional charges against her pending in other states might have an extra incentive to flee. On the other hand, a defendant with extensive business and social ties to the community might be less likely to flee.

- ◆ What risk does the defendant pose to the community in general and the victim in particular? This is usually based on the seriousness of the charges.

When setting bail, the judge takes the police report and the complaint filed by the prosecutor as valid, assuming for purposes of this early arraignment proceeding that they are true. The prosecutor uses the police report to argue the factors that will make a particular defendant a risk to the community or a flight risk.

Another tool that the prosecutor uses to increase bail is the defendant's criminal record, often referred to as a *rap sheet*. This includes how often the defendant has been arrested and convicted, whether she has violated any terms of probation, and whether the defendant has ever failed to appear or ignored a court order. A long rap sheet showing the defendant's pattern of criminal conduct can be a factor in deciding what risk the defendant would be to the community if released, and so in the amount of bail required.

def•i•ni•tion

A **rap sheet** shows a person's prior involvement with the criminal justice system, including prior arrests, convictions, probation violations, and so on.

Bail can be paid in two ways, which is called "making bail." The first is by putting up the full amount in cash. If paid in full, the bail will be refunded in full when the case is over, whether or not there is a conviction.

The second way to make bail is with the help of a bail bond service. For a nonrefundable fee, usually 10 percent, the bail bond service puts up the full amount of the bail. Before doing so, however, the bond service requires that the defendant or someone on his behalf provide enough collateral to cover the full amount of the bail. For example, if bail is $1 million, the defendant would need to pledge property valued at $1 million to the bond service. If the defendant does not show up at trial, the pledged property is turned over to the bond service.

For the Record

Bail bond companies sometimes use bounty hunters to find and return customers who have fled. In one notorious case, Max Factor heir Andrew Luster was released to house custody on $1 million bail during his trial on multiple charges of rape. He fled to Mexico, where he was later apprehended by Duane "Dog" Chapman of Duane Chapman's Bail Bonds. Meanwhile, the jury convicted him in absentia and he was sentenced to 124 years in prison.

Preliminary Hearing

The preliminary hearing is like a "mini" trial, with two key differences. First, instead of deciding the defendant's guilt or innocence, the court decides whether there is sufficient evidence to make the defendant stand trial. In essence, it is a judicial review of the prosecutor's decision to charge the defendant. Second, the standard is not "beyond a reasonable doubt," but the much lower one of "probable cause" to believe the defendant committed the crime.

In a preliminary hearing, witnesses come to court and answer questions from both the prosecutor and the defense attorney. The defense can call witnesses to show an affirmative defense (discussed in Chapter 12) but rarely does this. A judge (not a jury) determines whether there is enough evidence to make the defendant stand trial on specific charges.

The purpose of the preliminary hearing is basically the same as for a grand jury hearing; both review the prosecutor's case to make sure there is sufficient evidence to make the defendant stand trial. When there has been a grand jury hearing, there is usually no preliminary hearing.

Pretrial Motions

Since the judge will resolve any disputes over the admissibility of evidence at trial, the prosecutor or defense attorney, or both, often ask the judge to rule on the admissibility of key pieces of evidence before the trial.

For the Record

Pretrial motions are often time-consuming but have a couple important benefits. One is that they save the jury time. At trial, the jury has to wait in the jury room whenever an argument arises about the admissibility of evidence. Second, sometimes the court's pretrial ruling on the admissibility of a key piece of evidence helps resolve a case. For example, a defendant who is hoping to get his client's confession excluded, but hears the judge reject his Miranda violation claim and so will allow it in, may change his mind and decide to accept a plea bargain. More about plea bargaining in Chapter 18.

When evaluating which type of motions should be brought, defense attorneys and prosecutors assess which pieces of evidence are most damaging to their theory of the case. Then they evaluate any possible grounds for excluding that evidence.

The most common pretrial motions are those which allege a constitutional violation or challenge the qualifications or opinions of *expert witnesses*. Examples of motions to exclude evidence based on a constitutional violation include motions claiming that the evidence was obtained by an improper search in violation of the Fourth Amendment, or motions to exclude a confession obtained in violation of the Miranda requirements based on the Due Process Clause.

def•i•ni•tion

A lay witness is a fact witness, one who testifies to what he personally saw, heard, felt, and so on. An **expert witness** gives scientific opinions or conclusions based on factual evidence gathered by others, such as a forensics expert who examines fiber samples the police gathered from the crime scene and from the suspect's home, and concludes they are identical.

Some of the most difficult and complex pretrial motions are those testing the admissibility of expert witness testimony. Scientific experts with long and impressive resumes can be very persuasive to a jury, and few laymen have the background to assess the quality or reliability of the science involved. As a result, the criminal justice system makes the judge the "gatekeeper" for expert scientific evidence. As gatekeeper, the judge does not decide whether an expert's opinion is right or wrong, but whether the science on which his opinion is based is reliable and proven. Only then is an expert witness allowed to testify.

For example, most jurisdictions do not consider the accuracy of lie detectors sufficiently proven to permit expert testimony based on them. And it was years after DNA typing or matching was first discovered that courts began allowing the admittance of expert testimony based on DNA typing.

Jury of Your Peers

The Sixth Amendment guarantees the criminally accused the right to a trial "by an impartial jury."

> *In all criminal prosecutions, the accused shall enjoy the right to a speedy and public trial, by an impartial jury of the state and district wherein the crime shall have been committed, which district shall have been previously ascertained by law ....*

Without juries or the jurors who serve on them, our criminal justice system would not be able to function.

Being Called to Jury Duty

Juries consists of members of the surrounding community whose names are taken from voter's registrations. Many of you have probably been called to jury service or have even served on a jury. Usually, the call to jury service comes as a notice in the mail requiring you to come down to the courthouse for one week to be on-call for possible jury selection. This generally involves sitting around the courthouse all day, waiting to see if you are selected for a trial—be sure to bring a book, your current knitting project, or whatever. If you're not selected to sit on a jury, your jury duty is over—for at least a year. If you're selected, you are required to remain a juror until the trial is concluded.

Judges do everything they can to be considerate of jurors, realizing that their inconvenience can be great and the pay is generally lousy. But judges also know that jurors are essential to the functioning of the criminal justice system. For this reason, judges are reluctant to excuse people from jury duty for any but the most compelling reasons. An example of such a reason might be that a prospective juror is the primary caregiver of a sick relative. Excuses that generally aren't accepted include being busy at work and not wanting to lose the day's pay.

> **Objection**
>
> Whatever you do, don't try to avoid being seated on a jury by lying, like claiming there is no way you'd ever vote guilty, or that you always believe the police and prosecution and know they'd charge a person only if he or she were guilty. You might find yourself sent over to the civil side, seated on a much longer trial.

Voir Dire

The term *voir dire* (pronounced "vwah deer" with the first "r" nearly silent) is the fancy name for the process of questioning a pool of potential jurors to determine who should—or, rather, who should not—be seated on the jury. The purpose is to discover biases, beliefs, preformed conclusions from reading about the case in the newspapers, or other reasons a juror might not be fair and impartial.

During jury selection, a group of potential jurors—called a jury pool—is brought into the courtroom to be questioned. While most juries ultimately have just 12 members (6 in some states), the pool brought in to be questioned will be much larger, since many will be weeded out during *voir dire*. The questioning may be done by the judge, who often asks the attorneys to submit suggested questions, by the attorneys, or by both the judge and the attorneys.

For the Record

In addition to the 12 (or, in some states, 6) jurors, a judge may select 1 or 2 extra jurors called alternate jurors. Alternate jurors sit and hear all the evidence with the regular jurors, and so are ready to step in for a regular juror who becomes ill or otherwise unable to continue. Some judges excuse the alternates at the close of evidence; other judges allow the alternates to deliberate with the jury, although only the 12 regular jurors may vote.

Voir dire questioning starts out very general, such as name and occupation; then the questions become more specific. Typical questions include whether any juror has been a victim of a crime like that charged, whether one knows the defendant or a witness personally, whether one has a family member in prison, whether one has a family member in law enforcement, and so on.

If the questioning reveals that a prospective juror may be biased or hold some preju-dicial belief or attitude—something serious enough to keep her from being fair and impartial—either the prosecutor or the defense counsel may ask the judge to excuse the juror for cause. There is no limit to the number of jurors that may be dismissed for cause.

An example of a juror who would probably be excused for cause is one who, in a case involving the alleged murder of a child, reveals that her 6-year-old daughter was mur-dered in a random act of violence. The defendant's attorney would likely request that she be excused for cause, namely a possible bias against the defendant, and the judge would likely agree.

Preemptory Challenges

The other way potential jurors may be excused from the jury pool is through *pre-emptory challenges*. A preemptory challenge allows the attorney to reject a potential juror without giving any reason. However, each side is limited in the number of peremptory challenges each may make, usually three.

def•i•ni•tion

A **preemptory challenge** allows an attorney to have a juror removed even though no bias or other cause has been shown, and without giving the reason for the removal.

In a 1986 case called *Batson v. Kentucky*, the United States Supreme Court found that the Constitution imposes an additional limitation on peremptory challenges in criminal cases: a preemptory challenge may never be used to reject a potential juror because of their race, ethnicity, or gender. As you might expect, it is often hard to show that race or gender was the reason for an attorney's rejection of a juror. The judge does not put the attorney under oath and ask whether race was the basis for a challenge. However, under appropriate circumstances, the judge may require an attorney to identify some reason other than race, gender, or ethnicity for the preemptory challenge.

The Least You Need to Know

♦ The judge controls the courtroom and resolves disputes about the admissibility of evidence.

♦ At the arraignment, a magistrate judge reads the defendant the charges against her and advises her of her constitutional rights. She also gets discovery of the prosecutor's evidence and enters her plea of guilty or not guilty.

♦ To be released from custody between arraignment and trial, a defendant usually must post bail, a sum of money set by the judge at the arraignment that will be forfeited if the defendant does not show up at trial.

♦ Pretrial motions are brought to get early rulings on the admissibility of key evidence, which can shorten the trial and facilitate plea bargaining.

♦ *Voir dire* is the pretrial questioning of prospective jurors to uncover bias or other reasons the juror might not be fair and impartial.

Chapter 15

Evidence of a Crime

In This Chapter

- ◆ What is evidence?
- ◆ How the lawyers use different kinds of evidence to prove different issues in the case
- ◆ The process of deciding what evidence the jury will hear, and what will be excluded
- ◆ The privilege against being forced to testify about confidential communications in certain relationships

In this and the next chapters, we finally get to the meat of a criminal trial—the presentation of the evidence. At this point, the jury hears gut-wrenching testimony about the circumstances of the crime and its effect on the victims, experience the investigation as it is reconstructed and explained by the officers who conducted it, and watch witnesses examined and challenged during cross-examination.

Looming over the whole process is the momentous decision the jury has to make at the end: whether to acquit the defendant and let him go free, or to find him guilty and force him to take responsibility for the harm he has caused. To help the jury make the right decision, the criminal justice system is very careful about what evidence the jury hears during the trial. That's what this chapter is about.

Evidence 101

Throughout this book, we have talked about burdens of proof—the prosecutor has to prove guilt beyond a reasonable doubt, a defendant is presumed innocent until proven guilty, and a defendant sometimes has to prove a defense. So what's this "proof," and how is something "proven"? With evidence.

Basically, everything presented to a jury is considered evidence, except for the lawyers' statements and questions. The testimony of fact witnesses and the opinions of expert witnesses are evidence. Documents are evidence. Physical objects, like murder weapons, are evidence. Tape recordings, police reports, and photos are all evidence. Just about everything submitted to the jury that proves or disproves the charges against the defendant is evidence.

While evidence in general seems a simple enough concept, what the system permits to get to the jury is tricky. The Federal Rules of Evidence is a tome several hundred pages long, with over 300 rules—most with multiple subparts and sub-subparts. And then most of the rules have a whole host of exceptions. All of these rules and exceptions hinge on what kind or type of evidence is being offered and what the evidence is being used to show.

As you might expect, when you combine lots of complicated rules and a courtroom full of lawyers, you're going to get some arguments. Add to that the fact that admitting or excluding a key piece of evidence can mean the difference between winning and losing the case, and you've got a lot of *high-stakes* arguments. Add further that a lawyer must make an objection at trial in order to appeal the admission of any piece of evidence, and you can see why there are lots of objections.

So the lawyers raise objections; there are occasionally oral arguments to the court on the objections; and the judge rules. Getting evidence admitted at trial is sort of a dance—you have to bring the right stuff at the right time with the right support for its admission for things to go smoothly.

Basically, to be admitted into court, the evidence must be relevant, must be in the proper form, and must be presented in a way that complies with the evidence rules.

Hearsay
Professor and author H. Mitchell Caldwell, who was my trial advocacy professor, frequently told us that the lawyer who knows the evidence best wins. My experience as a prosecutor has shown this to be true, for the most part. But equally important is knowing the rules of evidence backward and forwards so that you can get helpful evidence admitted and damaging evidence excluded.

Relevance: What Does It Prove?

"Objection! Lack of relevance."

The first requirement for getting evidence admitted is that it must be *relevant* to the trial. Evidence is considered relevant if it tends to prove a fact that matters to the case. For example, evidence that the defendant owned the weapon used in a murder case is relevant because it connects the defendant to the murder weapon and so is one step toward proving that he committed the crime.

Evidence that, in addition to owning the murder weapon, the defendant has a knife collection probably isn't relevant in this trial because it doesn't prove anything about this crime. Taking that example a step further, evidence that one of those knives was used in another crime would be not only irrelevant, but also prejudicial.

def•i•ni•tion

Generally, evidence is **relevant** if it makes any material fact of the case more or less probable than it would be without the evidence.

If the evidence isn't demonstrated to be relevant, then the analysis doesn't go any further, and neither does the evidence. The burden of proving its relevance is on whichever side is trying to get the evidence in. That is to say, if I make a lack-of-relevance objection, I don't have to prove the evidence is irrelevant. The objection will be granted (called "sustained" in court) unless the attorney offering the evidence meets the burden of proving its relevancy.

The question of relevancy necessarily involves the question of what the evidence is being used to show. Sometimes, the relevance is obvious, such as, "This is the gun used to murder the victim," or, "This is a blow-up of the fingerprint found on the gun."

But relevance and what the evidence is being offered to prove can be hard questions that require drawing some pretty fine lines. For example, evidence that, just two weeks before a murder, the defendant told the victim, "I'm gonna kill you!" is not proof that he later did, in fact, kill the victim, so would be irrelevant if offered to prove that. But if the evidence were offered to prove there was bad blood between the defendant and the victim, it would be relevant and admissible.

Character Evidence

"Objection! That question calls for character testimony."

Many people would consider evidence of the defendant's bad character to be relevant to whether he committed a crime. If the crime is burglary, for example, shouldn't evidence that the defendant is shifty, couldn't keep a job, and got fired frequently for petty theft be admissible?

With a couple of important exceptions that we'll get to, the answer the criminal justice system gives is "no." The reason is that proof a defendant is the "kind of person" who might commit a crime is not proof he actually committed the crime of which he is charged.

> ### Hearsay
>
> You may be surprised to find that evidence of a defendant's prior convictions cannot be used as evidence of her guilt in the current case—even if the convictions are for the same crime. The prior convictions may be admissible to prove something else, but not the defendant's propensity to commit the crime charged. Some states—such as California—make an exception to this rule in rape cases: convictions for prior rapes may be used as evidence of the defendant's propensity to rape again.

If the defendant "opens the door" to character evidence, however, the prosecutor may then respond with her own character evidence. This happens in a couple of ways. First, if the defendant offers evidence of his good character, the prosecutor may offer evidence of his bad character.

For example, if a defense witness testifies that the defendant is known for being a nonviolent person, the prosecution may answer with evidence that the defendant has a prior conviction for armed robbery.

The second way the defense can "open the door" is by attacking some aspect or trait of the victim's character. The prosecutor may then show the defendant has the same negative trait. For example, say the defense calls witnesses who say the victim likes to pick fights. The prosecutor may respond with evidence that the defendant himself is a violent hot-head. The prosecution could not go beyond that particular trait and offer, for example, evidence that the defendant was a liar and a thief.

Objection

Evidence of a defendant's violent proclivities may be inadmissible as a reflection of his character, but it may be admissible if it is relevant to some other issue. For example, evidence that the defendant was involved in a violent barroom brawl with the victim a week before the victim was murdered might be admissible to prove that the defendant had a motive for murdering the victim.

Another character evidence issue comes up when a lawyer tries to show that one of her witnesses has an honest character. Such evidence is generally not admissible unless, again, the other side opens the door by first challenging the witness's credibility in some manner.

For example, the defense might attack a prosecution witness with evidence the witness got a reduced sentence in return for testifying against the defendant. In turn, the prosecutor might answer with evidence that the witness told the same story to the police before any deal was offered, or with other examples of the witness's honesty.

Prior Convictions and Bad Acts

"Objection! The prosecutor is trying to prove her case with propensity evidence."

Closely related to bad character evidence is evidence of specific bad acts the defendant has committed in the past. These bad acts may have led to convictions, but that's not required. Even with no conviction, and even if no charges were filed, a prior bad act that could have been charged as a crime can often be used. (DAs like to call this "the good stuff.")

However, like bad character evidence, the prior convictions or bad acts may not be used to prove that the defendant committed the crime charged, with a couple of exceptions. This is because the criminal justice system considers the probative value of such evidence to be outweighed by its prejudice. This concept is important in understanding how the criminal justice system handles evidence.

def•i•ni•tion

Probative value means how valuable some piece of evidence is for proving that a fact is true. **Prejudice** occurs when a jury considers some piece of evidence to have more probative value than it really has.

Probative value simply means how much the evidence helps prove that some relevant fact is true. *Prejudice* means that the jury may give the evidence more weight than it deserves. A good illustration is the set of photographs the police evidence team routinely takes at the crime scene of a murder victim. Such pictures can be grisly, gory, and otherwise extremely upsetting. In some cases, these photos can help prove the identity of the victim, her death, maybe the murder weapon, and so on. If these issues are truly contested and no other evidence exists to prove them, the photos may be admitted.

But if there's no real dispute over these issues or they can be readily proven with other evidence, the pictures likely will be excluded. The reason is that the minimal proof they add is outweighed by the chance that the emotion and horror such pictures generate may improperly sway the jury toward a guilty verdict.

def•i•ni•tion

Propensity evidence is evidence used to show the defendant had a tendency or propensity to commit the instant crime, because he has a history of committing criminal acts in the past.

Such evidence is called *propensity evidence*. While evidence of prior bad acts or convictions is usually excluded when offered to prove the defendant committed the instant crime, such evidence may sometimes be allowed in to prove something else. For example, prior convictions or even prior bad acts may be relevant to prove intent, identity, opportunity, and/ or motive. But even under these circumstances, the judge still has the option to keep out propensity evidence if he or she feels it will be unfairly prejudicial.

In addition, prior convictions for crimes that involved moral turpitude may be used as evidence of bad character, if the door to such evidence has been opened. It may also be used to impeach the defendant's credibility, if he testifies.

The term "moral turpitude" harkens back to what we learned in Chapter 2: that historically, there were two main classes of crimes: *mala in se* and *mala prohibita*. *Mala in se* crimes were those considered evil or inherently wrong. These are the kinds of crimes that involve "moral turpitude." Examples include murder, rape, assault, theft, and so on.

Objection

If the defense attorney asks the defendant whether she was ever convicted of a crime involving moral turpitude and she admits it, the defendant is no longer impeachable with evidence of that conviction because she honestly told the court/jury about it. Now, if the defendant tries to explain away the conviction by saying something like, "I was pressured by the police to confess" or "I was nervous because I'd never had to speak to the police before," the prosecutor then may impeach her by showing that the confession was free and voluntary, and that on numerous prior convictions and even arrests she had spoken to the police.

Prior Bad Acts Evidence in Sexual and Domestic Abuse Cases

"Objection! The prosecutor is trying to prove her case with propensity evidence."

"Objection overruled."

As I mentioned, there are a couple of very significant exceptions to the general rule barring prosecutors from using propensity evidence to argue that, because the defendant did it once, he probably did it again. That exception is in sexual assault and domestic violence cases.

Why does the criminal justice system make an exception for these kinds of cases? One reason is that these crimes often happen "behind closed doors," meaning there often isn't much other evidence. A second reason is that studies have shown that perpetrators of these crimes have a higher likelihood of reoffending.

Opponents of these laws argue that juries tend to give propensity evidence more weight than it deserves. They also question how reliable such evidence is, since the defendant need not have been convicted or even charged for the prior bad act. Most foes of propensity evidence are particularly opposed to statutes (like California's) that allow a prior bad act to be proven by only a preponderance of the evidence—the standard applicable in civil trials—rather than proof beyond a reasonable doubt, which is the normal criminal standard.

Rape Shield Laws

Another protection for victims whose character is attacked on the stand are rape shield laws. Before such laws, defendants would sometimes try to prove that the victim was promiscuous or had a reputation at school for being "easy," to support a claim that the victim had consented to the sexual encounter.

The specific wording of rape shield laws varies from state to state. Generally, however, they restrict such evidence to specific instances of the victim's past sexual behavior that prove one of two things. First, the defense can prove a specific instance when the victim had sex with another person, to show that the other person is the actual source of semen or injury. Second, when consent is at issue in a rape trial, the defense can prove specific instances of prior consensual intercourse between the defendant and the alleged victim.

Testimonial Evidence

When a person takes the witness stand, swears to tell the truth, and then describes what he or she saw, that is called testimonial evidence. It's one of the most frequently used types of evidence. We'll get more into the direct and cross-examination of witnesses in the next chapter, but we need to cover here what determines whether testimonial evidence will be admitted or excluded.

The basic requirement for getting a witness's testimony admitted is showing that the witness is *competent* to testify. As you might expect, competency requires that the witness be physically capable of testifying and mentally able to recall and communicate. In addition, competency requires that the witness be under oath, and that he or she is basing the testimony on personal, first-hand knowledge. Children and even an insane person can be competent to testify, so long as they are capable of understanding their legal duty to tell the truth (which includes the ability to distinguish fact from fantasy) and meet the other requirements.

def•i•ni•tion

Competent to testify means that the witness is physically and mentally capable of recalling events and describing them; is under oath; and is basing his or her testimony on personal, first-hand knowledge.

Personal knowledge is often the most difficult requirement to satisfy. It seems straightforward enough: the witness must have personally perceived the events with his or her own senses. But things can get tricky. For example, let's say a blind person hears a gunshot then hears the victim cry, "Johnny shot me!" The blind person can testify to hearing the shot, may or may not be permitted to testify to what she heard the victim say, but cannot testify that Johnny shot the victim.

The blind witness personally heard the gunshot, so is competent to testify to that perception. She did not, however, personally see Johnny shoot the victim, so is not competent to testify to that. She did personally hear what the victim cried out so is competent to testify about that, but whether she will actually be permitted to testify brings us to the fascinating but even more tricky world of hearsay.

Hearsay

Most people know that calling something hearsay means it isn't credible, but they may not know why—for good reason. What is and isn't hearsay, and when it is or is not admissible, presents some of the most complex issues in the law of evidence.

Again, the basic rule is easy to state, but the devil's in the details. Hearsay is basically one person's testimony about what another person said—the witness *heard* what another person *said*, hence *hearsay*. When the testimony is offered as evidence that what the other person said is true, it is generally not admissible. But there are exceptions galore, along with many other things such out-of-court statements could be offered to prove.

Suppose a witness testifies that she overheard the defendant in a bar complaining that the victim had double-crossed him and that he was going to get even by killing her.

If the testimony about the statement in the bar is used to prove the statement is true, that the defendant was going to kill the victim, then it's hearsay and inadmissible. But if the testimony is offered to prove something other than the truth of the out-of-court statement—say, to prove that the defendant had a motive for killing the victim—it's not hearsay and is admissible.

Other examples of avoiding a hearsay objection by offering it to prove something other than the truth of what was said include statements offered to show why the listener reacted the way he did, or the emotional state of the speaker, or the speaker's knowledge of certain facts.

> **Hearsay**
>
> Hearsay doesn't have to be words. Gestures can also be meant to express something, so a witness's description of someone else's gesture might be hearsay.

> **For the Record**
>
> What if the witness testifies to her own prior out-of-court statement? As long as it's offered to prove the truth of the prior statement, it is still hearsay.

Another common example is statements used to impeach a witness. Let's go back to the previous example, with the prosecution witness testifying against the defendant after reaching a plea-bargain deal. The defense could use evidence that the witness previously said the defendant was innocent. If the evidence of that previous statement was offered to prove that the defendant was indeed innocent, it would be inadmissible hearsay. But because it is offered to impeach the credibility of the witness, it is admissible. See what I meant about it being important to know the rules of evidence?

Even if the out-of-court statement is offered to prove the truth of what was said, and so is hearsay, a number of exceptions to the rule make such hearsay inadmissible as evidence. Consider these frequently occurring examples. A common thread runs through them—can you pick it out?

- The "excited utterance" exception applies to statements made as immediate reactions to a startling event, like a car crash.

- A statement against the speaker's own interest, such as a confession by a suspect, is admissible hearsay.

- Business records kept as part of the normal operations of the business are also admissible hearsay, as are public records such as recorded deeds, court documents, and so on.

- A present-sense impression is similar to the excited-utterance exception, and refers to an immediate response to some physical sensation, such as, "Ow! That's hot!"

- A prior inconsistent statement is allowed only if the person who made the prior statement is a witness; the idea is that the witness is there to explain the prior statement.

- A dying declaration is a statement made just before a person passes away, and is considered reliable because there is probably no motivation to tell a falsehood.

These are just a few of the exceptions to the hearsay rule of inadmissibility in the federal and states' rules of evidence. I've included several more in Appendix D.

What's the common thread? Each of these exceptions (and the others in Appendix D) has a secondary reason to believe the statement is credible: a business needs to keep accurate records to stay in business, people usually don't say things damaging things about themselves unless they are true, and someone reacting to a sudden event doesn't have time to make up a falsehood.

Privileges Against Testifying

Most people have heard somewhere that an attorney can't be forced to testify about what her client told her in confidence. This is called the attorney/client privilege, and a number of other privileges apply to other confidential relationships. Each involves a trade-off. On one hand, the criminal justice system is deprived of possibly relevant evidence. On the other hand, full communication in the privileged relationship is encouraged.

Let's take a look at the ones most frequently encountered in the criminal justice system. Pretty much any confidential communication between a client and her attorney is considered privileged, as long as the communication is made to facilitate legal services. The communication has to be confidential—if the defendant brings a buddy to the meeting with the lawyer, there is no confidentiality and so no privilege.

Some narrow exceptions also apply to the attorney/client privilege. If the communication was for the purpose of furthering some ongoing criminal activity or threatened the life or safety of another person, the privilege is overriden. An example is a defendant who talks to his lawyer about his intent to kill or threaten a witness against him into silence. Also an attorney may break confidentiality to defend himself against a claim brought by the client.

Doctors and psychotherapists similarly need full and candid information from their patients, so communications made to get medical treatment or those related to diagnosis and treatment are privileged. However, if the patient's injuries are at issue in the case, the medical provider may be examined about the injuries but not about what the patient told the doctor about them. Again, the communication is privileged, not the underlying facts. As with attorney/client privilege, if the medical treatment is sought as a means to further criminal activity (for example, if the defendant also talked to his therapist about his plans to kill the witness), the privilege does not apply.

Our society also recognizes the need to protect communication between spouses, which has led to two kinds of spousal privilege. The first applies to confidential communication between spouses. These may not be revealed unless both spouses agree to their

Objection

Only the communication between attorney and client is privileged, not the underlying facts communicated. For example, if the defendant tells his lawyer he sent a threatening letter to the victim, that statement to the lawyer is privileged, but the letter itself is not.

disclosure. The fact they have had a falling-out since the communication or even have gotten divorced doesn't change the privilege—unless both consent, the communication remains confidential.

The second privilege arises when one spouse is asked to testify against the other about something other than a confidential communication between them. If the wife is asked whether her husband was home with her on the night the crime occurred, she may refuse to testify, invoking spousal privilege, or she may choose to testify against her spouse. If she wants to testify against her husband, he can't do anything to stop her—unlike the privilege for private spousal communications.

Why the difference? The reason goes back to the purposes behind privileges like this. To encourage full communication between spouses, both need to know that what they say won't be used against them sometime later—just as with communications with one's lawyer, doctor, or therapist.

In contrast, the other spousal privilege isn't about protecting communications, but is intended to avoid forcing a spouse to give testimony that might damage the relationship. If that spouse doesn't think the testimony will damage the relationship or doesn't care, the protection of a privilege isn't necessary.

 Objection _____

The spousal privileges apply only in a legally valid marriage. So a boyfriend and girlfriend who live together would not have these privileges, nor would two gay persons in a state that doesn't recognize gay marriage. However, communications made during a marriage remain confidential even if the couple later separates or divorces.

The Least You Need To Know

- Evidence must be relevant before it will be admitted, which means that it makes some material fact in the case more (or less) probable than it would be without the evidence.

- Evidence of past bad acts or convictions offered to prove the defendant committed the current charge is not admissibly, except in sexual assault and domestic violence cases.

◆ Similarly, evidence of the defendant's bad character isn't admissible unless the defense "opens the door" to character evidence by attacking the character of the victim.

◆ Before a witness may testify, it must be shown that the witness is competent, meaning he or she is physically capable of testifying, mentally able to recall and communicate, under oath, and testifying on personal, first-hand knowledge.

◆ Hearsay is one person's testimony about what he heard someone else say. When the testimony is offered as evidence that what the other person said is true, it is generally not admissible. But there are many exceptions, usually where other circumstances indicate it is safe to rely on the statement's truth.

◆ Statutes grant confidentiality or privilege against testifying to communications made in certain relationships, such as between lawyer and client, doctor and patient, and husband and wife. The reason for such privileges is to promote full, open communication in these relationships.

Chapter 16

Opening Statements, Witnesses, Objections, and Closing Arguments

In This Chapter

- ◆ Prosecution and defense lay out their cases in opening statements.

- ◆ The witnesses take the stand.

- ◆ Building your case during direct examination and attacking your opponent's case during cross-examination.

- ◆ Objection! Why the lawyers make objections and what they mean.

- ◆ The lawyers argue their view of the evidence and what the jury's verdict should be in their closing arguments.

After the pretrial motions have been decided and the jury is in the jury box, the trial begins. Each trial has basically three parts: the prosecutor and defense attorney frame their case in their opening statements, then present evidence through examining and cross-examining the witness, then sum up and argue for the result they want in their closing arguments. That's what this chapter is about: how the trial actually plays out.

Opening Statements

During opening statements, the lawyers get their first chance to speak to the jury about their case. Since the jury will hear the evidence bit by bit, one detail at a time, lawyers use their opening statement to give the big-picture view of what the evidence will show.

One overused but good description of an opening statement is that it gives a roadmap of the case. Of course, each side thinks that map leads to a different place. So the opening statement is also often used to create a story and a theme that each side uses to summarize its view of the case.

> ### Hearsay
>
> Not all criminal cases are tried before a jury. Of course, the defendant has the right to a jury if desired, as we discussed in Chapter 13. However, if both the defense and the prosecution choose and the judge approves, the case can be tried before only the judge, without a jury.

One big difference between TV trials and real trials is that attorneys in an actual courtroom must follow the "no argument rule" when giving their opening statements. This means the lawyers can only preview the anticipated testimony, exhibits, and other evidence—they are not permitted to argue what they think the evidence means.

Let's consider an example of the no argument rule. Suppose the defense counsel thinks the prosecution's star witness is lying. It's okay for her to describe in her opening the evidence she expects will show the witness is lying, but she may not say, "He's a liar" or "His own mother wouldn't believe that."

To avoid running afoul of the no argument rule, both prosecutors and defense attorneys often preface a statement in their opening by saying, "The evidence will show …."

For the Record

Attorneys may argue what the evidence means in their closing arguments, since at that point the jury has heard the evidence and can weigh that against the attorneys' arguments. But in neither opening nor closing arguments, or at any other point of the trial, is either attorney permitted to argue what they personally believe. The attorneys aren't witnesses, and their personal opinions are not relevant.

I mentioned that skilled lawyers use their opening statements to give an overview of their case and to develop a theme. A theme is a single thought or idea that captures the essence of either the prosecutor's or the defense's case. It grabs the jury's attention and pulls together the various bits of evidence into a single, persuasive theme for the jury to consider throughout the trial. The lawyer later argues this theme during closing statements.

For example, a prosecutor trying a DUI case might say, "This case is about failing to take responsibility for one's actions" and then point out all the times that the evidence will show that the defendant didn't take responsibility for his actions. Maybe he lied about his drinking, or claimed someone else was driving, or refused to cooperate in the field sobriety tests.

Defense counsel sometimes use theme to deflect the jury's natural anger about a violent crime away from the defendant by focusing on a different theme. Consider a rape case, for example. Defense counsel might say something like, "This is the case of a brutal rape, just like the prosecutor said, but my client, Mr. Smith, is not the one who committed it." This type of opening statement gives immediate credibility to the defense by conceding the rape and lays out the defense theme: the wrong man has been charged, and the real rapist is still on the streets.

The Witnesses

Witnesses can play a huge role in a criminal case. Sometimes witnesses are the only evidence available, such as when physical evidence is lacking. As we discussed in the previous chapter, testimonial evidence requires that the witness be competent and that he or she testify based on their own personal knowledge.

But witnesses who testify about their personal perceptions of the facts of a crime—who did what to whom, when, where, and how?—aren't the only kind of witnesses that testify at criminal trials. Expert witnesses are also important—and are growing increasingly important as the techniques and technology of forensic science advance.

Regardless of whether the witness is an expert or a lay person, it's up to the attorneys to ask the right questions the right way and at the right time to pull out the information the jury will need. And believe me, the attorney on the other side isn't going to make that easy.

Fact Witnesses

As we saw in the last chapter, fact witnesses (also known as lay witnesses, to distinguish them from expert witnesses) can testify only about what they personally know—what they themselves saw, heard, and felt firsthand. The jury must decide whether to believe them and how much to believe them.

It's rare, but some witnesses lie. Others may shade the truth, some are honestly mistaken, most carry some kind of bias or preconception, and still others have been influenced by what they've read in the papers or heard from others. The lawyers have to bring this out as much as they can, but the fact is that the buck stops with the jury. They are the ones who have to assess how much weight to give each witness's testimony.

The jury instructions of most states help the jurors by suggesting factors for them to consider in assessing a witness's credibility. For example, California jurors are told:

Every person who testifies under oath is a witness. You are the sole judges of the believability of a witness and the weigh to be given the testimony to each witness.

In determining the believability of a witness you may consider anything that has a tendency reasonably to prove or disprove the truthfulness of the testimony of the witness, including but not limited to any of the following:

- The extent of the opportunity or ability of the witness to see or hear or otherwise become aware of any matter about which the witness testified;

- The ability of the witness to remember or to communicate any matter about which the witness has testified;

- The character and quality of that testimony;

- The demeanor and manner of the witness while testifying;

- The existence of nonexistence of bias, interest or other motive;

- The existence or nonexistence of any fact testified to by the witness;

- The attitude of the witness toward this action or toward the giving of testimony;

- A statement previously made by the witness that is consistent or inconsistent with his testimony;

- The character of the witness for honesty or untruthfulness;

- An admission by the witness of untruthfulness;

- The witness' prior conviction of a felony;

- Past criminal conduct of a witness amounting to a misdemeanor;

- Whether witness is testifying under a grant of immunity.

—California Jury Instructions—Criminal, 2.20 (2007–2008 Ed.)

Fact witnesses can testify to more than just facts. They may also give an opinion when it is based on something they perceived firsthand and requires no special expertise, or when the witness's opinion is helpful in making his whole testimony more clear.

For example, a witness might testify that she observed the defendant prior to the crime and that the witness was yelling words that made no sense to someone who wasn't there. The defense counsel might then ask, "Did you form any opinion about the defendant's mental state based on what you observed?" The witness might then answer, "The opinion I formed is that he was crazy as a loon." This isn't an expert medical opinion about the defendant's sanity, but rather is simply the witness's opinion about what she perceived.

As with factual testimony, many states' jury instructions have suggestions to help the jury evaluate how much weight they should give a lay witness's opinion. Again using California's as an example (hey, they're handy and besides, they're pretty typical):

In determining the weight to be given to an opinion expressed by [a nonexpert] witness …, you should consider:

1. Believability,

2. The extent of the opportunity to perceive the matters upon which the opinion is based and the reasons, if any, given for it.

You are not required to accept an opinion but should give it the weight, if any, to which you find is entitled."

—California Jury Instructions, Criminal, 2.81 (2009).

Other examples of opinions a lay witness might offer are a mechanic offering an opinion about the value of car repair services, the owner of property giving an opinion on its value, and the witness offering an opinion about his own mental state or physical condition. In all of these areas, the witness would know about these things firsthand, and his opinion would be based on that information, so his opinion is admissible. However, any opinions based on facts not perceived by the witness are the exclusive province of expert witnesses.

Expert Witnesses and Scientific Evidence

Expert witnesses are paid to appear in court and testify. In contrast, it is improper and unethical to offer any other witness payment for testimony. Expert witnesses also need not have firsthand perception of the facts upon which their opinions are based, unlike fact witnesses. In addition, many restrictions govern when experts may testify, and these restrictions do not apply to any other kind of witness.

Expert witnesses are brought in specifically to give their opinion on some specialized subject that is beyond the common experience of a jury of laymen. For example, a doctor may give her expert medical opinion on what caused the victim's death, what kind of weapon caused that fatal wound, and what time of day or night the death occurred. A chemist might give his opinion on the toxicity of a certain substance. A lab technician might give her opinion that trace fibers found on the side of the defendant's shoes matched those of the carpet in the victim's apartment. As you can see, some of the most critical and persuasive evidence can come from expert witnesses.

Hearsay
An expert witness does not need a Ph.D. or an M.D. or other evidence of high academic achievement. Anyone with specialized knowledge or experience may qualify as an expert witness. For example, an experienced longshoreman might provide expert testimony about standard procedures for loading and unloading a ship's cargo. A policeman who has spent years dealing with street gangs might provide expert testimony about gang behavior, markings, and so on.

Before an expert witness may testify, three thresholds must be met. The first is the determination that the jury needs to hear from an expert. The jury does not need an expert to tell them that a gun is a deadly weapon, or that a fall from the top of a 30-story building can be fatal. If a fact is within the common knowledge of a layperson, the judge will not allow either side to put special emphasis on that fact by calling an expert to opine about it.

The second threshold is that the expert is, in fact, an expert in this specialized field. The attorney puts the expert on the stand and asks her about her qualifications. As I mentioned, an advanced academic education is not necessarily required. A witness may qualify as an expert because of special knowledge, skill, training, education, or experience in the subject. The judge decides this question and has broad discretion.

For the Record

As a practical matter, judges often find that doubts about the qualifications of an expert "go to the weight." This means that the jury can weigh how qualified the expert is as they consider how much credence to give to his testimony. Some lawyers leave it to opposing counsel to bring out any weaknesses in the expert's qualifications on cross-examination, but I prefer to get them out on the table myself during direct questioning—it takes some of the sting out of the weakness.

The third threshold applies particularly to expert witnesses who use advanced scientific techniques as the basis for their opinions. The criminal justice system allows evidence based on solid science but carefully guards against the use of experimental, unproven, or simply "junk" science. Again, the judge is the gatekeeper assigned the task of deciding what scientific evidence will be allowed in the courtroom.

Federal and state courts use different tests to determine whether scientific evidence is reliable enough to be used or is based on techniques too new to be trusted. Federal courts use a balancing test that is known as the *Daubert* test (from the name of the Supreme Court case that established it) and a motion to exclude scientific evidence as a *Daubert* motion. The *Daubert* test looks to four factors:

- Can the scientific theory or technique be tested, and, if so, has it been?
- Have other experts in the field published and reviewed the scientific theory or technique?
- What is the known or potential rate of error for the scientific theory or technique?
- Is the scientific theory or technique generally accepted in its field?

The federal court judge looks at all these factors to determine whether the scientific evidence is sufficiently reliable to be used as a basis for convicting a defendant.

State courts do not have to follow the federal rule here; *Daubert* is not based on the Constitution, and the states can and do come up with their own criteria for admitting or excluding scientific evidence. For example, California uses the *Kelly* test instead of the *Daubert* test. The *Kelly* test asks only whether the scientific technique or theory is generally accepted by scientists in the field. If it is accepted by a cross-section of the appropriate scientific community, the technique is considered sufficiently sound and expert opinions based on it will be admitted.

Objection

Tests like Daubert and Kelly that look to whether a scientific theory is generally accepted may be the best tests available, but the history of science is replete with instances in which what was "generally accepted" was subsequently proven wrong.

Sometimes, I get my best expert testimony from cross-examining the defense's expert. A good, well-researched plan to cross-examine and discredit the opposition's expert can be even more effective than a motion to exclude his testimony as a whole, or calling my own expert, which only creates a "battle of the experts."

In preparing to cross examine an expert, skilled attorneys consider a number possible weaknesses to attack:

- ◆ Insufficient expertise in the specific subject matter of the opinion testimony

- ◆ Bias, such as large expert fees, always testifying for the defense, or never once believing police testimony

- ◆ Basing the opinion on iffy facts and/or questionable data

- ◆ Incomplete review of all the information available, instead focusing only on the information that supports his opinion

- ◆ When an expert has taken samples to examine, failure to prevent contamination and or corruption of the samples

- ◆ Reliance upon a single test or two, when other tests could have been done to confirm the expert's conclusions

- ◆ Other possible scenarios that would lead to the same opinion

- ◆ Any subjective or judgmental aspect of the opinion

◆ How other qualified experts/learned treatises have used different approaches or have reached different conclusions in similar situations

◆ Prior inconsistent statements in other testimony the expert has given, or in articles the expert has published

◆ Hypothetical questions that ask the expert to assume slightly different facts to test the reasonableness of his opinions.

As with lay witnesses, most states' jury instructions offer help in evaluating expert testimony. In addition to the other factors to consider for any witness's testimony, instructions (such as California's) suggest that the jury:

Consider the expert's knowledge, skill, experience, training, and education, the reasons the expert gave for any opinion, and the facts or information on which the expert relied in reaching that opinion.

You must decide whether information on which the expert relied was true and accurate. You may disregard any opinion that you find unbelievable, unreasonable, or unsupported by the evidence.

—California Jury Instructions, Criminal, 2.80 (2009).

Direct Examination and Cross-Examination

When one of the lawyers asks the witness on the stand questions, it is called an examination of the witness. Two kinds of examination occur: direct examination and cross-examination. When an attorney is questioning a witness she called to the stand, it is direct examination. When she is examining a witness that the other side called, it is cross-examination.

When an attorney calls a witness whose interests lie with the other side—say, the prosecutor calls the mother of the defendant to test on the defendant's alibi—the lawyer may ask the judge's permission to treat the witness as an "adverse" witness, and so use the rules of cross-examination when questioning her.

One big distinction arises between the rules of direct examination and those of cross-examination. On direct examination, the attorney's questions cannot be

def•i•ni•tion

A **leading** question is one that suggests the answer. Leading questions are proper when examining an adverse witness, such as on cross-examination, but are improper when examining a friendly witness called by the side doing the examining.

leading. A leading question is one that essentially tells the witness what answer the lawyer wants. Often such questions call for only a "yes" or "no" answer. For example, "Isn't it a fact that when you came into the house, you saw the defendant pointing a gun at the head of the victim?" is a leading question.

Leading questions do more than suggest the answer. They also confine the witness's answer, often to a simple "yes" or "no." This inhibits the witness's ability to frame his or her answer in a way favorable to the other side. It also forces the witness to answer the question the attorney asked instead of answering the question the witness wants to answer. Leading questions are as much about controlling the witness as they are about eliciting specific information.

Hearsay

A question that calls for just a "yes" or "no" answer isn't always leading. For example, "Did you go out to dinner on the night in question?" isn't leading because it doesn't suggest the answer. On the other hand, "You went out to dinner on the night in the question, right?" is leading because the question not only suggests, but actually has the answer within it.

Making Objections

Anyone who has watched courtroom dramas on TV or at the movies is familiar with an attorney leaping to his feet and exclaiming "Objection!" An objection is made when an attorney believes a question asked by the opposing counsel either is improper in the way it is asked (such as a leading question on direct examination) or calls for evidence that is not admissible or privileged (such as hearsay or an attorney/client communication).

Unlike on TV, however, most judges don't let lawyers get away with "speaking" objections, those that argue the point and are meant more for the jury than the judge. The lawyer needs to state briefly the legal basis for the objection, and no more. "Objection, leading" is a proper objection; "Objection! Judge, he's trying to put words in the witness's mouth!" isn't. I've put together a glossary of common objections and what they mean in Appendix D.

Evidence Objections

As we've discussed, different kinds of evidence must pass different tests before it may properly be submitted to the jury. Evidence objections are made when an attorney questions whether the evidence meets one of these tests.

For example, an attorney may object because a question asks for irrelevant evidence. A prosecutor might ask a teacher at the defendant's school whether the defendant often got into fights at school. Even if the charge is assault and battery, the defense counsel may properly object that this question is not relevant to whether the defendant committed the specific assault and battery charged. If the question were restated as "Did you ever see the defendant and the victim fighting?" The question might well be relevant and an objection to it denied.

For the Record

The judge responds to an objection by either sustaining it or overruling it. Sustaining an objection means the judge agrees that the question is improper, and the witness is not allowed to answer it. Overruling an objection means the judge disagrees with the objection and, consequently, instructs the witness to answer it.

A common objection to the evidence is that the attorney offering it has failed to lay a foundation for its admissibility. For a fact witness, for example, the necessary foundation is that the witness was in a position to perceive firsthand the facts about which she is asked to testify.

For an expert witness, a foundation objection might be based on a failure to show why the witness is an expert, or to show the "general acceptance" of the scientific theory or technique. These may seem like legal technicalities, but they're not; using evidentiary rules like these is how the criminal justice system ensures the reliability of the evidence on which a defendant's guilt or innocence is decided.

Physical evidence must also have a proper foundation, which means there must be evidence that the physical exhibit is what the witness claims it is. For example, if a police officer identifies a gun as the murder weapon, there must be evidence not only that a gun caused the murder, but also that the gun the officer identifies is that same gun.

This requires proving something called the chain of custody of the gun, from the time it was found at the crime scene to when it is offered as evidence in the courtroom.

The prosecutor must put people on the stand who can confirm that the gun was taken from the crime scene by police, held at the police station in a locked evidence locker, and then brought to the courtroom. Without evidence of this chain of custody, there is no foundation for the exhibit, and no way to be sure that the gun is the same gun as was found at the crime scene.

Hearsay is another common evidentiary objection. As you saw in the earlier discussion, unless an out-of-court statement fits one of the exceptions to the rule that hearsay is not admissible or is offered for something other than the truth of the statement, an objection to its admissibility will be sustained on the grounds that it is hearsay. Only evidence submitted in open court and subject to cross-examination is considered sufficiently reliable.

Objections to the Lawyers' Questions

Attorneys can raise numerous objections to the way the opposing counsel asks questions during an examination. We've already discussed a common basis for such objections, namely that a question asked on direct examination is improperly leading. But several other objections arise regarding the way an attorney asks her questions.

An attorney may object to a question that is ambiguous or is compound, which means it contains two questions (or more) in one. With such vague questions, it is unclear which question the witness is answering or what the witness's answer really means.

Another common objection is that a question "calls for a narrative answer." If a question asks the witness to give a long answer covering multiple events, this objection would apply. The problem with a narrative answer is that it may include inadmissible things like lay opinion or hearsay, and opposing counsel will have no opportunity to object before that improper testimony is presented to the jury.

"Asked and answered" is an objection used when the opposing counsel asks a question that has already been answered, but rephrases that answer in subtly different ways. Sometimes the examining attorney is trying to elicit an inconsistent answer; other times he is trying to hammer on an issue to keep the jury's attention on the favorable parts of the witness's testimony. Either purpose is improper, so the opposing attorney may object.

An attorney may object to the examining counsel's question as "argumentative." Do you remember our discussion about attorneys not being allowed to express their opinion on the evidence? When an attorney argues with or badgers the witness, the attorney may, by implication, express her views about the truthfulness or reliability of the testimony. Argumentative questioning may also be used to fluster the witness. Such questioning is improper and usually draws an objection.

A common examination technique is for an attorney to repeat the witness's answer back to him, but with a slight change in content or emphasis. For example, a witness may say, "I don't remember seeing the defendant that day," and the attorney may respond, "So you're saying you didn't see the defendant that day?" This is not an accurate restatement of the witness's testimony and will draw an objection claiming that the question "misstates the witness's testimony." If there is any doubt, the judge may ask the court reporter to read back the disputed question and answer for clarification.

A subtle but particularly effective form of improper question is one that "assumes facts not in evidence." The classic example of such a question is "When did you stop beating your wife?" The assumption in the question is that the witness beat his wife at some point, yet the question asks only when the witness stopped such beatings. Such a question that contains an unsupported assumption is improper and usually draws an objection.

One final example of an objectionable question is a question that "calls for speculation." This is a kind of foundation objection—there has been no showing that the witness has firsthand knowledge with which to answer the question, so any answer she gives is no more than a guess. A common question that draws this objection is one that asks the witness what the defendant meant by something she said, or what she intended by some act. Since the witness cannot read the defendant's mind, any answer would be speculation.

Judge and Counsel Conferences Without the Jury

One aspect of trials that may confuse and, frankly, often irritate jurors is when an objection is raised and the attorneys ask for permission to "approach the bench" to discuss it out of the hearing of the jury. Sometimes the jury is even "excused" from the courtroom so the arguments about such objections may be heard and resolved without the jury hearing anything about it.

The reason for this is a concern that the jurors may be prejudiced if they hear the arguments made by the attorneys, or the judge's ruling in favor of one side or the other. Remember that statements and arguments of counsel are not to be considered as evidence, and rulings of the judge are not to be interpreted as expressing the judge's opinion on the merits of either side's case. Holding such legal arguments outside the presence of the jury is an attempt to insulate the jurors from improper influences.

Closing Arguments

Closing arguments give the prosecutor and the defense attorney a chance to tell the story of their case in its entirety. Closing arguments are meant for argument, theory, and pure advocacy.

For the Record _____

While most everything is fair game in a closing argument, a prosecutor must still refrain from commenting on a defendant's exercise of his right to remain silent. A comment from the prosecutor like "Why didn't we hear the defendant's version?" is reversible error. Another limitation is that the lawyer can't give her personal opinion, like, "I'm a D.A., and I never would have tried this case if I didn't believe the defendant's guilty." This may or may not be grounds for reversal, depending on how prejudicial the judge and court of appeals feel it was.

Like opening statements, effective closing arguments use the attorney's theory and theme of the case to show why the jury should return a favorable verdict. Closing statements also can explain difficult legal issues in the instructions on the law the jury will receive from the judge, like what "reasonable doubt" really means. In addition, closings can show how specific facts and evidence support the attorney's case, the reasons for believing or disbelieving certain witnesses, the evidence that refutes the opposing side's theory of the case, and favorable facts that are undisputed.

The Least You Need to Know

- Lawyers use opening statements to give an overview of their case and the evidence that will support it.

- Fact witnesses are limited to testifying about what they have personally perceived, while expert witnesses may—if properly qualified—offer opinions about the meaning or significance of facts they have not personally perceived.

- The primary difference between direct examination of a witness (examination of a witness the attorney has called) and cross-examination of an adverse witness is that leading questions may be used in cross-examination but not in direct examination.

♦ Attorneys make objections when they feel a question has been improperly stated, or that it calls for inadmissible testimony.

♦ Conferences between the judge and the attorneys are sometimes held outside of the presence of the jury in order to prevent the jury from being improperly influenced by the arguments.

♦ Closing statements are the opportunity for the attorneys to sum up what their evidence has shown, explain confusing questions about the instructions that the judge will give to the jury, point out evidence that supports their favorable witnesses and impeaches unfavorable witnesses, and otherwise summarize their case.

Jury Instruction, Deliberation, and Verdict

In This Chapter

◆ Instructing the jurors on the law they are to apply

◆ What happens in the jury room during deliberations

◆ What if the jury has a question?

◆ Juror misconduct, discharging a juror, and seating an alternate juror

◆ The verdict

I am dying to sit on a jury. I know that's the opposite of what most people think when they get that official-looking envelope calling them to jury duty. But not me. I want to know firsthand what really goes though jurors' minds, to be there to see how they deliberate, to discuss the evidence with them, to cast my vote to convict or acquit, and then to work and argue to get the votes necessary for a verdict.

But I've never been on a jury. Why? Well, if you were a defense attorney, would you let a full-time prosecutor sit on your jury? I'll talk about how defense attorneys avoid that in a minute.

From what jurors have told me, and the many scholarly articles I've read on the subject, I know that a lot of things influence a verdict besides the evidence and my impassioned closing arguments. After all, jurors are people. They have to be thinking, feeling human beings to do their job, and do it well. It's simple human nature that sometimes prejudice and opinions infiltrate the objectiveness of a juror's thinking.

Jurors can be influenced, sometimes without their knowing it, by things like how the defendant does his hair, how the lawyers are dressed, or an accent with which a witness speaks. Even more influential are things like whether the jury liked the defendant, felt deep compassion for the victim, or disbelieved a witness because the lawyer on cross-examination indirectly communicated her distrust of the testimony. Sure, such influences are improper and the system strives mightily to avoid them, and the judges instruct their juries not to be motivated by passions for or prejudice against the defendant. But the reality is that it happens.

Most of the time when we think of a jury, it seems like a fairly straightforward job. In reality, matters like defining the precise wording of the instructions on the law from the judge, handling questions during their deliberations, dealing with juries that can't reach a verdict, and finally accepting the verdict are neither simple nor precise issues.

The Judge Instructs the Jury

After the prosecution and defense attorneys finish their closing arguments and sit down, all eyes turn toward the jury—it is time to see what they will decide. But of course they don't decide then and there. First they must *deliberate*, discuss the case among themselves in the jury deliberation room. And before they are excused to deliberate, they're given very specific instructions about the law and how they are to make their decisions.

How the Instructions Are Worded

The prosecuting and defense attorneys often disagree on the precise wording of the instructions the judge should give the jury. Before the trial even begins, each side will have presented the judge with jury instructions that reflect their view of the law. The judge may pick one or a combination of the two, or may draft her own. The judge's job is to make sure the instructions accurately state the law and are not prejudicial to either side.

Criminal cases generally have two types of nonpattern or *tailored* instructions. *Amplifying* instructions clarify an aspect of a pattern instruction that may be vague as applied to the particular circumstances of the case. *Pinpoint* instructions reconfirm that the prosecution has the burden of proof on a particular issue involved, such as premeditation. These tailored instructions are rarely used. Since errors in jury instructions are often asserted as a basis for appeal, it is safer to stick with the pattern instructions.

For the Record _____

All but two states use pattern jury instructions for many of the routine or frequently used matters on which a jury is instructed. Some of these pattern instructions are fairly simple, maybe with a couple of blanks to be filled in, but many are more complex and must be tailored to the facts of the individual case.

The jury instructions are delivered orally by the judge presiding over the case; some, but not all, courts also provide a written set of the instructions for the jury to take into the jury room. The instructions are taken down verbatim by the court reporter and become part of the court record, which is important because defendants sometimes claim on appeal that an error was made in the instructions.

The judge's instructions begin by stating the law that governs the case, as well as any important terms in the law with which the jury may be unfamiliar. This is when the jury is told what we covered in Part 2—all of the elements of each crime charged. Remember how specific the elements of crime can be? Well, the judge's instructions explain each of them and remind the jury that each must be proven beyond a reasonable doubt for the defendant to be found guilty.

The judge will also address things that have come up during trial. For example, if the credibility of a witness is called into question, the judge may instruct the jury on how to evaluate credibility, considering such factors as these:

◆ The character and quality of the testimony

◆ Demeanor while testifying

◆ Ability to perceive and recollect the event

◆ Ability of the witness to remember

◆ Any motive to be untruthful, such as bias or interest

There is even a pattern instruction that says, in effect, that if a juror thinks a witness's testimony was materially false in one area, the juror may disbelieve everything that witness said.

If the defendant didn't take the stand, the judge will probably explain that it is his right not to, and that this can't be used against him or taken as evidence of his guilt. If there were only one or two witnesses for the prosecution, the judge will tell the jury that there is no requirement for any specific number of witnesses—one witness is enough if her testimony proves the prosecutor's case. Similarly, simply calling a parade of witnesses who say the same thing doesn't add to the weight the jury should give their testimony. In fact, the judge often instructs the jury not to decide a case based on the number of witnesses on one side versus the other.

Explaining "Beyond a Reasonable Doubt"

Not just jurors have trouble wrapping their minds around these four seemingly simple little words. Judges and everyone else trying to come up with instructions that explain the concept have trouble, too. California judges define "beyond a reasonable doubt" as the level of certainty that leaves jurors with an abiding conviction of the truth of the charge.

Here's my favorite way to explain "beyond a reasonable doubt" to the jury, one I frequently use in my closing arguments. I bring a can of Diet Coke to the last day of trial but keep it in my wheelie briefcase until I get permission from the court to take it out and set it beside me on the prosecution's table. The jury members, of course, have never seen any kind of drink but a pitcher of water on either counsel's table, so they're wondering what the heck is going on.

During my closing argument, I take the Diet Coke can and shake it, really hard, right in front of the jury box. Up and down the can goes, and the jurors' eyes go up and down with it as their wonder starts to turn to worry. After a good 15 seconds of hard shaking, I lean in really close to the jurors and ask them if it's okay for me to pop the top of the can. As one, they lean back in their chairs shaking their heads, "No," often with a vocal juror or two exclaiming, "No way!"

I ask, "Why not?" and the answer is clear: "Because the Coke will explode all over everything!" I say, "How do you know that, for sure? Maybe I punched a little hole and drained all the soda out. You heard no testimony from experts giving scientific proof it will explode. Yet you know it will, because all of you know that when you shake a soda can and open it, it'll spew like a geyser. That, ladies and gentlemen, is proof beyond a reasonable doubt. Can your imagination come up with some crazy reason the can might not explode? Sure, but the ability to imagine some crazy reason isn't the standard. If it were, no one would ever get convicted of any crime, anywhere. Your doubt has to have a reasonable basis."

For the Record _____

Many a case has been overturned for poor or inaccurate explanations of what "beyond a reasonable doubt" means. Any definition must not shade in favor of the prosecutor by easing her burden of proof, or increase it as the defense may wish. As a result, once a definition gets approved by the state's highest court, it tends to become the pattern instruction even if some possibly clearer alternative is proposed.

Instructing on Lesser Included Crimes

In certain cases judges are also required, even if neither side asks for it, to give jury instructions on *lesser included crimes,* those that were necessarily committed as part of the greater crime but not separately charged. The judge's instruction will define the lesser included crime and tell the jury that it may find the defendant guilty of the lesser crime if the jury doesn't find sufficient proof of the more serious crime.

def•i•ni•tion _____

A **lesser included crime** is one that could have been charged, since it was a necessary part of the more serious crime, but only the more serious crime was charged. Prosecutors may decide to charge only the more serious crime because the penalties are more severe, and to prevent the defendant from avoiding those more severe penalties by pleading guilty to the lesser crime.

A legal distinction exists between a lesser included crime and a lesser related crime, one that is related to the greater crime but not necessarily part of it, such as receiving stolen property. If the defendant was caught red-handed with stolen property, but there is a reasonable doubt whether he himself stole it, receiving stolen property might be a lesser related crime.

The judge must instruct on lesser included crimes but has discretion on whether to instruct on lesser related crimes. If the lesser crime is closely related to the greater crime and there is evidence to support the lesser charge, the judge will probably instruct on the lesser related crime.

As you might imagine, keeping track of lesser included crimes and lesser related crimes can be tough. In practice, however, judges and lawyers use lists of these in pattern jury instructions, judge's bench books, or the complaint or other accusatory pleadings.

Jury Deliberations

As you probably are aware, juries have special jury rooms outside of the courtroom, where they deliberate. Jury rooms are locked and guarded, and the jury members are left to deliberate. All of the jury's deliberations that occur in the jury room are kept completely secret.

One of the first steps for the jury is to choose a foreperson to preside over the deliberations, which means he encourages the jury to go over all the evidence, makes sure all jurors have the chance to express their opinions, handles jury voting, and delivers the jury's verdict in court.

The judge determines what the jurors take with them into the jury room and what was admitted into evidence. Usually jurors are allowed to take any paper exhibits that have been received into evidence, their own notes, and any other physical exhibits—unless the court rules they should not go to the jury room. Judges may decide that particularly gruesome pictures, weapons, or anything dangerous should not go to the jury room. Drugs admitted into evidence in drug cases are generally not allowed in a jury rooms. Knowing this, prosecutors make sure they have pictures of the drugs, and the pictures are allowed into the jury room instead.

For the Record

Jurors can be taken to the crime scene if the judge agrees they need to see it for themselves. For example, in the trial of Phil Spector for allegedly murdering Lana Clarkson, a key issue was where Spector was standing at the time Clarkson was shot. The jury was taken to Spector's home and allowed to stand in the foyer and view the alleged crime scene.

During deliberations, the jurors discuss the evidence, the instructions they received, whether the prosecutor has proven her case, and whether the defendant has proven his defense, if one was argued. The jurors will not have transcripts of the trial testimony, but they may have transcripts of 911 calls, interviews, and so on, if admitted.

Periodically during their deliberations, the jurors will vote—seeing whether enough of them agree to reach a verdict. We'll get to that part in a minute.

For the Record _____

If the jury deliberations last longer than one day and there are particular reasons to be concerned about outsiders influencing the jury, the jury may be sequestered. Sequestering usually involves putting the jury members up in a hotel, where they have limited or no access to outside news sources or contacts with others. Sequestering is expensive and not at all popular with juries, especially for long trials. It's not very common and generally occurs only in high-profile cases where there is a lot of publicity and/or a plausible risk of jury tampering.

Handling Jury Questions

As I've said, the jurors' job is to evaluate the evidence presented to them. Their role does not require them to prepare questions—that's the lawyers' job. However, sometimes a juror has a question, either during the trial or during jury deliberations.

Here's the usual protocol for dealing with a juror's question: first, the question is submitted to the court in writing, usually via the deputy or bailiff. The judge then assembles both lawyers and, on the record, reads them the question. The attorneys make their recommendations about how the question should be answered, the judge accepts one side's recommendation or drafts her own, and the lawyers make their objections on the record. The judge then addresses the jury as whole (not just the juror who asked the question) and reads the response.

If there is a question during deliberations pertaining to the law, the judge often refers back to the jury instructions, highlighting which instruction to read, rather than drafting a new response. This tends to keep the jury on the right path with the law.

Hearsay

Lawyers and jurors aren't the only ones who can ask questions. Sometimes the judge may have a question for a witness during the trial. As long as the question doesn't suggest that the judge favors one side, she is usually permitted to ask the question. However, an attorney who feels the question improperly indicated bias from the judge should put his objection on the record, to preserve the issue for appeal.

Discharging a Juror

Sometimes it becomes necessary to discharge a juror. However, if this means there will be less than the required number of jurors (usually 12, but in some states 6) to deliberate and reach a verdict, the judge must declare a mistrial and begin the whole process again.

To avoid this, it is customary in most trials for judges to seat at least two extra jurors, called alternates. The alternates sit in the jury box with the others, hear all the same evidence, and basically are treated just like the other jurors. Two is usually sufficient, but when the attorneys and judge anticipate a long trial (a month or longer), the judge may decide to seat more than two alternates.

One obvious reason for needing an alternate to replace one of the original jurors is when a juror dies. Some other reasons why a judge might discharge a juror include the following:

 ◆ The juror becomes ill.

 ◆ Good cause is shown that the juror cannot perform her duties.

 ◆ The juror requests to be discharged because he is too emotionally involved in the case and can no longer be impartial.

 ◆ The juror becomes a victim of a crime similar to that charged in the case.

 ◆ The juror is inadvertently exposed to outside information about the case, which may later give rise to a presumption of prejudice.

 ◆ Juror misconduct occurs.

Handling Juror Misconduct

Juror misconduct doesn't refer to hanky-panky in the jury room. Rather, it means any improper juror action that could potentially prejudice the fairness of the proceeding. Juror misconduct could be sleeping during the trial, failing to answer a voir dire question truthfully, reading newspaper accounts of the case, talking with another juror about the case outside of the jury deliberation room, or engaging in any other prejudicial behavior.

Once possible juror misconduct is raised to a judge, the judge must investigate it and, if the misconduct occurred, address what should be done about it. Juror misconduct does not always require discharging the juror. The judge may decide the risk of prejudice can be handled by admonishing the individual juror, reinstructing all of the jurors about proper behavior, and obtaining renewed promises to follow the court's instructions.

If misconduct is too severe to be handled by an admonishment, the judge must decide whether to just replace the individual juror with an alternate, or whether the misconduct has tainted the entire panel. If the potential prejudice from the misconduct has spread to the whole jury (or to more jurors than there are alternates), the judge must declare a mistrial and begin the case anew—with a new jury.

The Verdict

Any lawyer, defendant, or interested party will tell you that waiting for a verdict can seem insufferably long. Minutes seem like hours, hours like days. However, no matter how long it takes, no one is allowed to put time pressures or deadlines on the jury. No one is allowed to sit in with them to "help speed things up." No one is allowed to tell them how long their deliberations "should" take.

The jury must decide whether they find the defendant guilty or not guilty—these are the only two verdicts available. Once the jury finishes deliberations and comes to a decision, the foreperson will inform the bailiff. The bailiff then tells the judge that the jury has reached a verdict, and the judge calls everyone back into court. At that point, the judge asks the foreperson what the jury decided, and the jury's verdict is entered as the final judgment.

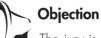 **Objection**

The jury is allowed to render only a verdict—no explanation of the reasoning behind their decision is required or allowed.

The Vote to Convict or Acquit

Contrary to popular opinion, the Constitution does not require that a jury's verdict be unanimous, nor does it require 12-person juries. Some states use 6-person juries; others use 12. Almost all require a unanimous verdict, while a few require only 11-to-1 or 10-to-2 to convict or acquit. The Supreme Court has even upheld one state's law, Louisiana's, that requires only 9-to-3. The Court has also held, however, that with six-person juries, the verdict must be unanimous.

Getting 9 out of 12 people to agree on anything is tough; getting all 12 to agree is a daunting task. But this is what our criminal justice system requires—and, if you think about it, disagreement in the jury room suggests reasonable doubt, which is an argument that proponents of the unanimity rule make.

Whatever majority the particular state's law requires, that majority must be present not just for a vote to convict, but also for a vote to acquit. Many times, the foreperson will take a vote several times throughout deliberations to see where the jurors stand. Only verdicts supported by the requisite majority are taken to the judge and read onto the record.

Hung Jury

If, after extensive deliberation, the requisite unanimity or majority cannot be reached, the foreperson tells the judge that the jury is deadlocked. Typically, the judge instructs them to keep trying and may emphasize the importance of listening to and considering every juror's input. If this doesn't work and indications are that the differences of opinion among the jurors can't be resolved by any further deliberation, we have what is called a *hung jury*.

def•i•ni•tion

A **hung jury** is one that cannot, after extensive deliberation, reach the unanimous or required majority agreement to either acquit or convict.

A hung jury means the judge must declare a mistrial and dismiss the jury. It's up to the prosecutor whether to retry the defendant. If she decides to go ahead with a new trial, the whole case goes back to square one—starting with a rearraignment and new trial date. In deciding whether to retry a case, the prosecutor weighs factors like the likelihood a second trial would result in a conviction, the seriousness of the crime, and the expense of another trial.

Need for a New Trial

A new trial typically happens in three ways. One is what we just discussed—when the judge declares a mistrial for juror misconduct, a hung jury, or some other reason. Another is when the judge grants a motion for a new trial. The third is when a guilty verdict is overturned on appeal.

A motion for a new trial is made by the party that lost at trial. To win such a motion, the losing party has to show that substantial legal errors occurred during the trial.

Most of the contested legal issues involved in the case, such as the admissibility of a piece of evidence or the wording of a particular jury instruction, will have already been argued and ruled on by the judge. So a new trial motion basically asks the court to change its mind—and, as you might expect, such motions are rarely granted. Occasionally, however, some newly discovered issue arises, such as when post-verdict juror interviews reveal jury tampering or juror misconduct. Although it does happen occasionally, getting a new trial by this means is rare.

The third way to get a new trial is by appeal. If the defendant is found guilty at trial, he can appeal the verdict. On appeal, the defendant cannot reargue the facts or submit new evidence. The defendant may only argue that some legal error occurred and was serious enough to prejudice the fairness of the trial. Such legal error might be an incorrect evidentiary ruling or jury instruction, failure to declare a mistrial after some juror misconduct, or court misconduct—or the defense may argue that there was so little evidence to support the verdict that it must have been the result of bias or prejudice.

If the court of appeals finds that any of these errors occurred, it then decides whether they were prejudicial to the fairness of the trial. The court might find that an error was not prejudicial—that it was harmless, if it was minor, adequately addressed by a *curative instruction* from the court, or that other, properly admitted evidence amply supported the verdict. But if the court of appeals finds that an error was prejudicial, it reverses the conviction and sends the case back for a new trial.

def•i•ni•tion

A **curative instruction** is one the judge gives the jury to correct or "cure" some mistake made during the trial. For example, a witness might unexpectedly include some hearsay evidence in one of his answers. Upon objection to the hearsay, the judge instructs the jury to disregard the part of the answer that was hearsay.

The Least You Need to Know

◆ When the evidence is in and the closing arguments have been given, the judge instructs the jury on the law to apply, the elements of the crime that must be proven, and what "beyond a reasonable doubt" means.

◆ Once instructed on the law, the jury retires to the jury room to deliberate. The jurors select a foreperson, discuss the evidence, and attempt to reach a verdict.

◆ Juror questions during deliberations may be sent in writing to the judge, who discusses them with the attorneys and then either refers the jury to the instructions for the answer or answers the question herself.

◆ Most states require all jurors to agree before reaching a verdict of guilty or not guilty, although some allow 11-to-1 or 10-to-2.

◆ If enough jurors cannot agree, after full deliberations, the jury is considered "hung" and a new trial is ordered.

Part 5

The Post-Trial Criminal Justice System

The trial is over. If the verdict is not guilty, the defendant is released, and he's out of the criminal justice system. But what happens next for a defendant who is convicted? We delve into the concepts and theories of criminal punishment, and we compare them to the penalties of the civil system.

Part 5 closes with an important chapter: the role victims play in the criminal justice system and what happens to them. Sometimes a conviction means the victim gets restitution; other times it simply means punishment for the defendant. At the extreme, participating in the criminal justice process can force victims and their families into witness-protection programs. Although the investigation and trial focus on the defendant, victims of crimes are often more deeply affected—and never made whole.

Chapter 18

Conviction and Sentencing

In This Chapter

◆ *Why* the criminal justice system punishes

◆ What happens at the sentencing hearing

◆ The factors that go into setting the length and terms of the sentence

◆ The pros and cons of plea bargaining

◆ Where, when, and how the death penalty is applied, and its constitutionality

The evidence is in, the jury has deliberated, the foreperson has announced the verdict—"We find the defendant guilty, your Honor"—and the bailiff has cuffed the defendant and escorted him from the courtroom. Now what?

One more critical step comes in before we're done: the sentencing. Here we look at the purposes for sentencing (you may be surprised!), how the length of the sentence is determined, sentencing terms other than prison time, the pros and cons of plea bargaining, and probation and parole. We close with a look at the death penalty—the ultimate punishment—and whether it is "cruel and unusual" under the Eighth Amendment.

The Purposes of Sentencing

The reason for sentencing is punishment, right? Well, yes, no, and maybe so. To illustrate, think about why a parent punishes a child for misbehaving, say after she draws a picture of the pony she didn't get for her birthday on the living room wall. Sending her to the corner for a "timeout" is simple retribution punishment, at least in part. But the goal of the timeout is also to change her behavior—to deter her from drawing on the wall again. And the timeout keeps her from getting into trouble for at least a little while, perhaps long enough for Mommy to cool down.

If, instead of the timeout, the punishment is for the child to clean the wall, then another goal is added—to have the child undo some of the damage and perhaps better appreciate the consequences of the misbehavior.

Believe it or not, each of these goals—retribution, deterrence, prevention of reoccurrence, and restoration—or a combination of them can be the purpose for sentences imposed by the criminal justice system. Let's take a look at each.

Retribution

Probably the harshest theory of punishment is retribution. Retributive punishment is your basic "eye for an eye" scenario. The more serious the harm caused by the crime, the more severely the system should punish the criminal. Retribution focuses on proportionality between the crime and the sentence, and basically seeks revenge.

The retributive theory of punishment gets a lot of flack because it is so tunnel-visioned in its focus on just the one act and its harm. Sometimes these are not accurate indicators of the "badness" or moral depravity of the offender.

For example, consider a driver who is distracted by a bee in the car and swerves onto the shoulder, striking and killing a mother walking with her child. Now compare that act to another that also results in two deaths: an estranged husband who breaks into his ex-wife's apartment with a gun, waits for her to come home with their child, and shoots them both. While the damage from the two events are equally tragic, the depravity of the offender's conduct is not. The goal of retribution alone fails to consider the whole character of the offender or the broader circumstances of the crime.

Incapacitation

Unlike retribution, which looks only backward at the crime, the incapacitation theory of punishment is forward looking. The goal of incapacitation is to keep the offender from committing another crime.

In other times and cultures, incapacitation is translated into cutting off a thief's hand so he cannot steal again. A less drastic example from our own culture is suspending one's driver's license after a conviction for driving under the influence of liquor or drugs. The offender is rendered incapable of committing the same crime again—at least, in theory.

Another form of incapacitation is removing the offender from society. What historically was accomplished by banishing criminals from society is now achieved by putting them in prison. But incapacitation is, at best, a temporary fix, and the costs of building and running prisons is high. For these and other reasons, incapacitation has received a good deal of criticism as a theory of punishment.

Deterrence

Also a forward-looking theory, deterrence takes a bigger picture of preventing future crimes than does temporary incapacitation. This theory looks at punishment as a way to discourage a person from choosing to commit a crime, generally through fear of punishment.

Deterrence can be specific or general. Specific deterrence tries to dissuade just the defendant being sentenced from committing more crimes. Under this theory of deterrent punishment, the goal is to make the sentence just bad enough to convince the offender that he never wants to go through that experience again.

General deterrence tries to dissuade the overall population from committing the same crime by making an example of the offender. Critics of general deterrence argue that it overpunishes the individual, with little done to prevention future criminal behavior.

For the Record _____

Some people felt that Paris Hilton's 45-day jail sentence for violating her probation on a drunk-driving conviction was excessive and an attempt to send a message that celebrities aren't above the law—that it was an example of general deterrence. Her lawyer, Howard Weitzman, was quoted in the press as saying, "I think she was singled out because she's who she is."

def•i•ni•tion

Recidivism is when a defendant who has served a sentence for one crime commits an additional crime or crimes after his release.

Whether or not you agree with the deterrence theory of punishment, statistics paint a somewhat bleak picture about its effectiveness. The high level of *recidivism*—that is, criminals returning to a life of crime after their release—suggests that the deterrence theory of punishment may not be doing a very good job.

Rehabilitation

As a theory of punishment, rehabilitation is a far more ambitious and complicated approach. Like deterrence, rehabilitation aims to prevent and reduce criminal activity, but it seeks to instill much more than just the fear of being punished again.

Rehabilitation takes a good look at the offender and tries to fashion a sentence that will help that particular defendant "go straight"—that is, to not commit more crimes. Rehabilitation can include jail time, but it can also involve a number of alternative sentences, such as interventions, drug treatment, and counseling.

A great example of a rehabilitative sentence was illustrated in the movie *Anger Management*, in which Adam Sandler's character is sentenced to anger-management therapy after lashing out at a stewardess on a plane. Although it's comedic and over-the-top, the movie demonstrates how a rehabilitative punishment can be effective.

Rehabilitation can be especially effective for criminal behavior linked to drug use. The need for money to support a drug habit is a common cause of crime. Sentencing a drug offender to a drug treatment program provides the tools necessary for the offender to break the habit.

Rehabilitation has proven to be most successful for nonviolent offenders and first-time offenders. This makes sense, since these offenders haven't yet been caught up in a cycle of criminal behavior. Repeat offenders show a far lower success rate from rehabilitative punishment. Another drawback to rehabilitative sentences is that the services they call for are expensive and require a great deal of funding.

Restoration

A recent trend in criminal justice is toward a restorative theory of punishment. Instead of fitting the punishment to the crime, or even fitting it to the criminal, restoration looks at righting the wrong done to the victim by having the offender make amends.

Restorative justice programs often include several steps. The victim and offender are brought together to discuss the harm caused by the crime. A plan is developed for the offender to amend and repair the harm he caused. Then steps are taken to restore both the victim and the offender as positive members of their community.

In my experience, restoration can bring the victim and the offender a great deal more closure than any of the other theories of punishment. Being able to interface with your offender can ease a lot of the psychological effects of the crime. In the same way, being able to apologize and explain yourself to your victim can bring peace of mind to the offender—and bring home the real human harm caused by crime. Unfortunately, because crimes, offenders, and victims vary so greatly, restorative justice is not always a possibility.

Cruel and Unusual Punishment

Another right given defendants in the Constitution is the Eighth Amendment's protection against cruel and unusual punishment.

> *Excessive bail shall not be required, nor excessive fines imposed, nor cruel and unusual punishments inflicted.*

At one time, the method of putting a person to death was deliberately cruel. Unfortunately, many examples exist: burning at the stake, impaling, drawing and quartering, and crucifying are just a few.

Today there's no doubt that such forms of execution would be considered "cruel and unusual." However, debate still arises over other methods of execution, such as hanging, electrocution, firing squad, and lethal injection.

The historical roots of this right, like many of our Bill of Rights, extend back to the seventeenth century, when the English parliament passed its Bill of Rights. But despite this long history, the precise meaning of "cruel and unusual" is not fixed. The reason is that the meaning changes as our society's sense of what is cruel and unusual evolves.

Perhaps the most debated issue under the Eighth Amendment is whether the death penalty is cruel and unusual punishment. About 40 years ago, in the case of *Furman* v. *Georgia*,

---

Hearsay

Punishment doesn't have to be of a physical nature to be cruel and unusual. For example, taking away someone's national citizenship is considered cruel and unusual.

the Supreme Court held by a 5-to-4 vote that the death penalty was being applied in an arbitrary and capricious manner, and so was a cruel and unusual punishment. The opinion listed four factors courts should consider when determining whether a punishment is cruel and unusual:

- ◆ Is it so severe that it degrades human dignity?
- ◆ Is the severe punishment given in an arbitrary manner?
- ◆ Does society completely reject the punishment?
- ◆ Is the punishment patently unnecessary?

In addition to punishment that is cruel or unusual by its very nature, an otherwise normal kind of punishment—such as a prison sentence—can be cruel and unusual if it is grossly disproportionate to the offense, or because of the lessened competence of the criminal. Thus, for example, the Eighth Amendment bars execution of minors and mentally incompetent persons. As you may recall from our discussion of the insanity defense in Chapter 12, it would be unconstitutional to give the death penalty to a legally insane person who thought he was killing a monster bug when, in fact, he was murdering his neighbor.

The last word has not been written on whether the death penalty is cruel and unusual punishment. States have acted to remove or lessen the "arbitrary and capricious" way in which the penalty is imposed, which is all the Supreme Court found unconstitutional in *Furman* v. *Georgia*—not the punishment itself. Meanwhile, societal attitudes appear to be in flux. Fourteen states and the District of Columbia have banned the penalty entirely, and the European Union refuses to admit any country that does not ban or impose a moratorium on it.

The Sentencing Hearing

After a conviction, a sentencing hearing takes place. The purpose of the hearing is to allow various interested parties to present evidence and argument about what the appropriate sentence should be.

The sentencing hearing generally takes place anywhere from 10 to 30 days following judgment. State statutes set the maximum time limit, but as with most rights given defendants, the defendant can waive the time limit to allow defense counsel more time to prepare for the hearing.

At the sentencing hearing, the prosecutor may present evidence of aggravating circumstances, and the defense counsel may present evidence of mitigating circumstances. State courts also often rely on testimony and reports from pre-sentence investigations by probation agencies or other designated authorities. The defendant is given the opportunity to make a statement, if he wishes. Courts may also consider statements from the victim or his family about the impact the crime has had on their lives, particularly in cases involving serious or particularly violent crimes.

Objection

The defendant's right to make a statement doesn't always mean it will do him any good. At O. J. Simpson's 2008 sentencing hearing for his Las Vegas armed robbery, he remorsefully explained to the judge that he was only trying to get back sports memorabilia he felt had been stolen from him. Nonetheless, the judge sentenced him to 33 years in prison, with no chance of parole for the first 9 years.

Sentencing Options

Let's go through the sentencing choices that may be available to a judge (or jury). These include one or more of the following:

◆ Fines (primarily used in minor offenses)

◆ Restitution (requiring the offender to pay compensation to the victim)

◆ Prison or jail time, with or without probation

◆ In some states, death

In addition, the incarceration time (jail or prison) part of a sentence has variations. The one defendants lobby hardest for is probation. Here, the judge sentences the defendant to a certain amount of incarceration time but suspends the sentence as long as the defendant complies with the terms set out in his probationary sentence.

For the Record

Each state has laws regarding which crimes are eligible for probation and which are not. For example, in some sex cases or extremely dangerous cases, a court cannot legally sentence someone to probation.

Certain standard terms of probation apply. For example, the defendant must be gainfully employed or in school, must violate no laws, and must report regularly to a probation officer. Other terms may be specific to the crime, such as drug treatment and testing, no contact with an abuse victim, anger management, marriage counseling in a domestic violence case, and so on.

If the defendant violates the terms of his probation, the suspended sentence becomes active and he could be sent to prison for the maximum punishment possible for the crime, even if his original sentence was less severe. A defendant is entitled to a hearing on whether he has violated the terms of his probation or parole, but the standard of proof is no longer beyond a reasonable doubt. In most states, revocation of parole or probation may be ordered if the court is reasonably satisfied that a violation occurred.

Objection

When a prosecutor believes a parolee has committed a new crime but doesn't think she has enough evidence to prove the new crime beyond a reasonable doubt, she may institute a parole revocation hearing instead. If the judge finds that a parole violation has been proven under the lower standard, the parole is revoked and the defendant incarcerated for up to the maximum term possible for the original crime.

Some jurisdictions offer alternatives that fall between probation and prison time—that is, more severe than probation but less severe than a prison term. These alternatives often implement the rehabilitative theory of punishment discussed earlier and can include "boot camps"; house arrest with electronic monitoring, rigorous supervision, and often drug treatment and testing; denial of federal benefits; and community service.

Another form of incarceration time is an indeterminate sentence. With these sentences, courts rely on the board of prisons, parole board, or mental health officials to assess a defendant's progress toward rehabilitation and thus decide how long the defendant should stay in custody. This form of incarceration sentence is rare.

The most common form of incarceration sentence is an indefinite sentence. This sets a minimum and maximum amount of prison time the defendant is to serve. Once the minimum time has been served, the defendant becomes eligible for parole. A parole board then decides whether the defendant has reached behavior goals and may allow release in advance of the maximum term (often subject to conditions similar to those imposed in probation).

The final form of incarceration sentence is a determinate, or definite, sentence. For these, a defendant is sentenced to a single, specific prison term. As part of the sentence, the judge may specify that after the term is served, the prisoner is to be released on parole. As with parole after an indefinite sentence, violating the terms of the parole can result in being returned to prison.

For many years, incarceration was the preferred method of punishment. It served the goals of the retribution and incapacitation theories of punishment, and offered a chance to rehabilitate offenders through education and services while incarcerated.

However, the Justice Department reports that, in mid-2007, there were 2,299,116 inmates in American prisons and jails. More studies show these huge numbers tend to defeat the goals of incarceration. Other critics argue our prisons are merely the "training ground" where nonviolent or first-time offenders are turned into hardened criminals and make connections to networks of other criminals

Setting the Terms of the Sentence

In most states, and in all federal courts, the judge decides what sentence is to be pronounced, called the *pronouncement of sentence*. A few states allow the jury to recommend the sentence, which the judge may or may not follow. These states are Arizona, Indiana, Kentucky, and West Virginia. A few other states—Arkansas, Missouri, Oklahoma, Texas, and Virginia—go further and allow the jury to actually set the sentence. Death penalty cases are a special category, and many states ask the jury to decide whether the death sentence is to be imposed.

def•i•ni•tion

Pronouncement of sentence is synonymous with final judgment. This is when the right not to be tried twice for the same crime—double jeopardy—attaches.

How much discretion the judge (or jury) has in setting the length of the sentence varies by state, versus the federal government, and sometimes even by crime. Most jurisdictions give the judge discretion to set the sentence length within certain minimum or maximum limits. It is not uncommon for states' laws to require that a person convicted of a particular crime serve at least some time in prison. Other statutes remove this court's discretion altogether and mandate that a specific sentence length must be served for a particular crime and that the judge or, later, a parole board cannot alter this. These are called mandatory sentences.

States often have a mix of mandatory sentencing for some crimes and discretionary sentencing for others. For example, in California, a defendant can face mandatory minimums, discretionary minimums, either, or both. Consider this example: a person has a prior robbery conviction and then is faced with a new burglary charge. Under California law, this would be considered a "second strike," making the defendant subject to a mandatory sentence of double the midterm or normal sentence if there are no aggravating or mitigating circumstances. However, a judge who wanted some discretion could find a legal basis to strike the prior robbery and thus avoid the "second strike" sentencing requirements—striking a strike, so to speak.

For the Record

A defendant convicted of more than one crime is sentenced for each, and the judge decides whether the multiple sentences will be served concurrently (all at the same time) or consecutively (one after another). This can make a big difference. For example, consider a defendant who is convicted of 20 counts of mail fraud and sentenced to six months on each count. Served concurrently, the sentence term is six months; served consecutively, the term is 10 years. Most multiple sentences are served concurrently. However, if the multiple offenses involved different victims, many courts will order that the sentences be served consecutively.

Federal courts handle sentencing much differently than state courts. While states must make sure that sentencing is equal in all the courts in the state, the promise of "equal justice for all" means that federal sentences must be uniform throughout the country.

To ensure this uniformity, federal judges are under the scrutiny of the U.S. Sentencing Commission and must strictly follow the sentencing guidelines established by the commission. As a result, federal judges have less flexibility in sentencing than most state court judges.

Plea Bargaining

A plea bargain is an agreement between the prosecution and the defense in which the defendant agrees to plead guilty (or no contest) and the prosecutor agrees to drop any additional charges, lower the remaining charge, and/or recommend to the judge a lighter sentence.

The Pros and Cons of Plea Bargaining

Roughly 90 percent of all criminal cases are resolved by plea bargains. Without them, the criminal justice system would have a difficult time functioning. Even if it could stay in business, the system would require far more tax dollars than it does now. Can you imagine 10 times the number of trials and judges to hear them, courtrooms in which to hold them, juries to decide them, and the prosecutors, public defenders, and witnesses to present them?

Yet for many people, plea bargaining seems like "cutting a deal" with justice and/or letting defendants off easy. Why is there such a poor perception of this important tool of the criminal justice system? The cons of plea bargains tend to be more dramatic and newsworthy, so they're better known. But the pros are very real, too. Let's take an even-handed look at both.

Every criminal trial involves a risk of losing, for both the prosecution and the defense. A prosecutor faces the risk that the jury will dislike or not believe the victim, the investigating officer, the key forensics witness, and so on. Some feel this is why O. J. Simpson was not convicted of the murders of Nicole Simpson and Ronald Goldman. It is possible that jurors may confuse "beyond a reasonable doubt" with no doubt at all, and acquit on the faintest of possibilities. The media coverage may affect the outcome, despite the best efforts of judge and jury to prevent it. Any or all of these factors could result in an acquittal, meaning the defendant is back on the street.

The defense faces a similar risk. Of course, the defendant would welcome an acquittal, but there is also a risk that he will be convicted on all counts and receive a heavy sentence. When a death sentence is possible, the decision to turn down a plea bargain and go to trial is very difficult indeed.

Of course, more goes into the plea-bargaining decision than fear of losing and hope of winning. For most cases, the outcome is far from certain and those few that are certain rarely get plea-bargained. Why? Well, if a conviction looks like a sure thing, I'm likely to take it to trial rather than settle. On the other hand, if the case is so weak a loss seems certain, I wouldn't file it in the first place.

> ### Hearsay
>
> A guilty plea is fundamentally no different than a jury verdict of guilty. The plea is an admission to every element of the crime or crimes to which the defendant pleads, and the judge enters final judgment against the defendant on the basis of his guilty plea, just as the judge would on a jury verdict.

The vast majority of cases fall somewhere in between—both the prosecutor's case and the defense's case have their strengths and weaknesses. Each side must carefully weigh the likelihood of winning against the likelihood of losing, and determine the consequences of each. Lawyers sometimes use a risk/benefit analysis to help make decisions like these. Simply put, the maximum benefit possible is discounted by the estimated chance of losing. For example, say the defendant is charged with first-degree murder in a particular state where the sentence is 10 to 20 years. A first-degree murder conviction is the best result possible, from the prosecution perspective (and the worst, from the defendant's perspective).

However, the prosecutor's case has some problems. A defense motion is pending to exclude the murder weapon from evidence on the grounds that it was the fruit of an illegal search. A key witness for the prosecution is the defendant's cellmate, who says the defendant admitted the crime to him. But the cellmate is a convicted child abuser who agreed to testify against the defendant only after being promised a reduced sentence in return. The jury may well not believe this witness, and if the judge excludes the murder weapon, the prosecutor will not have much of a case left.

The prosecutor considers the risks of the jury not believing the witness and of the judge excluding the murder weapon, and estimates that she has a 60 percent chance of winning and getting the maximum sentence. Applying 60 percent to the maximum 10- to 20-year sentence yields a risk/benefit assessment of 6 to 12 years. If the defendant will plead guilty to a lesser charge that results in a sentence of 7 to 15 years, the state may actually come out ahead by making the plea bargain—and have eliminated the possibility that the defendant would be released with no jail time at all.

Objection

Just because the prosecutor and defendant agree on a recommended sentence as part of the plea bargain, there is no guarantee that the judge will go along. For example, after Al Capone bragged about what a light sentence he got as part of his plea bargain, the judge rejected the recommended sentence and instead sent Capone to Alcatraz for seven and a half years.

Plea bargaining also involves other, less direct benefits. Perhaps the most important is that it frees up the resources of an already congested criminal justice system. This benefits not only the judges, attorneys and other participants in the system, but also the taxpayers, who have to pay for it all. And it saves witnesses, victims, others time away from work and school, not to mention the stress and hassle of coming to court, preparing for trial, and testifying.

But plea bargaining also has cons. The biggest one is that innocent people may be so fearful of a long prison term or of the trial process itself that they take deals for crimes they did not commit. Opponents of plea bargaining also argue that it undermines fundamental constitutional rights, such as the defendant's right to a jury trial, to confront his accusers, and to be considered innocent until proven guilty beyond a reasonable doubt.

On a final note, it is important to remember that a plea bargain doesn't mean that the defendant escapes punishment entirely. For example, James Earl Ray's plea bargain for assassinating Martin Luther King got him a sentence of 99 years. So why did he agree to it? Because it took the possibility of a death sentence off the table.

> **For the Record** _____
>
> Another important con to plea bargains is their effect on victims. A person harmed by a crime, perhaps severely, who is personally convinced that the defendant is guilty often finds a plea bargain to a lesser charge unsatisfying and hard to accept.

The Consequences of a Plea Bargain

Before a defendant pleads guilty by way of plea bargain, he must be informed of the constitutional rights he is waiving by doing so. The key ones are the right to a jury trial, the right to remain silent (the right against self-incrimination), the right to confront and cross-examine witnesses against him, and the right to be represented by an attorney.

While it is mandatory to advise the defendant of the constitutional rights he is waiving, it is also prudent for prosecutors and/or judges to make sure the defendant understands the direct and collateral consequences of a guilty plea. The direct consequences include these:

- ◆ How long a sentence he may receive

- ◆ Whether probation is possible

- ◆ Whether he will be required to register as a sex, narcotics, gang, or arson offender

- ◆ What restitution and fines he may be ordered to pay

- Whether his driver's license may be suspended or revoked

- What parole or probation periods are possible

The collateral consequences of a plea about which the defendant should be advised include these:

- Immigration consequences (if he is not a citizen, the defendant may be deported, excluded from entry, or denied naturalization or amnesty)

- The possibility that future sentences, if any, may be increased based on this guilty plea

- If the plea is to a crime of moral turpitude, the conviction may be used to impeach or attack the defendant's credibility if he appears as a witness

- The inability to own, use, or possess a firearm

- The inability to vote

Some courts use written waivers that the defendant must read, discuss with his counsel, sign, and then orally confirm to the court or prosecutor that he has understands and agrees to the waiver of rights. In other courts, this is done orally, on the record.

The Ultimate Punishment: Death

Death penalty, capital punishment, and execution are all names for the most severe and final punishment a criminal justice system can impose for a crime. Its use is controversial. Currently, 93 countries have abolished it, while 60 countries still use it.

> **Hearsay**
>
> Having the death penalty on the books is different from actually using it. In the year 2007, the greatest number of executions were carried out in China, Iran, Saudi Arabia, Pakistan, the United States, and Iraq—in that order. Sixty-two percent of the U.S. executions in 2007 occurred in Texas.

The term *capital* derives from the Latin *capitalis*, meaning "regarding the head." So the historical origin of the term *capital punishment* bears some relation to the penalty of beheading. Accordingly, the term *capital crimes* refers to crimes that may incur a death sentence.

In ancient history, death penalties were synonymous with death by torture. Many of the old means of execution were deliberately made as cruel and inhumane as possible. Stoning, disembowelment, crucifixion, quartering, and burning at the stake are just a few examples of how gruesome and painful executions were used for retribution and to deter criminal conduct.

As time when on, and especially after World War II, there was a worldwide movement away from the death penalty. Countries that retained it tended to reserve it for particularly heinous or serious crimes, like aggravated rape or murder, espionage, or treason. In addition, efforts were made to make the means of execution more humane.

In the United States, some states permit the use of capital punishment; others do not. The federal government does use it, but only for the most serious offenses. These include treason, use of a weapon of mass destruction, terrorism, espionage, federal treason, and certain violations of the Geneva Conventions that result in death.

Each state using the death penalty decides the crimes it considers serious enough to warrant that penalty. Some examples include aggravated rape, in Louisiana, Florida, and Oklahoma; extortionate kidnapping, in Oklahoma; aggravated kidnapping, in Georgia, Idaho, Kentucky, and South Carolina; aircraft hijacking, in Alabama; drug trafficking resulting in a person's death, in Connecticut; and causing a train wreck in which people die or perjury that leads to a person's death, in California.

The method of capital punishment also varies in the United States. Of the 36 states that currently use the death penalty, all but one of them use lethal injection. Only Nebraska uses electrocution. The electric chair once was more widely used, but concerns over malfunctions and cruelty caused its decline. No matter what method is used, executions are completed in private; neither the public nor the press are invited to witness them.

After a death sentence is entered, actually executing it is a drawn-out process. Let's look first at what happens in state courts. After the trial court enters the sentence, the case automatically goes to the state court of appeals for review. The appellate court may affirm the conviction and the sentence, affirm the conviction but order a new sentencing hearing, or acquit the defendant entirely based on errors during the trial.

For the Record _____

When the death sentence is given for a federal crime, the method of execution is the form used in the state where the sentence will be carried out.

If the appellate court affirms the conviction and sentence, the defendant may seek review by the state supreme court and then by the United States Supreme Court. If these appeals are unsuccessful, the state court defendant may attack the judgment and sentence by State Collateral Review in the state court of appeals. During this process, the defendant gets the chance to present a new reason for attacking his sentence. This has to be some reason that could not have been raised at court, such as ineffective assistance of counsel.

If the defendant fails to get a reversal at the State Collateral Review, he may try a third avenue of review: filing a petition for a *writ of habeas corpus* in federal district court. According to the Constitution, Article I, Section 9:

> *The privilege of the writ of habeas corpus shall not be suspended, unless when in cases of rebellion or invasion, the public safety may require it.*

def•i•ni•tion

The Supreme Court has called the **writ of habeas corpus** "the fundamental instrument for safeguarding individual freedom against arbitrary and lawless state action." It is an order (another word for "writ") from a court finding that the state is holding a person illegally, and ordering that he be released. The Latin habeas corpus translates to "you [shall] have the body," meaning that the prisoner shall be delivered to the custody of the court issuing the writ.

Such a petition may be based only on a claim that the state court proceeding violated one or more of the defendant's constitutional rights. The defendant may also try to offer new evidence of his innocence at this stage, but such new evidence has to be very compelling for the federal court to consider it. If the district court denies the habeas corpus petition, the defendant may appeal so the federal court of appeals will review his claims of constitutional violations, and then again request Supreme Court review.

If the federal court of appeals affirms the conviction and sentence, and the Supreme Court does the same or declines review, the defendant's next step is a habeas corpus petition and further appeals if it is denied.

If all avenues of challenging the conviction and death sentence fail, a date is set for execution. At this point, only a clemency hearing before the pardon and parole board can save the state court defendant. If the board recommends to the governor that the defendant's death sentence be commuted (a legal term meaning to reduce the severity of a sentence) to life in prison, then it's up to the governor. But pardon and parole boards rarely recommend clemency, and governors rarely grant it.

The course of review of a death penalty case tried in federal court is similar to that in state cases, except there is no State Collateral Review and no clemency hearing. As for commutation of a sentence or a pardon, Article II, Section 2 of the Constitution vests that power in the President. The Office of the Pardon Attorney within the Justice Department reviews most requests for commutation or pardon and recommends a response to the President, who may or may not follow the recommendation.

> **Hearsay**
>
> Although presidential pardons have been much in the news after the Bill Clinton and George W. Bush administrations, the number of presidential pardons has actually decreased since World War II.

The Least You Need to Know

♦ The primary reasons the criminal justice system punishes are retribution, deterrence of future crimes, rehabilitation of the offender, and restoration of the victim and offender.

♦ At the sentencing hearing, the views of the parties, social agencies, and often the victim are heard regarding what sentence the defendant should receive.

♦ State and federal statutes control the discretion the judge has to set the terms of the sentence, its duration, and whether probation is available.

♦ Through plea bargaining, the prosecution and the defense assess their chances of victory and reach compromise agreements if the issue is in doubt. This process has both pros and cons.

♦ The death penalty is controversial. Where it is allowed, it is restricted to the most serious of offenses, and special review procedures apply to cases in which it is imposed.

19

The Juvenile Criminal Justice System

In This Chapter

- ◆ Why we have a juvenile criminal justice system
- ◆ The differences between the juvenile and adult justice systems
- ◆ Juvenile corrections—where to place minors
- ◆ When and why a juvenile case may be transferred to adult criminal court

In just one year, 2000, almost two and a half million minors were arrested in the United States. In the past 20 years in California, there have been over 6,000 killings by persons between the ages of 4 and 17. This chapter focuses on how the criminal justice system functions when the accused is a juvenile. As you'll see, our system treats children who become involved in crime differently than their adult counterparts.

The specifics of these differences vary state to state, even as to who is a "juvenile," but there is a consensus that children are different from adults when it comes to both culpability and punishment. And one factor that is relatively consistent from state to state is that of all the possible goals for punishment—whether retribution, deterrence, or restoration—the focus of the juvenile justice system is on rehabilitation.

Why We Have a Juvenile Justice System

Traditionally, parents had sole discretion and power over their children. They decided everything about raising, educating, and disciplining them, and often putting them to work.

Around the late nineteenth century, at about the same time the state began to encroach on parents' rights by becoming involved in the welfare of children, the juvenile justice system began to evolve. Advocates fighting for better treatment of minors at home also began to advocate for the better treatment of children in the criminal justice system. This included the transition from a system designed to punish, to a more lenient criminal justice system for juveniles whose goal was to rehabilitate.

Until the late nineteenth century, minors whose behavior amounted to a crime were dealt with through the same criminal justice system that handled adults. The only difference was that some minors could use the *defense of infancy* against criminal charges. The rationale for treating juveniles differently from adults in the criminal justice system is simply that children are not equipped to weigh decisions and make adult choices. This same thinking is behind rules that contracts with juveniles are not binding on them, and juveniles cannot vote, drink, consent to sex, or drive cars.

def•i•ni•tion

Like the insanity defense, the **infancy defense** is based on the rationale that a person who is unable to understand the nature and repercussions of his decisions and actions is not culpable for them, and so is immune from criminal prosecution. Infancy as a complete defense is no longer available in most states, but the rationale for it continues to shape the criminal justice system.

But in passing laws regarding juveniles and crime, legislators cannot be sensitive only to the cognitive abilities of a child—they must balance the potential harm a child can cause to others and to society as a whole. While the most common public policy focus is to promote rehabilitation and change in a child's delinquent behavior, some states adhere to the punitive goals of the adult criminal justice system.

One such example is the state of Washington. Washington went to great lengths to revise its criminal code to "provide for punishment commensurate with the age, crime, and criminal history of the juvenile offender." The purpose of the revision, according to its legislative history, was for a juvenile offender to be "held accountable for ... his criminal behavior."

For the Record _____

Courts have generally held that state statutes creating juvenile courts and providing methods for dealing with juvenile delinquency are an acceptable extension of the state's police power, the same power that authorizes states to provide the adult criminal justice system. Juvenile statutes are also supported by the doctrine of *parens patriae* (literally, "father of the people"), which authorizes the state to legislate for the protection, care, custody, and maintenance of children within its jurisdiction.

Who Is a Juvenile?

Most states define juveniles as persons between the ages of 10 and 18, but the specific minimum and maximum ages for the juvenile courts to get involved vary from state to state. While some states allow juvenile *dispositions* (as sentences are known in the juvenile justice system) to last all the way until the defendant is 25 years old, some states prohibit juvenile dispositions that extend beyond the minor's 18th birthday.

The Federal Juvenile Delinquency Act defines any act that is otherwise a crime but is committed by someone under 18 years of age as juvenile delinquency, and sets rules that states must follow with regard to juvenile court procedures and punishments.

def•i•ni•tion _____

In the juvenile justice systems of most states, "sentences" are referred to as **dispositions**.

Differences in Juvenile Justice

The statutes dealing with juvenile crime are generally referred to as the law of juvenile delinquency. Some states have specific penal codes for juveniles. (A code is a collection of laws dealing with a particular subject.) Other states use a combination of their adult penal codes, which define the offenses, and welfare codes plus court rules that set the procedures for handling juvenile cases.

Status Offenses

Certain behaviors are legal for adults but criminal for minors. These are referred to as status offenses, since they are offenses only because of the status of the offender. Examples of status offenses include curfew violations and the purchase or possession of cigarettes or alcohol.

Some offenses may frequently be charged in juvenile court and may seem like status offenses but really aren't. Consider, for example, the charge of possessing a weapon on school property. While the crime itself may seem aimed at the actions of minors, since they make up most of the people on school grounds, this type of crime is not a status offense. Anyone, adult or juvenile, who carries a weapon on school grounds may be charged for this violation.

For the Record

The federal role in the juvenile justice field is largely one of funding programs to assist the states in dealing with juvenile delinquency. For example, a law originally passed in 1968 and now known as the Juvenile Delinquency Prevention Act assists states and local communities in providing community-based preventative services to youths in danger of becoming delinquent, trains individuals in occupations providing such services, and provides technical assistance in the field.

Public vs. Private Proceedings

One of the biggest differences between the adult and juvenile systems is in the area of public access. You may remember from our discussion of constitutional rights that a defendant has the right to an "open and public" trial. In contrast, juvenile proceedings and records are generally kept private and confidential. However, a tendency has arisen in recent years to eliminate some of the differences between the adult and juvenile court, and public access is a changing area. More states are granting the media access to the identity and sometimes the physical images of juveniles involved in delinquency proceedings.

Juvenile Justice Terminology

Another notable difference between the juvenile and adult justice systems is their terminology. For example, instead of calling an offender the "accused" or "defendant," juvenile offenders are usually referred to as "minors" or "juveniles." Instead of being "arrested" for committing a "crime," a juvenile is "taken into custody" for committing a "delinquent act."

The language differences go on. In adult criminal courts, prosecutors file charges by a complaint, information, or indictment; in juvenile courts, prosecutors file a petition with the court. Minors "admit or deny" a charge rather than plead "guilty" or "not guilty." Instead of a trial, juveniles have an "adjudication" (or adjudicatory hearing), which determines the truth or falsity of the petition.

This chart summarizes the differences between the two systems:

Differences in the Adult and Juvenile Justice Systems

	Adult System	Juvenile System
Purpose of the system	Punish, deter, rehabilitate, restore, incapacitate	Rehabilitate
The offense	Crime	Delinquent behavior
Apprehending a suspect	Arrest	Taken into custody
Document setting out the charges	Indictment, complaint, information	Petition
Terms of release, pending trial	Payment of bail, unless released on own recognizance	Placed into parental custody
Hearing to decide whether the accused will be held until trial	Bail hearing	Detention hearing
Trier of fact	Jury	Juvenile judge
Proceeding to determine guilt	Trial	Adjudication
Standard of proof	Beyond a reasonable doubt	Beyond a reasonable doubt

continues

Differences in the Adult and Juvenile Justice Systems (continued)

	Adult System	Juvenile System
Decision on responsibility	Verdict, which either convicts or acquits	Finding of delinquency, which either sustains the petition or dismisses it
Proceeding to determine the outcome	Sentencing hearing	Disposition hearing
Court proceedings	Public	Private

Similarities in Juvenile Justice

Minors have the right to an attorney at their adjudication hearing. They also have the right to confront and cross-examine their accusers. Probationary sentences are common sentencing tools used in juvenile cases as well adult cases. This type of sentence allows minors to stay in school and otherwise continue with their lives, while monitoring their behavior. Juvenile court judges have wider latitude with respect to probation than adult court judges, and may grant a probationary sentence regardless of the severity of the underlying crime.

Most states apply the same rules of evidence in both adult criminal cases and juvenile adjudication hearings, so rules like hearsay and the exclusionary rule control both kinds of proceedings. Similarly, the standard of proof is the same in both adult and juvenile courts: the prosecutor must prove her case beyond a reasonable doubt.

Finally, the discovery rules are similar or the same in most states. In particular, obligation for reciprocal discovery, where both parties have an obligation to turn over evidence to the other, usually applies in juvenile as adult courts. And prosecutors in juvenile cases have the same added obligation of turning over evidence that might be helpful to the defense.

Objection

A juvenile's right to be free of unreasonable searches and seizures varies in some ways from an adult's. At school, for example, a student's locker may be searched without his consent. And a parent can give consent to a search of a juvenile's room at home.

Pros and Cons of the Juvenile System

Some people criticize the juvenile system for not affording minors all the constitutional rights that are available to adults, primarily the rights to an open and public trial and to a jury. But there are some benefits to the juvenile justice system.

Making juvenile adjudications private prevents publicity that may sensationalize a crime and publicly brand a child for life. Perhaps the greatest advantages are the juvenile court system's shorter sentences and avoidance of state prisons as the most-used correctional facility, meaning minors are usually better off staying in the juvenile court system.

Juvenile Corrections and Placement

The first juvenile placement center was known as the "House of Refuge." It was founded in 1825 in New York State by a Quaker reformer who wanted a place to house vagrant juveniles who committed crimes. It provided food, shelter, and education—all of which were probably absent from the juvenile's life and likely played a part in his turning to crime.

Today juveniles are placed in youth detention centers or juvenile hall. These detention centers serve the same function as prisons, in that they remove offenders from society. However, there's an effort to make more of a homelike environment in detention centers so juveniles can transition more easily back into society. For example, juveniles continue to receive the same education they would under the public education system "on the outside."

Each state has its own juvenile sentencing laws. The maximum time period is calculated much like in adult court, where the judge has the discretion to sentence the juvenile up to the maximum stated in the statute.

If the confinement period of a juvenile's sentence extends beyond his eighteenth birthday and he is in under the jurisdiction of the state's Department of Corrections (which typically means he is being held in the state's youth authority, the highest level of juvenile incarceration), the state has the authority to keep a juvenile incarcerated

For the Record _____

Juvenile sentencing statutes rarely have mandatory minimum periods of detention, unlike those applicable to adult defendants.

until it feels that the appropriate amount of time has been spent in a custodial environment (keeping in mind that community restoration and victim restoration can be achieved during the confinement period).

The maximum age for a juvenile to stay in most youth authorities is 25 years of age. When a child who is considered particularly dangerous reaches the maximum age in the juvenile system, he or she may be transferred to the adult system if the prosecutor applies to the court for further detention.

Transfer to Adult Court

Even though there is a special justice system for juvenile offenders, there is still the possibility that the youth offender will be tried as an adult in the criminal system. A juvenile can be transferred to criminal court in three ways: judicial discretion, prosecutorial discretion, or statutory exclusion. Depending on the state, one or a combination of these transfer methods may be used.

Judicial discretion allows the juvenile court judge to waive jurisdiction over the juvenile's offense when the juvenile's record and/or the seriousness of the crime warrant. This waiver causes the juvenile's case to be transferred to adult criminal court.

Prosecutorial discretion allows prosecutors to file the criminal charges against a juvenile defendant directly in adult criminal court. This is called "direct filing" and is most often done when the crime is especially serious or violent. Individual states set limits on how young the offender can be for direct filing in adult criminal court. For example, in California, juveniles who commit serious crimes over the age of 14 years may be tried as adults at the prosecutor's discretion.

Some states provide for "fitness hearings," which are held when a prosecutor asks that a case originally filed in juvenile court be transferred to adult court. In California, the prosecutor need only prove by a preponderance of the evidence, not beyond a reasonable doubt, that the transfer to adult court is appropriate. The factors typically considered include how close to the age of majority the juvenile is, the seriousness of the crime, and his prior juvenile adjudications and dispositions.

Finally, statutory exclusion (also called legislative exclusion) occurs when a statute excludes juvenile defendants from juvenile court when certain factors are present. For example, some states use statutory exclusion to automatically transfer juveniles to adult criminal court when they are both over a certain age and charged with a felony or drug crime.

Some statutory exclusion laws get quite detailed. Here's one from California (§ 707(a)(1)) of the California Rules of Court) that mandates transfer of juveniles to adult criminal court:

---

1. The child was a particular age, 16 years or older at the time of the alleged offense.

2. The child would not be amenable to the care, treatment, and training program available through facilities of the juvenile court, based on an evaluation of all the following criteria:

    a. The degree of criminal sophistication the child exhibits

    b. Whether the child can be rehabilitated before the expiration of jurisdiction

    c. The child's previous delinquent history

    d. The results of previous attempts by the court to rehabilitate the child

    e. The circumstances and gravity of the alleged offense

The Least You Need to Know

♦ The rationale for having a separate juvenile justice system is the belief that children are not equipped to weigh decisions and make choices like adults.

♦ Rehabilitation of the offender is the main goal of the juvenile criminal justice system.

♦ Some of the major differences between the adult and juvenile justice systems are that in the juvenile courts there are no juries and no public trials, and the terminology is generally toned down from that used in adult courts.

♦ However, the same high standard of proof—beyond a reasonable doubt—applies in juvenile court, as do the rules of evidence.

♦ Juveniles may be tried in adult criminal justice courts when the circumstances warrant. Those circumstances vary state to state but generally involve serious, violent crimes and older juveniles.

Chapter 20

Victim's Rights

In This Chapter

- ◆ Bringing the victim's experience of the crime into the courtroom
- ◆ Making the defendant pay the victim back for the damages he caused
- ◆ Programs to protect victims and witnesses

So far, we've spent a lot of time discussing the rights of the accused, before and during trial. We've covered what the police do and the roles of the lawyers, judge, witnesses, and jury in the criminal justice system. So you may be wondering, what about the victims? They are the ones most directly harmed by the crime. Shouldn't the victims have some role in what goes on? Don't they have rights, too?

The answer is, yes. Most states are increasingly providing victims with a number of rights, responding to growing concerns about the welfare of victims in a justice system that focuses heavily on the rights of defendants. In addition to suffering the effects of the crime, victims are seeing an increase in retaliatory actions when their offenders are released from prison. Because of these concerns, and to correspond with rights defendants enjoy, many states now have what are known as a victim's bill of rights.

The Victim's Bill of Rights

Victims' rights are generally about showing the victim dignity, respect, courtesy, and sensitivity throughout the criminal justice process. Although numerous rights center on these concepts, they typically fall into one of three categories—the right to be present, the right to be heard, and the right to be informed. Each of these categories gives victims a voice and allows them to be proactive regarding their own well-being.

The Victim's Right to Be Present

Victims generally have a blanket right to be present during criminal proceedings. Victims can watch the trial and make their presence known to the defendant. In capital murder cases, a victim's immediate family members have the right to be present at the offender's execution. These experiences can be very important to victims psychologically. Testifying and being present throughout a trial allows victims to face their offenders and witness the system's efforts to avenge the crimes they suffered. Watching a jury announce a conviction and being present during sentencing or an execution can bring a sense of closure.

Naturally, exceptions arise. The defense counsel may bring a *motion to exclude* the victim from part or all of a trial. The most common reason is a concern that the victim's testimony may be affected by hearing the testimony of other witnesses. The victim does, however, have the right to attend all of the sentencing or other hearings that do not involve taking evidence at the guilt phase of the trial.

def•i•ni•tion

A **motion to exclude** seeks to keep a witness or victim from hearing another witness's testify by excluding him from the courtroom. Two witnesses are usually not subject to exclusion: the prosecutor's investigating officer and the defense's private investigator.

As another exception to a victim's right to be present, a victim who is a minor might be excluded for her own protection. Occasionally, a victim also must be excluded to maintain order in the court room. But these exceptions are rare, and it is far more common for the victim to be present during the trial of the accused.

The Victim's Right to Be Informed

The right to be informed is one of the key components of a victim's bill of rights and is one of the main reasons such bills of rights were instituted. Understandably, victims want to know everything about "their" case: how the investigation is going, when an arrest is made, whether the defendant is released on bail, and so on. Just about anyone who has been through the trauma of a crime wants to know this information.

The victim has the right to be informed of all the steps as the case makes its way through the criminal justice system, not just the trial. She should hear from the district attorney or prosecutor if there is a plea bargain. She should be advised how the trial concluded, if she chooses not to attend.

The victim has the right to be notified of sentencing hearings and parole hearings. She is entitled to know if the offender's sentence has been reduced in return for becoming an in-custody informant. And every victim has the right to be notified when the offender is released from prison, whether it's through parole, a work program, completion of the sentence—or a jail break.

The Victim's Right to Be Heard

As you may have noticed, the right to be informed and the right to be present tend to work together: the right to be told about an upcoming hearing gives the victim a chance to be present. And both the right to be informed and the right to be present tie into the third right—the right to be heard.

In several phases of a criminal action, it is important to hear from the victim. When setting the bail amount, the judge may consider the victim's situation and the nature and extent of injury allegedly caused by the accused. Any threats made to the victim can increase the bail amount significantly.

Victims may also make statements at sentencing and parole hearings. Often these statements describe how the quality of their lives has been affected since the crime. And the parole board can consider the likelihood that the offender might go after the victim again if granted parole.

For the Record

Most often, victims make statements in an effort to keep the offender in jail. But sometimes victims have forgiven the offenders and actually make a statement to their benefit.

Victim Impact Statements

One of the most effective ways victims get their voices on record is through victim impact statements. Victim impact statements are made by the victims themselves and also by the victim's family members, especially in murder cases. The statements are recorded by audio, through video, in writing, or by being read into the official court record.

No exact formula or specific rules govern how a victim impact statement should be written or what it should cover. The statement may be long or short, express anger or hurt, run hot or cold. The purpose is to give the judge (and sometimes, in a penalty phase of a proceeding, the jury) a firsthand account of how the crime has affected the victim, his family, his friends and associates, and his community.

Most statements cover not only the economic harm the victims have suffered, but also the emotional trauma and long-lasting psychological effects the experience has caused. The statement may describe the victims' hopes and aspirations for the future—and how the crime has hindered these. The statements may also express how the victim or family feels about the proposed sentence and, if they do not feel it is adequate, what outcome they would like to see instead.

It is important to point out that victim impact statements become part of the permanent court record. And because these statements are in a recorded format, they can be used not only at the sentencing hearing, but also at later parole hearings.

When victims of a crime I am prosecuting ask me what to include in their victim impact statement, I offer the following questions as guidelines:

- How have the defendant's actions (before, during, and after the crime) changed your day-to-day life?

- Did you suffer any physical injury or property damage? Any emotional or psychological injury?

- How long do you think the damage, of whatever kind, will last?

- Has the crime affected others in your family? Your friends? Has it changed how you relate with them?

- What are the financial effects of the crime, including time taken off from work or school to go to court, to testify, to participate in the investigation, and so on?

- Describe what you think would be a "just" sentence. Don't consider just jail time—think about restitution, rehabilitation, community service, and so on, if you wish.

◆ Keep your statement personal, candid, and from your heart. Don't hold back—this is your chance to make sure the judge, the defendant, and everyone else knows exactly how you feel.

Hearsay

Not all victim impact statements simply tell the court they want the offender thrown into prison and the key lost. Some victims use the opportunity to "save face" by explaining their own actions, to tell the defendant the case was prosecuted only because the authorities chose to, or to express forgiveness of the offender.

Victim impact statements are especially important in murder trials. Obviously, the victim cannot appear before the jury. Impact statements from the victim's family and friends may be the best way to tell the jury who the victim was and convey the impact of her loss. And such witness impact statements "by proxy" can be incredibly compelling.

For the Record _____

Victim impact statements can be so effective that a recent Supreme Court case addressed a claim that they are *too* effective. Two murder defendants appealed their conviction and death sentences, arguing that videos shown to the jury chronicling the victim's lives, accompanied by poignant music, were overly persuasive, prejudiced the jury against them, and resulted in their death sentences. The Supreme Court rejected their argument, ruling that even this type of victim impact statement may be used in the sentencing phase of death penalty trials.

I want to share with you one of the most compelling victim impact statements I've ever heard. I quote it at some length not only because it shows how powerful these statements can be—how they can bring the persona of a murder victim to life in a courtroom—but also because it does a far better job than I ever could to give you a bottom-of-the-heart appreciation and understanding of the victim's perspective on crime.

Erin Runnions delivered her victim impact statement at the sentencing of Alejandro Avila, the man convicted of kidnapping and murdering her 5-year-old daughter Samantha. Her statement began by thanking the judge, the jury, the District Attorney's team, and the spectators who had shown so much care and compassion throughout the trial.

Then she turned to the defendant, Alejandro Avila.

I have written and rewritten what I would say today to you.

Part of me doesn't want to speak to you or acknowledge you in any way, but I've decided that I have to address you because I hope to never see you again. I never want to hear your name or see your face. You don't deserve a place in my family's history. And so I want you to live. I want you to disappear into the abyss of a lifetime in prison where no one will remember you, no one will pray for you, no one will care when you die. Since Samantha's death, I have felt more hate and rage than I ever thought possible, but I love that little girl so much that it would be a horrible insult to her to let my hate for you take more space in my heart and head than my love for her.

I am supposed to speak to the impact of this crime on my life. There is no describing the impact, and I am not sure you're intelligent enough to ever comprehend it anyway. I wrote this state-ment on the third anniversary of the night you took my baby and hurt her and scared her and crushed her until her heart stopped. She fought. I know she fought. I know she looked at you with those amazing, sparkling brown eyes and you still wanted to kill her. I don't understand it. I never will.

It's like you never learned to think. You have absolutely no concept of how heinous, how egre-gious your crimes were. I can't help but wonder how it is you survived as long as you did being so stupid.

You killed a child with a loving and passionate heart. Samantha was outrageously bright and funny. She wasn't demanding, she didn't ask for everything under the sun, just to play and have fun as much as humanly possible. Why would you want to take that away? I have researched and really thought about pedophiles and your psychology. You're a human being, you've known pain and fear. Did you pretend that she wasn't real?

I want an apology. Someday I want you to feel the impact of what you did to Samantha. I want you to realize how much you stole. I have to take family photos, and my little girl isn't there; she will always be missing. Every happy moment of my life has a moment of gut-wrenching agony because she's not there. And I have to stop and acknowledge how much it hurts to live without her.

Samantha made me feel like I had a purpose on this planet. She was so incredible that I felt sure that if I just did what I could to give her every opportunity to become the best person she could be and I didn't mess her up in the meantime, she would have done something truly wonderful for this world. She wanted to be a dancer, a teacher, and a mother. She was a won-derful storyteller and she wrote all the time. Who knows what she would have become?

But you just don't care. You have no idea of what it is to love someone. You have no concept of what life is about, and yet you were so arrogant as to think you had a right to take it.

For me and my family, our lives were shattered. For the past three years we've been trying to paste it back together, but there's this huge void and the lack of her laughter, of art on the walls, of her dancing and singing and running and jumping and swinging and smiling. The lack of Samantha is actually a part of our life now. The pain is impossible to describe, the guilt I feel for bringing that sweet baby into the world only to be tortured and terrified. I am so sorry I let her down.

And you should be sorry you took her away. You should be so sorry. Not sorry you got caught; not sorry that your wasted life will be taken (as if its worth could ever compare), but sorry that you took a life, the life of a very special little girl.

While everything in me wants to hurt you in every possible way, when I'm very honest with myself, what I want more than anything is I want you to feel remorse. Everyone feels alone in our pain and confusion. There is so much misery built into being a human being that I can't fathom what would make you want to add to it.

In choosing to destroy Samantha's life, you chose this, you chose to waste your life to satisfy a sick desire. You knew it was wrong, but you chose not to think about it. Now you have a lot of time to think about it. Don't waste it. Write it down so that the rest of us might learn how to stop you people.

You are a disgrace to the human race."

Restitution

Another important victim's right is the right to obtain restitution for their losses suffered as a result of the crime. Restitution seeks to restore the victim to where she was before the crime, to make the victim or the victim's family as whole as possible. Courts in every state have the ability to order restitution for the victim from the offender. Some states go further and require restitution as part of the sentence, in addition to jail time and other punishments.

Losses or Damages That Qualify

Restitution may be ordered not just for economic, harm but for a variety of losses suffered by the victim or the victim's family. Each state's statutes define what kinds of losses can get restitution. Most—if not all—include medical expenses, lost wages, property loss or damage, and funeral expenses.

Objection _____

Medical expenses are not limited to treatment for physical injuries caused by the crime, but include physical therapy and counseling expenses. Property loss or damage restitution usually compensates the victim not only for the value of the property, but also for the time the victim was forced to live or work without it. For example, restitution for a car that was stolen and wrecked would include not just the replacement cost of the car, but also the cost of a rental during the search for a replacement.

Some states order restitution even though a victim has insurance that pays for her medical expenses or funeral costs. The courts of such states may require the defendant to pay restitution to the insurance companies for these costs.

Other states strictly limit restitution to losses suffered by the victim that were incurred prior to sentencing. Other states include future medical costs and other out-of-pocket expenses directly related to the crime. For example, an identity fraud offender may be ordered to compensate the victim for the costs of fixing his credit history. Some states include interest in their restitution payments, and some, like California, include attorneys' fees incurred in the effort to obtain the restitution payment.

When ordering restitution, the courts look at several factors. One of the most obvious is the financial damage the crime caused the victim. Many states take into account the defendant's economic situation and ability to pay. But this is becoming the disfavored view, and more states are limiting consideration to the victim's loss when determining the amount of restitution the defendant owes.

Even though more statutes are being passed to award victims restitution, surprisingly little restitution is ordered by the courts. Why? A couple of reasons. First, the victim must request (through the prosecutor) an order of restitution. Second, she must prove the loss. Many victims either don't ask for restitution or aren't able to produce evidence of their damages at the time of sentencing.

Collecting Restitution

Defendants are far from a reliable source for compensating crime victims. So what happens when the defendant can't pay the restitution amount? First, states go to some lengths to determine exactly what the defendant can afford to pay. Then payment plans are put into place based on this determination. Nonpayment is considered contempt of court.

For the Record _____

One view of restitution is that it's really not important whether the defendant can or does actually compensate the victim—it's more the principle of the thing. Advocates of this view argue that it is important enough to get an order confirming the victim is entitled to restitution, and putting a dollar value on the victim's suffering.

But some defendants simply cannot pay. Because of the state's concern for the toll crimes take from their victims, another means of compensation has developed. Instead of restitution funded by offenders, many states have created state restitution funds to aid victims of violent crimes.

State restitution funds operate with the same purpose as court-ordered restitution: to assist victims in paying for expenses directly related to the criminal act they suffered. But like all state funding, these restitution funds are limited. As a result, state-funded restitution is run a little differently than the court-ordered variety.

As a general rule, state-funded restitution focuses on personal injury rather any property damage caused by crimes. For this reason, state funds are usually available only to victims of violent crimes, including murder and domestic violence. And expectedly, the kinds of expenses that may be compensated are more limited those a court might order.

Medical expenses and funeral expenses for the victim are the most commonly available through state restitution. Lost wages are also usually available, but only for a limited period of time off a job. Then there are the more unique kinds of expenses that may be compensated, such as crime scene clean-up after a crime committed in a residence, or a security system installed in a home where a crime has taken place. And the state may pay for relocation expenses for the victim and any dependants, particularly in domestic violence cases.

How a state pays for its restitution program varies by state, but generally most of the funds come from fines paid to the court. These can be fines offenders are required to pay as part of a sentence, or any number of other court fees paid during a criminal proceeding. Some states require that some part of a prisoner's wages from a prison work program be paid into the restitution fund. Other sources include federal grants and even private donors. Although state-funded restitution is limited, it is the most reliable means of providing restitution to victims.

Victim- and Witness-Protection Programs

In the 1970s, Congress enacted the means for providing protection for victims and witnesses facing extreme danger. The main witness-protection program is run by the federal Department of Justice and administered by the U.S. Attorney General. Some states have developed their own protection programs to protect witnesses the federal program doesn't cover.

Most of the witnesses and victims in a protection program are at risk from organized crime, gangs, domestic violence, or high-level drug traffickers. These criminal organizations are often so expansive that it's almost impossible for a victim or witness to be safe anywhere. So it's understandable that witnesses threatened by such offenders will not come forward and testify without protection. And the only real means of protection is to change the witness's identity and location.

Before victims or witnesses are considered for relocation and protection, credible evidence must show that they are in substantial danger. Substantial danger can be shown in a number of ways, from the nature of the criminal organization involved, to threats that have already occurred. Because of the expense involved in relocating someone, this is a fairly high bar.

For the Record

Legislatures have made attempts to reduce the need for victim/witness protection by passing laws with stiff penalties for those who intimidate, hurt, threaten, or otherwise interfere with a criminal prosecution or investigation.

Going into witness protection is no easy task. The victim or witness must provide the authorities with all their personal information. Anything they omit could leave a thread that might enable someone to trace their new identity. Then the government creates a whole new identity for the witness, including new identity papers, such as a driver's license. The government also relocates the witness, providing housing and basic living expenses until the witness is able to support himself in his new life. As you can imagine, this is no inexpensive endeavor for one witness, let alone for a whole family that needs protection.

The burdens on the witness go beyond the trauma of being uprooted and making a new life. First and foremost, they must cooperate with the government and do everything possible to avoid detection. They are also required to regularly inform their witness-protection officer of their activities and any address changes. And they are required to not commit any crimes, especially because this could make them more detectable.

For all its costs and the burdens on witnesses, their families, and the government, witness-protection programs have been key to bringing some of the most dangerous criminals to justice.

The Least You Need to Know

- A victim's bills of rights ensures the victim's right to be informed about what is happening in the case, to be present at the trial and other proceedings, and to be heard about how the crime has affected his life.

- Victim impact statements tell the judge, defendant, the public, and sometimes the jury how a crime has changed the victim's life, and become a part of the formal court record.

- Restitution seeks to restore the victim to where she was before the crime, to make the victim or the victim's family as whole as possible. It may be ordered as part of the sentence or paid as part of a state program.

- Victim- and witness-protection programs relocate and provide new identities to witnesses at risk of violent retaliation if they come forward and testify.

Appendix A

Glossary

accessory after the fact   A person who receives, comforts, or assists the perpetrator in fleeing, covering up the crime, or otherwise avoiding prosecution. To share responsibility for the crime, the accessory after the fact must know the person that he is assisting committed a crime.

accessory before the fact   Also known as accomplices. Such a person may assist in the planning or preparations for the crime, or facilitate the actions of the person carrying it out. An accessory before the fact is liable for the crime, just like the person who commits it.

accomplices   Accomplices are often what the law calls accessories before the fact. Such a person may assist in the planning or preparations for the crime, or facilitate the actions of the person carrying it out. An accomplice is liable for the crime, just like the person who commits it.

affirmative defense   A defense that justifies or excuses the alleged criminal conduct instead of denying it. Examples include self-defense and insanity.

aggravating factors   Circumstances associated with a crime that increase its culpability under the law and, thus, justify increasing the severity of the punishment.

alternate jurors   Two or more jurors in addition to the 6 or 12 regular jurors are selected to sit and hear all the evidence. These alternate jurors step in to replace any regular juror who becomes ill or otherwise unable to continue.

anti-kickback statutes   Anti-kickback statutes criminalize a form of bribery that involves offering something of value (such as money) to an official to get or retain business.

arraignment   The first appearance that a defendant makes in the courtroom. He is formally notified of the charges against him, is advised of his constitutional rights, and pleads either guilty or not guilty. The judge also sets the amount of bail.

arson   The malicious burning of someone's dwelling place. Some states include places of business as well.

assault   Assault differs from battery, in that assault involves no physical contact. Assault is either trying to commit battery but not succeeding, or deliberately making the victim fear imminent bodily harm.

attorney/client privilege   An attorney can't be forced to testify about what her client told her in confidence.

bail   The amount of money a defendant must put up before he will be released pending trial. If he doesn't show up at trial, that money is forfeited.

bailee   Also known as a custodian. A person with whom some article is left, usually pursuant to a contract, who is responsible for the safe return of the article to the owner when the contract is fulfilled.

bailiff   The one in a police uniform, often carrying a gun and wearing a badge. The bailiff calls the court to order, announces the judge when she enters the courtroom, and is responsible for maintaining order in the courtroom.

battery   Most modern statutes define battery as any intentional, offensive touching of another person, whether or not it causes physical injury. Thus, battery extends from clubbing someone with a baseball bat to surreptitious fondling on a crowded subway.

battery, simple   Battery that does not have aggravating factors. They are usually charged as misdemeanors.

breaking and entering   The breaking part of breaking and entering means nothing more than removing some barrier to entry, such as pushing an ajar door farther open. Entering occurs when any part of the intruder's body enters the home.

bribery   Offering or requesting something of value with the intent to influence some action by a public official. Note that the offer or request may be turned down, but the act is still bribery; the offer or request is enough.

burden of proof—defendant   The defendant's burden of proof means that the defense counsel must submit enough evidence to prove the elements of a defense are more probably than not true.

burden of proof—prosecutor   The prosecutor's burden of proof with respect to the elements of the crime charged is to provide enough evidence to prove the elements beyond a reasonable doubt. In contrast, the burden of proof in a civil trial is a "preponderance of the evidence"—that is, proof that the fact is more likely true than not.

burglary   The traditional definition of burglary is the breaking and entering of someone's dwelling place with the intent to commit a felony inside. Some more recent statutes have dropped the "at night" element, some have expanded "dwelling place" to include any place people work or spend time, and some say the intent to commit a misdemeanor is enough.

chain of custody   Proof that only authorized persons have had access to some piece of evidence; thus, the evidence has not been altered, substituted, or changed.

child abuse, emotional   Typical language used to define emotional abuse of a child includes "injury to the psychological capacity or emotional stability of the child as evidenced by an observable or substantial change in behavior, emotional response, or cognition."

child abuse, neglect   The deprivation of adequate food, clothing, medical care, shelter, and supervision of a child.

child abuse, physical   Any nonaccidental, physical injury to a child. This can include hitting, pushing, shoving, slapping, kicking, burning, and so on.

child sexual offender   Anyone who has been convicted of one or more child sexual offenses.

chop shop   A place where a car is disassembled ("chopped" up) so the individual parts can be sold without revealing that the source of the parts was a stolen car.

closing argument   An opportunity for the attorneys to tell the story of their case from beginning to end, and to argue for the result they want the jury to reach.

cocaine, crack   Cocaine in its most potent and addictive form. Powder cocaine is converted into its solid form of crack cocaine; it is then smoked.

cocaine, powder   Cocaine snorted through the nose, a relatively less effective method of introducing it into the bloodstream than crack cocaine, which is smoked. Far more effective is converting powder cocaine into its solid form of crack cocaine and then smoking it.

commercial burglary   The burglary of a nonresidential building, such as an office or store. The penalties are usually less than for a residential burglary.

compassionate use defense   Prevents prosecution for marijuana possession when the possession is for medicinal use of the marijuana.

concurrent sentence   Multiple sentences are served at the same time. In a consecutive sentence, they are served one after another.

consecutive sentence   Multiple sentences are served one after another. In a concurrent sentence, they are all served at the same time.

consent   Most states define consent as "the positive cooperation by both parties where both people can appreciate both the nature of the act and the consequences of the acts they are agreeing to." Positive cooperation, in turn, means cooperation that is not influenced by fear, duress, or illegal substances.

conspirator   Someone who forms an agreement with another person to break the law.

contempt   Failing to comply with a court order is generally known as contempt, or contempt of court.

conversion   A term used in connection with the crime of embezzlement to refer to the act of converting ownership of property from the rightful owner to the embezzler.

court clerk   Person who keeps the court's schedule, makes sure every order or judgment is properly recorded, administers the oath to each witness to tell the truth, and takes care of all the exhibits that become part of the evidence at a criminal trial.

court reporter   Person responsible for taking down a verbatim record of everything said during court proceedings, including all attorney questions and witness answers.

crime against justice   Crime that undermines the integrity and effectiveness of the civil or criminal justice systems, or prevents justice from being served.

crimes against habitation   An offshoot of crimes against property. The most common examples are burglary, arson, and vandalism.

crimes against justice   Crimes that either disrupt or corrupt the justice system. Examples include perjury, failure to follow a court order, and bribery.

crimes against persons   People-on-people crimes, such as murders, rapes, kidnappings, and assaults.

crimes against property   Modern crimes against property stem from the historical crime of larceny. Larceny, simply defined, is the taking of property from its owner without the intent to return it.

crimes against society   Crimes that are harmful not only to the individuals involved, but also to the security and order of society itself. An extreme example is terrorism.

criminal negligence   Extreme carelessness. The defendant exercised an unintentional but extreme lack of care toward the harm that would probably result from his actions.

cross-examination   Part of a trial when an attorney is questioning a witness whom the other side called to the stand.

cross report   A report of a crime passed from one government agency to another.

cruel and unusual punishment   The Eighth Amendment bars cruel and unusual punishment, but the precise meaning of this phrase is not fixed; rather, it evolves as our society's sense of what is cruel and unusual changes.

curative instruction   Instruction the judge gives the jury to correct or "cure" some mistake made during the trial. For example, if a witness unexpectedly included some hearsay evidence in one of his answers, the judge might cure the error by instructing the jury to disregard the part of the answer that was hearsay.

custody   A police officer is exerting control over a suspect's actions in some significant way. This could be anything from locking the suspect in a jail cell, to making a motorist wait in his car while the officer runs his plates for outstanding traffic violations.

cycle of violence   The three phases in abusive domestic relationships: tension building, acute battering, and loving reconciliation.

Daubert test   Test to determine whether proposed scientific evidence is sufficiently reliable to be used as a basis for convicting a defendant.

deadly weapon   Anything that could kill another person. This includes guns, knives, automobiles, clubs and other blunt instruments, and even rocks.

defendant   A person formally accused of a crime.

definite or determinate sentence   Sentences a defendant to a single, specific prison term.

deliberations   Jury deliberations take place after the evidence is all in, the judge has instructed the jury on the law, and the jury retires to the jury room to consider whether the defendant is guilty.

delinquent act   The juvenile justice system's term for a crime.

deterrence punishment   Theory of punishment that seeks to discourage a person from choosing to commit a crime, generally through fear of punishment.

direct examination   Part of a trial when an attorney is questioning a witness she called to the stand. Leading questions are generally not allowed in direct exam.

direct filing   Term used when the prosecutor files charges against a juvenile directly in adult court, rather than filing in juvenile court and requesting transfer to adult court.

discovery   The defendant's right to see and review well before trial the documents, witnesses, and other evidence that will be offered against him at trial.

discretionary sentences   Most statutes allow the judge (or jury) to use some discretion in setting the length of a sentence, within certain minimum and/or maximum limits. These are referred to as discretionary sentences.

dismissed for cause   A potential juror may be dismissed for cause if the voir dire questioning reveals some bias or prejudice serious enough to keep her from being fair and impartial.

disorderly conduct   Anything that creates a public nuisance or disturbs the peace. Examples include playing excessively loud music or noise, displaying public drunkenness, or starting a brawl.

dispositions   In the juvenile justice system, plea bargains are referred to as "dispos," which is slang for dispositions.

district attorneys   State prosecutors. They are lawyers employed by the state to represent the state at trial.

domestic abuse   Usually defined as abuse committed against an adult in which the abuser is either a spouse, a former spouse, a cohabitant, a former cohabitant, or a person with whom the victim has or had a dating or engagement relationship.

double jeopardy   Being tried twice for the same crime—the second trial exposes the defendant a second time to the "jeopardy" of being convicted and sentenced.

driving under the influence   Driving under the influence (DUI) or driving while under the influence (DWI) means driving while one's his motor skills, reaction times, judgment, attention, and so on are impaired by drugs or alcohol.

duress   The defense of duress under most state statutes requires (1) an immediate threat of harm or death, (2) a reasonable belief the threat will be carried out, and (3) no reasonable means of escape.

embezzlement   Crime in which a person entrusted with something of value, frequently money, deliberately uses fraud to take ownership of it away from the rightful owner.

entrapment   The entrapment defense protects defendants who are tricked into committing a crime by the police. It requires proof that the defendant would not have engaged in the criminal conduct but for pressure or other conduct of the police.

evidence   Basically everything presented to a jury is considered evidence, except for the statements and questions from the lawyers. This includes witness testimony, documents, tape recordings, police reports, photos, and physical objects, like a murder weapon.

exclusionary rule   States that evidence obtained by the police in a manner that is inconsistent with the U.S. Constitution cannot be used at trial—it is excluded from evidence.

expert witness   Witness hired to give opinions at trial on some specialized subject that is beyond the common experience of jurors, based on the expert's special education, training, or experience.

extortion   The threat of harm versus the promise of a benefit is the primary distinction between bribery and extortion. For example, offering to buy a favorable ruling from a judge is bribery, while threatening physical harm to the judge unless she rules in your favor is extortion.

fact witnesses   Fact witnesses (also known as lay witnesses, to distinguish them from expert witnesses) can testify only about what they themselves saw, heard, felt, and so on first hand.

false imprisonment   The act of confining someone to a particular area against his will.

false pretenses   Knowingly or recklessly telling a falsehood to induce the victim to turn ownership of something of value over to the offender.

felony   The most serious category of crime, punishable by higher fines, longer sentences, and even death. Jail time is from a minimum of one year up to life, and is served at a state or federal prison instead of a local county jail.

fitness hearings   Term used in some states to refer to the hearing on a prosecutor's request for a juvenile case to be transferred to adult court.

foreperson   Foreperson, elected by the jury, to preside over the jury deliberations. She encourages the jury to go over all the evidence, makes sure all jurors have the chance to express their opinions, handles jury voting, and delivers the jury's verdict in court.

fruit from the poisonous tree   A corollary of the exclusionary rule. It means that when improperly obtained evidence leads the police to other evidence, that other evidence is also excluded as "fruit" of the improperly obtained evidence.

gangs   In prosecuting gang crimes, the criminal justice system focuses on whether a group with some kind of commonality was involved in committing the crime, to determine whether it was a gang crime.

general intent   General intent to commit a crime means the defendant had the intent to commit an act and either knew or didn't care that the act would likely cause injury to the victim.

hate crime   Any crime motivated by an intent to target persons in a particular class, such as race, religion, gender, national origin, sexual orientation, or handicap. A hate crime is not itself a distinct crime, but it escalates the sentence for the underlying crime.

hearsay   One person's testimony about what another person said—the witness *heard* what another person *said*, hence *hearsay*. Hearsay is generally not admissible, but there are a host of exceptions.

heat of passion   A killing in which the victim provokes or pushes the killer over the edge into an uncontrollable rage is legally referred to as a killing done under the heat of passion.

heroin   A highly addictive, illegal drug made from the opium poppy. It is usually injected into a vein with a needle and syringe, and creates a relaxed, euphoric state in its users.

hung jury   A jury that, after extensive deliberation, cannot reach the unanimous or required majority agreement to either acquit or convict.

identity theft   Using someone else's identity (or a fake identity) to obtain credit cards, loans, or goods in the victim's name.

impeach   To raise doubts about the credibility or believability of the witness's testimony, such as by showing the witness's bias or contradictions in his testimony.

incapacitation punishment   Theory of punishment that tries to protect society by eliminating an offender's ability to commit another crime for some period of time, usually by putting him in prison.

indefinite sentence   A sentence that sets a minimum and maximum amount of prison time the defendant is to serve. When the minimum time has been served, the defendant becomes eligible for parole.

indeterminate sentence   A rare form of sentence that directs the board of prisons, parole board, or mental health officials to assess a defendant's progress toward rehabilitation and, thus, decide how long the defendant should stay in custody.

indictment or information   The complaint or formal statement of charges against a defendant. An indictment is the charging document used after a grand jury has heard a case. An information is the name of the document when the case is reviewed and filed directly by the prosecutor.

infancy defense   Rare defense that makes children immune from criminal prosecution. It is based on the rationale that a child is unable to understand the nature and repercussions of his actions and, therefore, is not culpable for them.

infraction   The least serious type of crime. An infraction is punishable by fines only, not jail time, and the fines are usually less than $1,000.

insanity defense   The most common definition of the insanity defense is called the M'Naghten Rule, which requires proof that the defendant either did not know what he was doing or did not know it was wrong, as a result of a mental illness.

insider trading   A common type of securities fraud, in which someone relies on non-public information to buy or sell a security.

instructions   Instructions that the judge uses to describe the law the jury should apply, such as the individual elements of a crime that must be proven beyond a reasonable doubt.

joint   Slang name for a marijuana cigarette, or slang for a jail or prison.

judge   Often called a magistrate or commissioner. Judges decide all the legal issues in a case and instruct the jury on the law it is to apply.

juror misconduct   Any improper juror action that potentially prejudices the fairness of the proceeding. Examples include sleeping during trial, not being truthful and forthcoming during voir dire, and reading press accounts of the case.

jury   A group of 6 or 12 members of the surrounding community whose names are drawn from voter registrations. The jury decides whether the defendant is guilty or not guilty, based on the evidence at trial and the judge's instructions on the law.

jury pool   The group of potential jurors brought into court to be questioned during voir dire.

juvenile hall   Facility that serves the same function for juveniles as a prison does for adults. They usually also provide for continued schooling and rehabilitation efforts.

juvenile   Most states define juveniles subject to the jurisdiction of the juvenile justice courts as persons between the ages of 10 and 18, but the specific minimum and maximum ages vary from state to state.

kidnapping   While the precise definition of kidnapping varies in federal and state statutes, all contain the following elements: seizing, confining, and carrying away another person by force, fear, or deception, or otherwise without their consent.

larceny   *Larceny* and *theft* are often used interchangeably but mean the same thing: taking someone else's property with no intent to return it.

laying a foundation   Establishing the basis for admitting some testimony or other piece of evidence. For a fact witness, for example, this might mean showing she was in a position to observe the events to which she will testify.

leading question   A question that suggests the answer.

legal capacity   The ability to make a legally binding decision or act—for example, to consent to a sexual encounter.

lesser included crime   A crime that could have been charged since it was a necessary part of the more serious crime, but only the more serious crime was charged.

lesser related crime   A crime that is related to the greater crime but not necessarily part of it. For example, a defendant caught red-handed with stolen property might be charged with receiving stolen property as well as larceny, just in case the prosecution is unable to prove that the defendant stole the property.

life   Under most criminal justice statutes, life for purposes of homicide laws means the fetus can be born alive.

mail or wire fraud   Mail or wire fraud occurs when mail or wire communications are used as part of an attempted scheme to defraud.

malice aforethought   Malice aforethought distinguishes murder from manslaughter and means one of the following: intent to cause death or great bodily harm, knowledge that death or great bodily harm will occur, a gross indifference to the value of human life, or a death that follows a person's intent to commit a felony.

mandated reporting   Requirement that certain professionals must report when they have reason to suspect abuse, if the victim or someone else tells them about abuse, or if they observe child abuse.

mandatory sentence   Sentence that results when a statute mandates that a specific sentence must be imposed for a particular crime and cannot be altered by the judge or later by a parole board.

manslaughter   The killing of another person without malice aforethought. The lack of malice aforethought makes manslaughter a different crime than murder.

manslaughter, involuntary   An unintentional killing that is the result of criminal negligence.

manslaughter, vehicular   A killing caused by the operation of a motor vehicle. It may be a misdemeanor or a felony, depending primarily on whether the driver was under the influence of alcohol or a drug and was driving with gross negligence—that is, driving without caution or concern for the safety of others.

manslaughter, voluntary   A killing that would be first-degree murder except that it was committed in response to some sort of provocation on the part of the victim—for example, an "in the heat of passion" killing.

marijuana   Drug derived from the cannabis plant, which is dried and then smoked in a pipe or hand-rolled cigarette or "joint."

material   A material fact is one that could affect the outcome of the case or hearing.

mens rea   The mental state or level of intention with which a crime is committed.

methamphetamine   Commonly referred to as "meth." It is a stimulant drug that is extremely addictive. Meth can be taken in a number of ways, including smoking, swallowing, snorting, or injecting.

Miranda rights   Miranda rights get their name from the Supreme Court case that ruled that a suspect in custody must be read certain rights, such as the right to remain silent and the right to have an attorney present, before being questioned.

misdemeanor   Crime that falls between an infraction and a felony in severity, and can involve jail time as well as fines for punishment. Jail time for a misdemeanor, however, is generally less than a year and is served at a local county jail instead of a state prison.

mistrial   Declaring a mistrial means some problem has occurred that is so serious that the whole trial must be ended and started over, with a new jury. Problems might include a hung jury or juror misconduct.

mitigating factors   Factors that reduce the culpability of a crime and may warrant reducing the charge or lowering the sentence. They are the opposite of aggravating factors.

motion to exclude   A motion that seeks to keep the witness or victim from hearing another witness testify by excluding her from the courtroom.

motive   The reason for committing the crime. Intent, or mens rea, is the mental state or degree of intention with which it is committed.

murder, capital   A first-degree murder that qualifies for capital punishment (the death penalty).

murder, first-degree   A killing that is willful, deliberate, and premeditated.

murder, second-degree   Any murder with malice aforethought but without the "willful, deliberate, and premeditated" mindset of first-degree murder.

no argument rule   Rule that the lawyers can preview the anticipated testimony only in their opening statements and may not argue what they think the evidence means.

obstruction of justice   A broad crime that encompasses any attempt to interfere with virtually any part of the criminal justice system.

officers of the court   As officers of the court, attorneys have obligations to the court as well as to their clients, such as the duty to not offer evidence the lawyer knows is false, to refrain from giving personal opinions about the guilt or innocence of the defendant during trial, and so on.

opening statements   Presentations by the lawyers at the start of a case that summarize the evidence to come and give a big-picture view of the case.

opens the door   If the defendant opens the door, as lawyers call it, by voluntarily testifying on a subject, he loses the ability to assert the Fifth Amendment as to all questions on that subject.

ordinance   A law passed by a city or county as part of its city or county code, as distinguished from the state or federal code.

overruling an objection   The judge disagrees with the objection and, consequently, instructs the witness to answer it.

parens patriae   Doctrine, literally meaning "father of the people," that authorizes the state to legislate for the protection, care, custody, and maintenance of children within its jurisdiction.

pattern jury instructions   Instructions preapproved for use to explain many of the routine or frequent legal issues on which a jury is instructed.

perjury   Lying or giving false testimony under oath. Because it is an attempt to cause a miscarriage of justice—to cause the criminal justice system to reach a wrong result—it can result in a heavy punishment.

perpetrator   Also known as the principal. The person or persons who actually committed the crime.

plea bargain   An agreement between the prosecution and the defense in which the defendant agrees to plead guilty (or no contest) and the prosecutor agrees to (1) drop any additional charges, (2) lower the remaining charge, or (3) recommend to the judge a lighter sentence.

Ponzi scheme   A form of fraud in which artificially high rates of return are paid to early investors in order to attract new investors, with the capital invested by the new investors used to fund the high rates of return paid to earlier investors.

preemptory challenge   Allows an attorney to have a juror removed even though no bias or other cause has been shown, usually without giving the reason for the removal.

prejudice   The jury may improperly give the evidence more weight than it deserves.

preliminary hearing   Hearing in which the court decides whether there is sufficient evidence to make the defendant stand trial. A preliminary hearing happens only in jurisdictions that do not file a case by a grand jury indictment.

premeditation   Means "purposeful," "knowing," "deliberate," or "with intent." All reflect the mental state required for murder in the first degree.

pretrial motions   Motions filed by either the prosecution or the defense to get a ruling from the court on some issue before trial. The most common pretrial motions are those that seek to exclude certain pieces of evidence or that challenge the qualifications or opinions of expert witnesses.

principal   Also known as the perpetrator. The person or persons who actually committed the crime.

probable cause   Probable cause means that a police officer has sufficient objective, factual information to show that the suspect is most likely responsible for the crime.

probation   The judge sentences the defendant to a certain amount of jail time but suspends the sentence as long as the defendant complies with the terms set out in his probationary sentence.

probative value   How much the evidence helps prove that some relevant fact is true.

pronouncement of sentence   Synonymous with *final judgment*.

prosecutors   Lawyers employed by the government—federal or state—who represent the government at trial. State prosecutors are often called district attorneys.

protected classes   Groups of people who, because they share a particular racial, cultural, religious or other characteristic that has historically been the target of discrimination, receive specific protection against such discrimination through hate crimes.

public defenders   Government-employed lawyers appointed to represent defendants who cannot afford to hire a private attorney to represent them.

rap sheet   The defendant's criminal record.

rape shield laws   Laws that prevent (with a couple exceptions) attacks at trial on the character of victims of rape or other sexual assault.

recidivism   Term used in the criminal justice system to describe when a defendant continues to commit crimes after serving his sentence for an earlier crime.

reckless falsehood   A falsehood made by a person who doesn't know whether the statement is true, or does not have any information that would make her believe it's true.

regulation   A law promulgated by a government agency, either state or federal.

rehabilitation   The attempt to help a convicted person change his ways and to turn from a life of crime to one of law-abiding citizen.

rehabilitation punishment   Theory of punishment that tries to tailor a sentence to help the defendant "go straight"—that is, not commit more crimes.

relevancy   Evidence is considered relevant if it tends to prove a fact that matters to the case.

restitution   Seeks to restore the victim to where she was before the crime, to make the victim or the victim's family as whole as possible. Restitution may be ordered by the court as part of a sentence or paid under a state program.

restorative punishment   The restorative theory of punishment seeks to right the wrong done the victim by having the offender make amends for the harm caused.

restraining orders   Require a person to stay away from another person or place, often used in abuse and other domestic violence cases.

retribution punishment   The retribution theory of punishment is basically "an eye for an eye"—its philosophy is that the more serious the harm is caused by the crime, the more severely the system should punish the criminal.

rioting   More than just disorderly conduct on a grander scale—it is an unlawful assembly of three or more people (some states require only two) who have gathered to carry out an unlawful purpose in an unlawful way.

search warrant   Warrant obtained by the police from a judge, who issues the search warrant only if he finds probable cause to believe that relevant evidence is at the location to be searched.

securities fraud   The deliberate use of false or incomplete information in connection with the purchase or sale of securities. A common type of securities fraud is insider trading, in which someone relies on nonpublic information to buy or sell a security.

security   For purposes of securities fraud statutes, anything that gives an investor a piece of a company, whether that is a piece of a company's assets (such as stock) or a piece of its liabilities (such as a bond).

self-defense   Using reasonable force to protect yourself against an imminent threat of physical harm—harm that is about happen right away.

sentencing guidelines, federal   To fulfill the constitutional mandate for equal justice for all, the U.S. Sentencing Commission promulgates sentencing guidelines that federal judges must follow.

sentencing hearing   Hearing to allow various interested parties (including the victim and the defendant) to present evidence, make statements, and offer arguments about what the appropriate sentence should be.

sequestering   Putting up the jury members in a hotel where they have limited or no access to outside news sources or contacts with others.

serious bodily injury   Injuries that would warrant a felony charge of battery, including those creating a substantial risk of death, unconsciousness, extreme physical pain, disfigurement, or impairment. Small cuts, bruising, and other slight injuries are not serious bodily injuries and would support only charges of misdemeanor battery.

sexual assault   Involves physical contact—actual touching or other contact—and includes all kinds of contact, from groping to sodomy, to oral intercourse.

sexual exploitation   Occurs when an adult victimizes a child for personal advancement, sexual gratification, or financial profit.

sexual molestation   With sexual molestation, the focus is on the intent of the perpetrator to cause some sexually inappropriate behavior. This includes any act in which an adult engages in behavior that is not necessarily physical but uses a child for sexual gratification. Examples include Peeping Toms and flashers.

show-up   In a show-up, a police officer shows an eyewitness a single suspect and asks, "Is this the person who committed the crime?" It is considered the form of identification most open to suggestibility and so is generally used immediately after a crime has occurred, while the victim and police are still out in the field.

sidebar conference   When the attorneys ask the judge for permission to "approach the bench" to discuss an objection or other matter out of the hearing of the jury.

SODDI   Short for the common defense that "some other dude did it."

speaking objections   Objections that explain why the lawyer thinks a question is improper. They are meant more for the jury than the judge. Speaking objections are improper.

specific intent   Specific intent to commit a crime means the defendant purposely intended the result of his or her crime.

spousal privilege   Two kinds of spousal privilege are recognized. One protects confidential communications between spouses, and the other protects one spouse from being forced to testify against the other.

stalking   To qualify as criminal stalking, there must be a series (at least two) of such events or acts, and many states require some sort of credible (that is, realistic) threat to the victim.

status offenses   Offenses based only on the juvenile status of the offender. Examples include curfew violations and the purchase or possession of cigarettes or alcohol.

statute   A law enacted by a legislature, either federal or state. All have the force of law.

statutory exclusion   Also called legislative exclusion. Occurs when a statute excludes juvenile defendants from juvenile court when certain factors are present, and mandates prosecution in adult court.

statutory rape   Sexual intercourse with a female who has not reached the age of consent. Even if the underage female consents to the intercourse, it is statutory rape because of her age.

strict liability   Strict liability to commit a crime requires no intent or mental state.

subornation of perjury   To cause another person to commit perjury—that is, to lie under oath.

sustain an objection   When the judge sustains an objection made by one of the attorneys, the judge agrees that the question is improper, and the witness is not allowed to answer it.

terrorism   A violent or dangerous action meant to intimidate or devastate a society or government. Current statutes, such as the USA Patriot Act, specifically identify actions, weapons, targets, and locations in defining criminal terrorist activities.

trespass   Similar to burglary, but without the element of intending to commit another crime once inside the dwelling; it also usually applies to any structure, not just dwellings. All that is required is that a person enter a home, apartment, business, or other establishment of another without consent.

under oath   A witness is under oath when he swears (or solemnly affirms) to tell the truth.

vandalism   The intentional damaging of another's property. The property need not be physical—deliberately spreading a computer virus, for example, can be vandalism.

victim impact statements   Statements made by the victim and/or her family to the judge, the defendant, the public, and the sometimes the jury. The statement describes how the crime has affected the victim, her family, and others—not only the economic harm, but also the emotional trauma and long-lasting psychological effects the crime has caused.

victimless crime   A crimes in which no particular individual is the intended victim and no one is considered to have been harmed by it. But victimless crimes can cause extensive and serious harm and have many indirect victims. Probably the most common victimless crime is a traffic violation.

victim's bill of rights   Ensure that the victim is shown dignity, respect, courtesy, and sensitivity throughout the criminal justice process. The main rights are the right to be present, the right to be heard, and the right to be informed.

voir dire   (Pronounced "vwah deer.") The fancy name for questions that the lawyers or judge ask potential jurors before trial. These questions try to discover biases, beliefs, preformed opinions about a case, or other reasons a juror might not be fair and impartial.

warrant   A document issued by a court directing a law enforcement officer to arrest the person identified in the warrant.

wet reckless   A less serious alternative to the crime of driving under the influence. Prosecutors may allow a defendant to plead to this lesser crime if there are mitigating circumstances, such as if the defendant's blood alcohol was low, there was no evidence of impairment, or there was no accident.

white-collar crime   A crime can be considered a white-collar crime for one of two reasons. One is that the type of offense is associated with business activities. The other is that the perpetrator is of a high socioeconomic status; occupies a position of trust; or is a business, professional, or academic person.

wobbler   Crime that can be charged as either a misdemeanor or a felony, at the discretion of the grand jury or the prosecutor.

writ of habeas corpus   An order (another word for writ) from a federal court finding that the state is holding a person illegally and ordering that he be released.

youth detention center   Facility that serves the same function for juveniles as a prison does for adults, but usually provides for such things as continued schooling and rehabilitation efforts.

Sample Felony Plea Script

_____ Is that your true and correct name?

You are charged in complaint number_____, in count _____ with a violating _____ section _____ subsection, a felony, commonly known as _____.

Do you understand the charges against you?

Have you discussed the facts of this case with your lawyer, including any defenses you might have?

Waiver of Constitutional Rights

Before the court will accept your plea, you must be advised of your constitutional rights and must understand, waive, and give up these rights.

◆ PRELIMINARY HEARING

First, you have the right to a preliminary hearing. In a preliminary, a judge listens to the evidence presented and decides whether there is sufficient evidence to establish that there is probable cause to believe that you committed the charged.

DO YOU UNDERSTAND YOUR RIGHT TO A PRELIMINARY HEARING, AND DO YOU GIVE UP THIS RIGHT?

◆ JURY TRIAL

You have a right to a jury trial where 12 people are selected to hear the prosecution's case and your defense. These 12 people would make the decision of your guilt or innocence. You could be found guilty only if all 12 people agree that the prosecution had proven its case beyond a reasonable doubt.

DO YOU UNDERSTAND YOUR RIGHT TO A JURY TRIAL, AND DO YOU GIVE UP THIS RIGHT?

◆ COURT TRIAL

You also have the right to a court trial with the consent of the prosecution. The judge would listen to the evidence presented by the prosecution and the defense. You could be found guilty by the judge only if the judge was convinced that the prosecution had proven its case beyond a reasonable doubt.

DO YOU UNDERSTAND YOUR RIGHT TO A COURT TRIAL, AND DO YOU GIVE UP THIS RIGHT?

◆ CONFRONTATION/SUBPOENA POWER

If you had a prelim or trial, you would have the right to confront and cross-examine the witnesses against you. This means that witnesses would be brought into court, take the witness stand, and give testimony under oath. Your attorney would have the right to ask those witnesses questions.

You also have the right to an affirmative defense and would be able to use the subpoena power of the court to subpoena witnesses on your behalf at no cost to you.

DO YOU UNDERSTAND YOUR RIGHT TO CONFRONT AND CROSS-EXAMINE THE WITNESSES AGAINST YOU, AND DO YOU GIVE UP THIS RIGHT?

◆ SELF-INCRIMINATION

You also have the right to remain silent. This is referred to as the privilege against self-incrimination. By pleading guilty, you are giving up this right because you are, in fact, using your own words to incriminate yourself.

DO YOU UNDERSTAND AND GIVE UP YOUR RIGHT TO REMAIN SILENT?

Consequences of Plea

Before the court can accept your plea here today, you must also be informed of the consequences of your plea.

- ◆ SENTENCE

The maximum confinement in your case is _____.

However, due to your plea here today, we have agreed that you will receive

_____.

DO YOU UNDERSTAND THE PLEA AGREEMENT?

- ◆ PROBATION

There will be certain terms and conditions on your probation. If you violate the terms and conditions of your probation, you could be brought back to court, and after a hearing, if the judge determines that you, in fact, violated the terms of your probation, you could be sent to prison for the maximum term.

DO YOU UNDERSTAND THIS?

- ◆ PAROLE

If you are sent to state prison, once you have completed your sentence, you will be put on parole. There are certain conditions put on parole, and if you violate the terms and conditions of parole, you could be sent back to prison for up to one year for each violation.

DO YOU UNDERSTAND THIS?

If you are currently on probation or parole in another court or agency, your plea here today could constitute a parole or probation violation and could subject you to additional time in custody.

DO YOU UNDERSTAND THIS?

- ◆ CITIZENSHIP

If you are not a citizen of the United States, your plea here today will cause you to be deported, denied reentry, denied naturalization, or denied amnesty.

DO YOU UNDERSTAND THIS?

- ◆ RESTITUTION AND FINES

In addition to your jail/prison sentence, the court could impose a fine ranging from $200 to $10,000, a restitution fine of at least $200, a booking fine, and/or a fee. These fines can be paid over a period of time.

◆ FIREARMS

As a result of your plea here today, you can no longer own, use, or possess a firearm, as this will constitute a separate felony.

DO YOU UNDERSTAND THIS?

◆ IMPEACHMENT/MORAL TURPITUDE

This is a crime of moral turpitude. Therefore, your plea can be used to impeach or attack your credibility should you ever appear as a witness in court at some time in the future.

◆ STRIKE

You are pleading to what is considered a strike under the California 3 Strikes Law. As a result, if you are convicted of another felony in the future, ANY sentence you will receive will be doubled. If you are convicted of another serious or violent felony in the future, you will be considered a "3 Striker," which means that if you are convicted of another felony in the future, the minimum sentence you can receive is 25 years to life.

Violent Felonies in California:

Murder	Robbery
Mayhem	Arson
Rape	Kidnapping
Sodomy	Carjacking
Oral Copulation	Extortion
Lewd Act on a Minor	Criminal Threats

◆ SEX/NARCOTICS REGISTRATION

You are required by law to register as a narcotics/sex offender/arson/gang with the local law enforcement agency nearest your home. If you move, you are required to register in your new area within __ days.

◆ PLEA

Are you pleading guilty (no contest) freely and voluntarily, and because you feel it is in your best interest to do so?

Has anyone threatened you or anyone close to you to get you plead guilty or no contest today?

Other than the agreement as to your sentence as I have stated here in open court and on the record, has any other promise been made to you in order to get you to plead guilty or no contest today?

◆ NO CONTEST PLEA

Do you understand that a no contest plea will be treated exactly the same as a guilty plea?

◆ ARBUCKLE WAIVER

You have a right to be sentenced by the same judge who takes your plea. Do you understand this right? Do you waive and give up this right so any judge may sentence you?

You have the right to be sentenced within ___ court days. DO you understand this right? DO you give up this right OR DO you wish to be sentenced today?

◆ CRUZ WAIVER

If you are released from custody but fail to return to court on _____, your date of sentencing, do you understand that your plea today will be considered an "open plea" and the judge may sentence you to the maximum time?

DOES THE COURT WISH TO INQUIRE FURTHER? May I take the plea?

_____ in felony case #_____ to count _____ a violation of _____Code Section, commonly known as _____, how do you plead?

Does counsel join in the waivers, concur in the plea, and stipulate to a factual basis for the plea based on the police reports included with the complaint?

PEOPLE JOIN THE JURY WAIVERS.

SPECIAL ALLEGATIONS, PRIORS

Do you admit that you suffered the following prior conviction

CASE_____CODE SECTION_____SUBSECTION_____ ON _____
(DATE) IN _____COUNTY SUPERIOR COURT

667.5 PRIORS

... AND THAT YOU DID NOT REMAIN FREE FORM CUSTODY FROM PRISON FOR A PERIOD OF FIVE YEARS?

Is the court satisfied with the waivers and may I take the plea?

THE PLEA

_____ in felony complaint _____ you are charged with a violation of penal code section _____ subsection _____ a felony. HOW DO YOU NOW PLEAD?

Do you understand a no contest plea will be treated the same as a guilty plea?

Counsel, do you join in the plea, concur in the waivers and stipulate to a factual basis?

People join.

Online Resources

Children and Crime

National Center for Missing and Exploited Children
www.missingkids.com

The National Center for Missing and Exploited Children helps prevent child abduction and sexual exploitation; helps find missing children; and assists victims of child abduction and sexual exploitation, their families, and the professionals who serve them.

National Crime Prevention Council
www.ncpc.org/publications/brochures/children

The National Crime Prevention Council provides information on the prevention of crimes directed toward children.

Crime Prevention

National Crime Prevention Council
www.ncpc.org

The National Crime Prevention Council provides information about crime prevention, community building, and activities to reduce victimization and deter crime and criminals. The council addresses the causes of crime and violence to help individuals keep themselves, their families, and their communities safe from crime by learning crime-prevention strategies, engaging community members, and coordinating with local agencies.

Crime Stoppers International, Inc.

www.c-s-i.org

Crime Stoppers International offers cash rewards to individuals furnishing anonymous information that leads to the arrest of criminals, felons, and fugitives. Crime Stoppers programs enable the police, the press, and the public to work together, solving over half a million crimes and recovering over $3 billion worth of stolen property and narcotics to date.

Crime Statistics

Bureau of Justice Statistics

www.ojp.usdoj.gov/bjs/cvict.htm

The National Crime Victimization Survey is the nation's primary source of information on criminal victimization. It provides statistics regarding crime frequency, crime characteristics, and the consequences of victimization regarding assault, burglary, larceny, motor vehicle theft, rape, and robbery crimes experienced by U.S. residents and households each year.

City Rating

www.cityrating.com/crimestatistics.asp

CityRating.com offers crime statistics often used to measure the safety of a city in tabular and graphic reports, including violent and property crime rate information and crime reports on hundreds of cities and metropolitan areas in the United States.

Federal Bureau of Investigation

www.fbi.gov/ucr/ucr.htm

The Federal Bureau of Investigation administers the Uniform Crime Reporting Program, special studies, and database reports in order to publish, archive, assess, and monitor the nature and type of crime in the nation.

Sourcebook of Criminal Justice Statistics

www.albany.edu/sourcebook

The Sourcebook of Criminal Justice Statistics compiles data supported by the U.S. Department of Justice and Bureau of Justice Statistics into over 1,000 tables of many aspects of criminal justice characteristics, public opinion, crime and victims, arrests and seizures, court procedures, prosecution and sentencing, parole, jails, prisons, and the death penalty.

Cybercrime

Cybercitizen Partnership
www.cybercitizenship.org

The Cybercitizen Partnership Awareness Campaign offers approaches for teaching children about cyberethics, cybercrime information, and links to adult and youth resources.

Play It Cyber Safe
www.playitcybersafe.com

Funded by the United States Department of Justice, this program educates the public on cybercrime and intellectual property theft. It assists children, parents, and teachers in preventing cybercrime by helping them understand the law, showing them their rights, and teaching them how navigate cyberspace safely.

Death Penalty

Death Penalty Information Center
www.deathpenaltyinfo.org

The Death Penalty Information Center provides analysis, information, resources, and information about executions, and serves a resource to both the media and the public on issues concerning capital punishment.

Driving Under the Influence

Center for Disease Control and Prevention
www.cdc.gov/ncipc/factsheets/drving.htm

The Department of Health and Human Services provides information and statistics regarding the occurrences and consequences of impaired driving.

Domestic Violence

Women's Law
www.womenslaw.org

Women's Law provides information regarding state laws, court proceedings, and advocacy regarding domestic abuse, domestic violence, and sexual assault.

Drugs

Bureau of Justice Statistics
www.ojp.usdoj.gov/bjs/dcf/contents.htm

The U.S. Department of Justice summarizes statistics about drug-related crimes, law enforcement, courts, and corrections from Bureau of Justice Statistics reports and other statistical agencies.

Drug Policy Research Center
www.rand.org/pubs/occasional_papers/2005/RAND_OP121.pdf

RAND Corporation's Drug Policy Research Center analyzes trends in drug use and evaluates policies for responding to drug-related problems. This report presents objective information to assess the success of programs and choices for the future in the United States' "war on drugs."

United Nations Office on Drugs and Crime
www.unodc.org/unodc/en/illicit-drugs/index.html

The United Nations Office on Drugs and Crime presents international information on illicit drugs and abuse, human and illicit trafficking, law enforcement, crop monitoring, corruption, organized crime, and justice reform.

Forensics

DNA Initiative
www.dna.gov

The president's DNA Initiative provides extensive information on the uses of DNA, statutes and case laws regarding forensic evidence and post-conviction testing, DNA statistics, and research regarding forensic analysis, to ensure that forensic testing reaches its full potential to solve crimes, protect the innocent, and identify missing persons.

Forensic Science
www.library.thinkquest.org/04oct/00206/index1.htm

Forensic Science attempts to educate and intrigue, with concise and easy-to-understand language that explains many concepts used in forensics, demonstrates the key role forensic science plays in determining the innocence or guilt of a suspect, and illustrating the different techniques used to analyze a variety of crimes.

Handbook of Forensic Services
www.fbi.gov/hq/lab/handbook/forensics.pdf

The Handbook of Forensic Services provides guidance and procedures for safe and efficient methods of collecting and preserving evidence. It also describes the forensic examinations that the FBI Laboratory performs.

Gangs

Coroner's Report
www.gangwar.com

The Coroner's Report provides intervention and prevention resources on gang activities, including an in-depth review of gang history, identification symbols, characteristics, and warning signs.

National Gang Center
www.nationalgangcenter.gov

The National Gang Center provides training, survey information, and analysis on gang research and policy issues. It also provides practical trial strategies for prosecutors engaged in combating gang violence.

National Youth Gang Center
www.iir.com/nygc/gang-legis

The Institute for Intergovernmental Research provides a comprehensive compilation of gang-related legislation.

Gun Control

American Bar Association
www.abanet.org/gunviol

The Special Committee on Gun Violence provides information on the American Bar Association's policy on gun violence, facts about gun violence (including comparisons of the United States to other nations), guns in schools, and kids and guns.

Gun Violence Prosecution
www.ndaa.org/apri/programs/gun_violence/gvp_home.html

The American Prosecutors Research Institute's Gun Violence Prosecution Program seeks to dramatically reduce gun-related violence in America through professional training, technical assistance, and educational publications.

National Center for Policy Analysis
www.ncpa.org/iss/cri/i_selfdefense.html#guncontrolmyths

This site presents a compilation of articles on background checks, the Brady Gun Law, gun control myths, gun-related deaths, handgun restrictions, liability and guns, rifle bans, police and guns, safety requirements, self-defense, and the right to carry laws.

Hate Crimes

Anti-Defamation League
www.adl.org

The Anti-Defamation League fights hatred, extremism, and terrorism by gathering, analyzing, and disseminating intelligence on anti-semitism, extremism, and hate activity by various hate or fringe groups.

Federal Bureau of Investigation
www.fbi.gov/hq/cid/civilrights/hate.htm

The Federal Bureau of Investigation serves as the lead agency for investigating violations of federal civil rights laws; publishes various statistics regarding crimes motivated by biases based on race, religion, sexual orientation, ethnicity, and disability; and provides information regarding civil rights statutes, the history of hate crimes, abuses by public officials, and how to report hate crimes and acts.

Partners Against Hate
www.preventinghate.org

Partners Against Hate provides education and counteraction strategies for young people and the wide range of community-based professionals who work and interact with youth, including parents, law enforcement officials, educators, and community and business leaders.

Southern Poverty Law Center
www.splcenter.org

The Southern Poverty Law Center provides tolerance education programs, tracks hate groups, combats causes of hate, achieves legal victories against hate groups, and fights all forms of discrimination.

Identity Theft

Federal Trade Commission
www.ftc.gov/bcp/edu/microsites/idtheft

This national resource provides detailed information to help deter, detect, and defend against identity theft. Consumers can learn how to avoid identity theft and learn what to do if their identity is stolen. Businesses can learn how to prevent problems and help their customers deal with identity theft. Law enforcement can get resources and learn how to help victims of identity theft.

Privacy Rights Clearing House
www.privacyrights.org

Privacy Rights Clearing House provides information and guidelines for victims of identity theft, as well as information for legislators. It maintains a roster of consumers and experts willing to testify for legislation related to privacy and identity theft.

U.S. Department of Justice
www.usdoj.gov/criminal/fraud/websites/idtheft.html

This comprehensive site explains identity theft, identity fraud, and Internet and tele-marketing fraud, with advice for victims and information on how to prevent identify theft and fraud.

Juvenile Justice

Center on Criminal and Juvenile Justice
www.cjcj.org/blog

The Center on Criminal and Juvenile Justice provides research on juvenile criminal justice, detention and diversion programs, and alternative programs to incarceration that can reduce overburdened correctional facilities and recidivism rates.

Juvenile Crime
www.lawyershop.com/practice-areas/criminal-law/juvenile-law

This website provides a variety of information regarding juvenile crime, juvenile cases, juvenile crime demographics, and delinquency prevention. It also includes a glossary and gives an overview of the juvenile justice system.

Office of Juvenile Justice and Delinquency Prevention
www.ojjdp.ncjrs.org

The Office of Juvenile Justice and Delinquency Prevention collaborates with professionals from diverse disciplines to improve juvenile justice policies and practices. It also studies juveniles in crisis, from serious, violent, and chronic offenders to victims of abuse and neglect.

Laws, Legislation, and Statutes

House of Representatives
www.house.gov

This website includes an outline of issues currently on the House floor and access to the laws of the United States, including U.S. codes, bills, and amendments; congressional records; and voting information.

United States Department of Justice
www.ojp.usdoj.gov/BJA

As the primary federal criminal investigation and enforcement agency, the Bureau of Justice Administration supports law enforcement, courts, corrections, treatment, victim services, technology, and prevention initiatives that strengthen the nation's criminal justice system.

United States Constitution

www.usconstitution.net

The United States Constitution, Declaration of Independence, Articles of Confederation, and other historical topics are presented in a series of individual pages, in searchable text and using keywords hyperlinked to a quick-reference guide.

Law Enforcement

Bureau of Justice Statistics

www.ojp.usdoj.gov/bjs/lawenf.htm

This website presents law enforcement statistical information and publications about law enforcement in the United States justice system.

Officer.com

www.officer.com

This police source provides news and information for the police and law enforcement community.

Police Jobs and Law Enforcement Training

www.policeemployment.com

This website provides job listings and information on careers in criminal justice and law enforcement.

U.S. Department of Labor

www.bls.gov/oco/ocos160.htm

This information from the Bureau of Labor Statistics provides a detailed description of the occupational outlook for police and detectives.

Media

Justice Interrupted

www.justiceinterrupted.blogspot.com
www.justiceinterrupted.com

Justice Interrupted, LLC is a media consulting team whose goal is to highlight criminal cases that aren't receiving adequate media or law enforcement attention, and to help victims use media resources to find the justice they seek. The team consists of three experts whose experience covers the three components of criminal cases: police officer (Stacy Dittrich), violence expert (Susan Murphy-Milano), and prosecutor (Robin Sax).

The weekly radio show "Justice Interrupted Radio Network" is one of the highest rated shows on Blogtalk radio, and is currently being developed into a weekly television show. Guests have included top criminal justice professionals as well as many victims needing to have their voices heard. Examples include Mark Geragos, Mark Klaas, Diane Dimond, Joel Brodsky for Drew Peterson, David Dimond, Polly Franks, Shaw Chapman Holley, crime author Diane Fanning, former NYPD Detective Gil Alba, Dana Pretzer, criminal profiler Pat Brown, Tina Dirrman, and Joe Hosey.

The efforts of "Justice Interrupted" have contributed to denials of paroles for convicted murderers, front-page stories in newspapers such as *The Chicago Tribune* and *The Miami Herald*, and victim's stories brought to the television screen in shows like *48 Hours.*

Domestic Violence, Child Abuse, and Sex Crimes

Some wonderful organizations throughout the country not only provide educational information in sexual abuse prevention but also have a contact list showing to whom or where one can go to learn more or get help. Some of my favorite organizations are the following.

The Awareness Center
theawarenesscenter.org

An international organization addressing sexual victimization of both adults and children in Jewish Communities.

Beyond the Missing
24 hour Support and Business Phone: 415-339-0923
info@beyondmissing.com
www.beyondmissing.com

Founded by Marc Klaas after the kidnap and murder of his 12-year-old daughter Polly. Beyond Missing promotes an aggressive child safety agenda and provides many resources—including online tools to create "missing person" flyers for free.

Carole Sund/Carrington Memorial Reward Foundation
www.carolesoundfoundation.com
209-567-1059

This foundation is committed to raising public awareness of the issue of missing persons, many of whom are later found to have fallen victim to the most violent of crimes. The foundation offers support and resources to aggrieved families, and under qualifying circumstances may post rewards for information on behalf of families who lack the financial means to do so themselves.

Childhelp USA National Child Abuse Hotline
1-800-4-A-CHILD
(1-800-422-4453)
TDD: 1-800-2-A-CHILD
ChildLine (UK): 0800 1111

Childhelp USA is a nonprofit organization "dedicated to meeting the physical, emotional, educational, and spiritual needs of abused and neglected children. Its programs and services include a hotline children can call and talk to a Childhelp counselor about any kind of problem, with complete anonymity and confidentiality.

The Innocent Justice Foundation
innocentjustice.org
The Innocent Justice Foundation
132 N. El Camino Real #483
Encinitas, CA 92024
760-585-8873
1-888-698-8873
E-mail: info@innocentjustice.org

This foundation is dedicated to helping rescue children from sexual abuse, as well as to educate the public about Internet crimes against children, advocate victim legislation, and support law enforcement and governmental agencies that prevent, investigate, prosecute, and criminally adjudicate sex crimes against children.

i-SAFE
www.i-safe.org

Founded in 1998, i-SAFE Inc. is the leader in Internet safety education. Available in all 50 states, i-SAFE is a nonprofit foundation whose mission is to educate children on how to recognize and avoid dangerous, inappropriate, or unlawful online behavior.

The International Society for Prevention of Child Abuse and Neglect (ISPCAN)
www.ispan.org
245 W. Roosevelt Road Building 6, Suite 39
West Chicago, IL 60185, USA
Telephone: 630-876-6913
Fax: 630-876-6917

Founded in 1977, ISPCAN is the only international organization that brings together a multidisciplinary cross-section of professionals from different fields who work together towards the prevention and treatment of child abuse, neglect and exploitation. ISPCAN has been a global force combating cruelty to children in every nation, in every form: physical abuse, sexual abuse, neglect, street children, child fatalities, child prostitution, children of war, emotional abuse, and child labor.

National Children's Alliance
1612 K Street, NW, Suite 500
Washington, DC 20006
1-800-239-9950
202-452-6001
E-mail: info@nca-online.org

Call the Children's Advocacy Center nearest you for a referral to a nearby support group or therapist specializing in child sexual abuse.

National Domestic Violence/Abuse Hotline
1-800-799-SAFE
1-800-799-7233
1-800-787-3224 TDD

This is a 24-hour hotline staffed by trained volunteers who connect victims of domestic violence with emergency help and other resources available in their own communities. The hotline staff can provide information and referrals for a variety of services, including counseling for adults and children and assistance in reporting abuse. They have an extensive database of domestic violence treatment providers in all 50 states and U.S. territories. Many staff members speak languages besides English, and they have 24-hour access to translators for approximately 150 languages. For the hearing impaired, there is a TDD number. All calls to the hotline are confidential, and callers may remain anonymous if they wish.

National Missing Exploited Children (NCMEC)
Charles B. Wang International Children's Building
699 Prince Street
Alexandria, Virginia 22314-3175
Phone: 703-274-3900
Fax: 703-274-2200
Hotline:1-800-THE-LOST (1-800-843-5678)

The National Center for Missing & Exploited Children's (www.themissing.org or www.missingkids.com) mission is to help prevent child abduction and sexual exploitation, help find missing children, and assist victims of child abduction and sexual exploitation and their families, as well as the professionals who serve them.

Parents for Megans Law
www.parentsformeganslaw.org

A not-for-profit 501(c)3 community and victim's rights organization dedicated to the prevention and treatment of sexual abuse through the provision of education, advocacy, counseling, victim services, policy and legislative support services.

Rape, Abuse, Incest National Network (RAINN)
www.rainn.org
1-800-656-4673

RAINN has an automated service that links callers to the nearest rape crisis center. Rape crisis centers are staffed with trained volunteers and paid staff members who also understand sexual abuse issues and services (though sometimes they are not adequately prepared to refer male callers). All calls are confidential, and callers may remain anonymous if they wish.

Peace Over Violence
www.peaceoverviolence.org
24-Hour Hotlines
310-392-8381
213-626-3393
626-793-.3385
1-877-633-0044 (stalking hotline)

A non-profit, feminist, multicultural, volunteer organization dedicated to a building healthy relationships, families and communities free from sexual, domestic, and interpersonal violence. The agency manages five departments providing emergency, intervention, prevention, education, and advocacy services.

Texas EqquSearch
www.texasequusearch.org/

The Texas EquuSearch Mounted Search and Recovery Team was started in August, 2000 with the purpose to provide volunteer Horse Mounted Search and Recovery for Lost and Missing persons.

National Sex Offender Registry
www.familywatchdog.us

This website provides facts about sex offenses and gives detailed information about registered local sex offenders.

Registered Sex offenders
www.megans-law.net

This guide describes the problem of acquaintance rape of college students, addressing its scope, causes, and contributing factors; methods for analyzing it on a particular campus; tested responses; and measures for assessing response effectiveness.

White-Collar Crime

Federal Bureau of Investigation
www.fbi.gov/whitecollarcrime.htm

The Federal Bureau of Investigation investigates white-collar crime and fraud, insurance fraud, mortgage fraud, health-care fraud, mass-marketing fraud, money laundering, and securities and commodities fraud. It provides information about these crimes, including how to protect yourself from common scams and what to do if you think you've been victimized.

White Collar Crime—the Crash Course
profs.lp.findlaw.com/collar/index.html

This website provides a crash course in white-collar crime and information on the criminal procedure in the real-world defense of individuals during the preindictment stage of a federal white-collar crime investigation.

Common Objections in Criminal Trials

Argumentative: Usually a hostile question that forces the witness to accept the attorney's version of the facts, perspective of the case, or inference.

Asked and answered: A question that duplicates a question that was previously asked and responded to.

Assumes facts not in evidence: A question that includes a piece that has not been proven; it is necessary to be a predicate for a future question.

Compound question: A question that is really two questions in one, thus making a single answer misleading.

(Calls for) hearsay: A question or answer that refers to an out-of-court statement offered in a court case, to prove or be offered as being truthful.

Inadmissible opinion: A question or answer that goes beyond the expertise or knowledge of that person.

Lack Of foundation: Similar to speculation, with the necessary prerequisite facts or knowledge not yet proved.

Leading: A question that suggests the answer. (Available only on direct or redirect.)

(Calls for) narrative: A question or answer that is longer than a few sentences. (Usually cured by attorneys who say things like, "And then what happened?")

Nonresponsive: A response to a question that does not address the question.

Outside of the scope of direct exam: Asking a question that goes beyond the areas asked, implied, or inferred in direct examination. (Available only during cross.)

Relevance: Testimony in which the probative value is outweighed by the prejudicial effect.

(Calls for) speculation: A response to a question that either makes a layperson either go beyond their sensory perception or requires the witness to guess.

Vague: Also sometimes objected to as ambiguous; a question that is ambiguous or vague, or does not make sense.

Most Common Exceptions to the Hearsay Rule

Hearsay is nonetheless admitted into evidence a number of situations because there are special circumstances indicating it is truthful and reliable.

Business record: This is a document that was prepared and kept in the regular course of a company's business. The idea is that a company needs to keep accurate records to be in business.

Excited utterance: This an immediate, verbal reaction to a sudden surprise or emotional event, like "Oh, no!" Since a person has no time to think before making the utterance, it is considered reliable.

Medical diagnosis: This is similar to the business record exception, but for records generated in the course of providing medical treatment. The rationale is the same: medical providers need to keep accurate records.

Presentsense impression: This is similar to the excited utterance exception, and refers to an immediate response to some physical sensation such as "Ow! That's hot!"

Previous admissible conviction: This is the court record of a defendant's prior conviction for a different crime.

Prior inconsistent statement: This is allowed only if the person who made the prior statement is a witness; the idea is that the witness is there to explain the prior statement.

Public record/vital statistic: This is another variation on the business record exception; government agencies need to keep accurate records.

Reputation: This can be allowed to show one's character in a community; usually used to show that a witness is honest. While the statement may come in for honesty or good character, remember that the rules allowing good or bad character evidence are subject to their separate evidence rules, this exception is merely the exception to the out of court statement part

State of mind: This is a statement that is being used to show the declarant's mental state, not the truth of what was said.

Hearsay exceptions that apply only if the person saying it (the declarant) is not available to testify in the current case:

Dying declaration: This is a statement made just before a person passes away, and is considered reliable because there is probably no motivation to tell a falsehood.

Former testimony: This is earlier testimony given under oath and transcribed.

Statement against interest: This applies when someone makes a comment that is contrary to his financial or other best interest. An example might be a motorist who says, after an accident, "I wish I hadn't been going so fast." The idea is that a person wouldn't say something that is damaging to him if it weren't true.

Index